LOST WALLOWA

LOST WALLOWA
1869–1879

Book Three in the Saga of
Tall Bird and John Crane

BILL GULICK

A Double D Western

Doubleday

NEW YORK   LONDON   TORONTO   SYDNEY   AUCKLAND

A Double D Western
Published by Doubleday, a division of
Bantam Doubleday Dell Publishing Group, Inc.
666 Fifth Avenue, New York, New York 10103

A Double D Western, Doubleday and the portrayal of the
letters DD are
trademarks of Doubleday,
a division of
Bantam Doubleday Dell
Publishing Group, Inc.

Library of Congress Cataloging-in-Publication Data
Gulick, Bill, 1916–
The saga of Tall Bird and John Crane
A Double D western
Contents: bk. 1. Distant trails, 1805–1836—
bk. 2. Gathering storm, 1837–1868—
bk. 3. Lost Wallowa, 1869–1879
1. Nez Percé Indians—Fiction.   I. Title.
PS 3557.U43S24   1988   813'.54   87-34337
ISBN 0-385-24164-X (v. 1)
ISBN 0-385-24165-8 (v. 2)
ISBN 0-385-24166-6 (v. 3)

LOST WALLOWA

PART ONE

DISTANT THUNDER
1869–1876

Now that the treaty was ratified and its amendments approved, money for schools, buildings, and improvements on the Nez Perce Reservation began to move through government channels on a more dependable schedule. But along with the increased availability of funds, President Grant's administration wasted little time adopting two basic tenets on which care for Indian wards seemed to be based: (1) Do not tolerate an agent who is sympathetic to the people in his charge; (2) Dismiss any agent who shows signs of behaving honorably.

In June, 1869, Robert Newell, whose health was failing, was terminated. First he was replaced by an army officer, Lieutenant J. W. Wham, who soon was charged with embezzling Indian funds, then by Captain D. M. Sells, who in addition to being dishonest was also a drunk. In September, the Nez Perces lost their best white friend when William Craig died of a paralytic stroke. Two months later, Robert Newell passed away. With the Army in charge of Indian reservations now, John Crane saw no future for himself at Lapwai, left agency headquarters, and joined Tall Bird and his family in the Wallowa country.

"Talk is, the federal government is being pressured to take control of the reservations away from the Army and turn it over to the churches," he told Tall Bird. "The Catholics are favored to take charge of the Nez Perce Reservation, I hear."

"That seems strange to me," Tall Bird said. "The Christian Nez Perces have always had Presbyterian ministers and teachers."

"The Indian Bureau thinks in strange ways, brother. And the Catholics are pushing hard to get a foothold on the reservations."

As John expected would happen, both the Protestant Nez Perces on the Lapwai Reservation and the white American Board of Commissioners for Foreign Missions in Boston raised such an uproar over the arbitrary decision to assign the Nez Perces to the Catholics that it was quickly reversed and given to the Presbyterians. Much to the pleasure of the older Indians, who still revered him, the seventy-year-old Henry Spalding was returned as a teacher, though the more powerful post of

Agent was given to the scrupulously honest, well-intentioned, unbending forty-year-old son of a Presbyterian minister, John B. Monteith.

Blind, full of years, and content that his son would lead his people in the paths of peace, *Tu-eka-kas*—"Old Joseph"—died in August, 1871. He was buried on a knoll where the Lostine and the Wallowa Rivers came together, with a beautiful view of the towering mountains to the west, south, and east which separated this remote valley from the world outside. Though a fence was erected around the site of his grave, with one of his favorite horses being slaughtered and a bell hung on a pole to rock and ring in the gentle breeze, no care would be given the site in years to come, John knew, for it was the traditional way of the *Nimipu* to let burial places of their honored dead revert to their natural state in due course of time.

When late September frosts turned the aspen and tamarack of the high country to gold, with the first snow falling over the mountain peaks, the Chief Joseph band began its leisurely process of moving down to lower country, where the families and their livestock would winter. More and more in recent years, the Indians had given up living in longhouses set on sandbars at the juncture of the Grande Ronde with the Snake, preferring light, snug, portable skin tepees which could be used both as summer and winter homes. Pitching their lodges in small or large camps, they could move their herds of horses and cattle down from the high to the low country, where the best grass, water, and shelter from winter weather were available with a minimum of fuss and bother. Usually the moves were made in a northeasterly direction from the mile-high valley of the Wallowa country to the less than thousand-foot elevation of the broad, sheltered, grass-rich lower valleys of the Imnaha, Chesnimnus, and Grande Ronde. From these camps along the west bank of the Snake, whose flow was low and easily crossed at certain places in wintertime, the Wallowa *Nimipu* could and frequently did indulge their love for travel by going to see their relatives and friends living on the Lapwai Reservation.

For the past two years, John Crane had lived with Tall Bird and his relatives as an accepted member of the family. When he was hungry, he was welcome to food from any spit or pot. When he made a successful hunt, he shared the game he brought home with anyone who needed it. On warm, sunny days, Singing Bird's children—there were three of them now—pestered him to play games, take them hunting or fishing, or tell them tales of the *Suyapo* world far away. On cold and snowy winter days, they teased him to tell them *Nimipu* folktales about Coyote, Fox, and the monster-fish that lived in Wallowa Lake—tales they knew better than he did, for they took great delight in correcting him if his account varied in the slightest detail from the way they had heard these grandfather tales before.

When he wanted to go off by himself, as he sometimes did, Tall Bird insisted that he treat the log cabin on the homestead claim Tall Bird had filed as his own. As a contribution to its comfort, he installed a cast-iron cooking and heating stove with a flue that drew well, two bunk beds, and a lean-to under whose roof a winter's supply of wood could be stored. Within the lean-to, he constructed a one-hole privy at one end of the wood-storage space, while at the other end he built a solid log room where dressed game and dried fish could be hung and protected from marauding animals. Using a tin sink, faucet, pipe, and other plumbing materials he had purloined from supplies shipped to the Lapwai Agency —they were supposed to have been installed in his quarters but never had been—he piped water from a spring upslope into the cabin so that he would not have to go outside in zero weather, if he chose to stay here for a while in the wintertime.

Adjacent to the cabin, he erected a log-rail corral that would hold half a dozen horses, with an open-ended stable and a loft in which a supply of wild hay, scythed by hand off the native grass and sun-cured, could be stored. Like the other Wallowa Nez Perces, Tall Bird had built up a sizeable herd of beef cattle, which John helped him look after as they ranged along the lower slopes and across the broad valley during the spring, summer, and fall.

On his final trip to the Willamette Valley, John had packed his clothes, his tools, and a few dozen books, which he loaded on two packhorses. After selling all the rest of his livestock except three saddle horses he wanted to keep, he signed his rights to the rest of the property away to Felicia's daughters and their husbands.

"Always liked to travel light," he told Faith with a smile. "Man my age don't need much to keep him happy."

"You'll always be welcome here, Father John. Come see us any time."

"Sure," he said. "I'll do that."

They both knew that he would not, of course, for whatever home or blood ties left him now were in the Nez Perce country. Since he had not expected the subagent job to last long, he was not particularly disappointed when it ended. He did miss his old friends William Craig and Doc Newell, but their passing was part of growing older.

Though Tall Bird approved the creature comforts John had added to the cabin, he was concerned that his brother would be lonely during the long, cold, snowbound months of winter.

"Who will you talk to, brother?"

"The mountains, my horses, myself. What better company could I have?"

"If you want a woman, I can find one for you. There are several widows in our band who need a man."

"Singing Bird would scratch her eyes out. She thinks I'm her man."

"She loves you deeply, I know. But as a father, not as a husband, which she has. The woman I would find would cook and keep house for you, mend your clothes, look after your health, and keep you from being lonely. At your age, a man needs such a woman."

"I'm obliged for the offer, brother. Truly I am. But I really enjoy being alone. Gonna make me a pair of snowshoes so I can do some traveling around, come winter. Think I'll even make me a pair of Norwegian runners, like I've seen in the mining camps over Salmon River way, and try to slide down a hill like a big bird, the way the miners do."

"Snowshoes I know about," Tall Bird said, frowning. "Norwegian runners I do not. What are they?"

"A pair of smooth boards four or five inches wide and six or seven feet long, with their front ends curled up so they won't bury in the snow. What you do is, strap them on your feet, climb a hill, and slide down so fast you're almost flying. I've never tried it but I've seen it done. Looks like a lot of fun."

"Well, if you want company, put on your snowshoes or your Norwegian runners and come down to our village on the lower Imnaha River. You will be welcome there."

"That's where you plan to winter?"

"Yes. The grass is good, the weather mild, and no white men pass through that country. Ten lodges of our people with their horses and cattle will be in our village."

Lying on the Oregon side of the deepest part of Snake River's Big Canyon, the lower Imnaha was an ideal place to winter, John knew. Little more than fifty miles from Wallowa Lake over an easy trail which had been the route of traveling *Nimipu* from time immemorial, it led from the domain of the Lower Nez Perces living west of the Snake to that of the Upper Nez Perces living in the Salmon and Clearwater areas east of the Snake. Containing an extensive spread of grass-covered lowlands and sheltered sandbars, the region could sustain twenty or thirty lodges without strain. In contrast to the high Wallowa, where the snows came early and stayed late, the climate of the lower Imnaha was so mild that John had seen coveys of naked Nez Perce boys swimming in sun-warmed comfort on late November afternoons, and hordes of grasshoppers jumping about in lively fashion on mid-February mornings.

"Glad to hear you're going to winter there," he told Tall Bird. "Suppose any of your people will be visiting Lapwai?"

"They always do. It is easy to cross the Snake at Big Eddy when winter comes. If Swift Bird does not bring his family to visit us, we will go to Kooskia and visit him. When we do, we will pass through Lapwai."

"I'd be obliged if you'd check for my mail there."

"I will. What do you hear from your son?"

"He's finally gotten out of Washington, which he's been dying to do. First, he was headquartered at Jefferson Barracks, in Missouri, so he moved his family back to St. Louis. Most of the Army's problems in the West are with the Sioux, he says, so the government is building posts in strategic places on the upper Platte and Missouri Rivers, hoping they can impress the Sioux with their power."

"From what I hear, Red Cloud, Sitting Bull, and Crazy Horse will not be impressed by a show of military power. What would impress them would be for the government to honor the agreements it has made with them."

"They may have a long wait on that," John said dryly. "Anyhow, the last letter I had from Luke he was headed for Bismarck, North Dakota, where the Army is planning to build a new post called Fort Abraham Lincoln. He was happy about the assignment because it would let him rejoin his old Civil War buddy, Colonel Custer. But he was unhappy because he's going to be busy putting up buildings while Custer is riding to hell and gone chasing Sioux, maybe getting into a battle or two and covering himself with glory."

"Long and bloody as the Civil War was, I should think that would have been enough glory for your son."

Shaking his head, John said bleakly, "Among your people, is a war chief content in times of peace? Sure, Lawyer is a wise man and he's led his people in the path of peace for years. But what is his fondest memory? What does he brag about every chance he gets?"

"The time he fought on the side of the whites in the Battle of Pierre's Hole."

"Exactly! And your own son, Swift Bird—what is he proud of?"

"The time he and Young Looking Glass rode with Old Looking Glass as warriors for Governor Stevens, ready to protect him from the Blackfeet, Coeur d'Alenes, and Spokanes."

"What about his army service with Colonel Wright? Isn't he proud of that?"

Tall Bird shook his head. "This is a sensitive subject, brother, which he does not talk about much. In one way he is proud. In another way, he is ashamed."

"Why?"

"Because in war, the honorable thing for a man to do is to show bravery, fight fiercely beside his friends, and kill the enemy or make him run away. But when peace comes, it is a shameful thing to hang enemy prisoners, take whole families as hostages, and kill hundreds of horses with no other purpose than to degrade defeated enemies. He is ashamed of that."

"Does he still go to the buffalo country?"

"Yes. He loves to hunt buffalo almost as much as he loves to fight Blackfeet."

"Aren't things peaceful between the Nez Perces and Blackfeet these days?"

Looking concerned, Tall Bird shook his head. "From what I hear, the *Nimipu* have honored the treaties Governor Stevens made with us and the Blackfeet seventeen years ago. When we hunt in the buffalo country, we stay south of the Big Muddy, while the Blackfeet make their hunts to the north. But the Crows, who live in the Yellowstone country to the east, did not sign those treaties and refuse to honor them. They hunt buffalo and go on horse-stealing expeditions wherever they like. Now in retaliation for a defeat suffered by them in a battle against the Blackfeet, they want Looking Glass to lead two hundred *Nimipu* warriors across Lolo Pass, meet them in the buffalo country, and go to war with them against the Blackfeet."

"Seems a good way to get his band into a lot of trouble. Is Looking Glass interested?"

"I'm afraid he is," Tall Bird answered. "Since all his adult life he's been known as the son of a war chief, with no great victory achieved in his own name, he burns for a chance at glory, too. If he leads two hundred *Nimipu* warriors to join the Crows, I know Swift Bird will ride beside him. They have learned each other's death-songs and have sworn to fight together to the end."

2

When the stranger approached him that crisp, sunny, early November afternoon, John Crane had just finished loading a packhorse with the carcass of a deer he had killed and dressed out. From the elevation of the lower foothills on the north slope of the mountains, he'd gotten a clear view of the man as he came riding across the open valley floor. From the appearance of the horse the man straddled, the pack animal trailing behind him, his outfit, clothes, and weapons, John judged him to be a man used to camping out and familiar with the customs of the country, rather than another of the roughs increasingly infesting the mining settlements these days, who would rather steal than work.

Still, as the stranger halted a respectable fifty feet away, placing his left hand in plain sight on the saddle horn while he lifted his right hand to the brim of his gray slouch hat in a casual, friendly greeting, John stood close enough to his saddle horse to put the sheathed rifle on its near side within easy reach.

"Howdy," the stranger said. "Looks like you've had good luck hunting."

"Meat for the table. Lot of deer around."

"So I've noticed the past few days, wandering over the valley. Seems to be a paradise for game."

If he'd been wandering over the valley for a few days, John mused, that would account for his riding in from a northeasterly direction—the wilds of the Big Canyon and Snake River—rather than from the west, the direction of the upper Grande Ronde Valley and the white settlements along the Oregon Trail.

"Looking for anything in particular?" John asked.

"Grass, mostly," the stranger said. "Over Grande Ronde way, where I've been ranching, we've had a mighty dry summer. Sure like to find some new range for my cattle."

"You won't find it here. The Wallowa country belongs to the Nez Perces."

"If that's so, where are they? I've been riding and camping from one end of the valley to the other for almost a week. I haven't seen a single Indian."

"This time of year, they've all moved down to the lower valleys along the Snake, taking their horses and cattle with them to winter there."

The stranger was silent for a time while he digested this piece of information. Apparently feeling that he had asked questions enough before politeness required that he identify himself, he smiled and held out his hand.

"My name's Smith. A. C. Smith."

A slim, wiry, small-statured man, A. C. Smith looked to be in his early forties, quietly self-confident, and able to take care of himself. His manner was straightforward and open, his gaze penetrating and curious without being offensively aggressive, and he had the look of a man who knew what he wanted and would not be easily diverted from the course he took to get it. John extended his hand.

"Glad to meet you. I'm John Crane."

"Here on a hunting trip?"

"No. I live here."

Smith frowned. "Thought you said this country belongs to the Nez Perces?"

"It does. My brother and I filed a claim on a square mile of land under the Oregon Donation Act before the Stevens Treaty was signed back in '55. Since we're both friends of the Nez Perces and there's plenty of land in the Wallowa country, they've respected our rights."

"Mind telling me your brother's name?"

"Mark. Mark Crane."

"He with you now?"

"Right now, he's taken most of our horses and cattle down to winter pasture on the lower Imnaha River," John said lightly. "It's much easier to move them to mild weather than it is to feed them in bad."

"If the Indians are wintering their stock in that part of the country, isn't he afraid his will be stolen?"

"No, why should he be?" John said coldly. "There are no white men around."

Give A. C. Smith credit; he knew when he'd asked one question too many. Turning in his saddle, he waved an encompassing hand at the broad, open, grass-covered valley lying to the east, north, and west. "Lord, what beautiful grass! Looks like it's hardly been touched. But a lot of places it's burnt, I notice. Lightning set the fires?"

"No, the Nez Perces did. Just before they leave every fall, they torch the dead grass. Makes it come on richer next spring."

"Good God, what a waste! Over our way, we'd mow it, rake it, and put it up for winter hay."

"Why go to all that work, the Nez Perces say, when a few days' drive will move their livestock down to pasture they don't need to mow, rake, and put up?"

A. C. Smith chuckled. "From what I've seen of Indians, there's a lot to be said for the way they let Mother Nature do their work. But a white man can't live that way. Once he files a claim, the law says he's got to stay on it the year round, no matter what the weather. That's why I'm looking for a new place to live. So when I heard that the Wallowa country was open for settlement, I thought I'd ride over and look around."

"You heard the Wallowa country was open for settlement?" John said with sudden alarm. "Where did you hear that?"

"It's been in all the papers—the *Oregonian,* the La Grande *Union,* the Walla Walla *Statesman.* When the new treaty was ratified a few years ago, all the Nez Perce lands outside the new boundaries were thrown open for settlement by whites. The government is sending in survey crews next summer to lay out land grids and bench marks so that the settlers can identify the claims they're filing on. From what I hear, a land office will be opened in Union, the county seat of the Grande Ronde Valley."

"The whites can't file on the Wallowa country," John said heatedly. "This land belongs to the Indians."

"Not according to the federal government, it don't. When the Nez Perces signed the new treaty back in '63, they sold it to Uncle Sam. According to the Homestead Act, it's open to settlement by whites. I intend to be one of the first to file a claim."

What A. C. Smith represented, John mused with concern, was the vanguard of white settlers that would move into the Wallowa country as they had done elsewhere in the West, filing their homestead claims on choice quarter sections of land which controlled the best water rights, breaking ground for gardens and crops, building cabins, barns, bridges, toll roads, and towns, letting their livestock roam over increasingly large areas of Indian lands, sending word out to relatives and friends that they had found a new, fertile, virgin land, developing the country— as they called it—until eventually there was no room left in it for the natives who had long called it their own. This sort of man would not easily be turned aside from the course he had chosen, for land hunger was the strongest hunger of all.

"I've got a cabin in the foothills yonder," John said, gesturing toward the nearby mountains. "Come and stay with me a spell. We've got some things to talk over."

"Why, that's kindly of you. It'll be a pleasure . . ."

Because he knew A. C. Smith suspected it, John Crane told him the truth after supper that evening, admitting that his half brother, Mark Crane, usually went by the Indian name Tall Bird, and was a member of the Wallowa Nez Perces. Smith asked him how many people were in the Joseph band.

"Forty or fifty families, at best. The way they come and go visiting relatives on the Lapwai Reservation over in Idaho and the Umatilla Reservation in the Walla Walla country, it's hard to make an accurate count. At a rough guess, I'd say there are less than two hundred people in the band."

"Good Lord, John, in a country this big, you could hide them all in a single canyon. There's plenty of room for white settlers without crowding the Nez Perces."

"But it's *their* land, A. C., granted to them by the Treaty of 1855."

"Which was amended in 1863—and which they signed."

"That's the point I've been trying to make clear to you. Old Joseph and the chiefs of four other bands did not sign the 1868 Treaty. Rather than sign it, they agreed to disband the tribe."

"Like the South seceded from the North, you mean? You know that didn't work."

"What I know is that the Nez Perce way of governing themselves is different from the white man's way. We've recognized the fact that Indian tribes are sovereign nations ever since the government started dealing with them after the Revolutionary War. I was at Lapwai when the new treaty was made in '63, and I know which chiefs signed it and which chiefs didn't. Old Joseph never sold the Wallowa country. It still belongs to Young Joseph's band, no matter what the bureaucrats in Washington say."

"Well, so far as I'm concerned, my cattle can't wait for a silly argument over who owns this country to be settled. They need new pasture now. Come spring, I'll be driving a herd across the mountains—and I suspect a few neighboring ranchers will join me."

"Chief Joseph will make a strong objection. He doesn't want whites trespassing on his people's land."

"Will he fight?"

"He's a peaceful, religious, reasonable man, A. C. The last thing in the world he wants to do is to get his people involved in a hopeless war. But right is on his side. You've got to respect that."

"I do. And I respect Indians, John. So far as I'm concerned, they can have all the grass, water, wood, and land they need to live in this country as they always have lived. But after seeing how big and rich in grass, water, wood, and land the Wallowa country is, I'm going to claim my fair share. When Chief Joseph and his people come back next spring, I hope you'll help me make clear to him that my friends and I mean to live in this country with the Nez Perces in peace. But whatever their attitude, we *do* intend to live here . . ."

3

By late spring, when the first of the migrating Nez Perces began to return from their winter villages to the high Wallowa country, A. C. Smith and half a dozen other white men had driven strings of horses and herds of cattle across the mountains from the Grande Ronde Valley and turned them loose to graze on the rich green grass. Apparently cautioned by Smith that they would be sharing the country with the Indians, the settlers avoided filing claims and building cabins on such traditional *Nimipu* campgrounds as the juncture of the Lostine with the Wallowa and the shores of Wallowa Lake.

Called "Indian Town" by the whites, the circle of tepees pitched within sight of Old Joseph's grave, where the skeleton of the horse killed in his honor was still visible, and the bell hung on a pole nearby still tinkled in the breeze. This central village was where Joseph, his younger brother, *Ollokot,* and other leaders of the band pitched their tepees every year, and where all council meetings were held.

When the main body of Wallowa Nez Perces returned in early summer, Chief Joseph was disturbed to find half a dozen white ranchers taking squatter's rights on choice pieces of rich grassland scattered across the wide valley, where they had turned their cattle loose to graze and were building cabins, corrals, and barns at sites with access to year-round streams. Also camped in the valley was a team of surveyors employed by the federal government, sent there to establish bench marks, lay out grids, and map the region so that homestead claims filed in the Land Office could be properly registered and recognized.

"Can they do this?" Tall Bird asked John with concern. "Is there no way to stop them?"

"They claim the federal government bought the country. If that's true, there's not much we can do."

"Joseph wants to talk with A. C. Smith. He feels there has been a misunderstanding which can be straightened out by discussion."

"From what I know of A. C. Smith, he's not an unreasonable man, brother. If Joseph wants to talk to him, I'll set up a meeting at Indian Town."

When the two men met, Chief Joseph was polite.

"We want to be friends with the white man," he told Smith. "We are not greedy and do not object to the white man coming into the Wallowa country to hunt, fish, and camp in tents. But this is our country. We do not want the white man to build houses and barns, plow up the land, or put fences around it to keep our people out."

"According to the federal government, the Wallowa country has been opened to settlement by the whites," A. C. Smith said patiently. "It is a big country, with plenty of room for all. I have told my friends that they should respect your rights to whatever portions of the country you traditionally use. So far, they have done so."

"I have observed that. I appreciate it. Still, you and your friends have built houses and barns, plowed up the land, and put fences around it."

"The only claims we have filed have been merely to give us title to the place where we've made our homes. We have plowed up only enough land to plant grain for our cattle and a vegetable garden for our families. The only fences we have built have been to protect our grain and vegetables from livestock, our own as well as yours."

Silent for a time as he carefully weighed what the white man had said, Chief Joseph at last turned, motioned with his left hand at the wide expanse of valley floor visible from this height, and asked, "When a white man files a claim, how much land does he take?"

"According to the Homestead Act, he's entitled to one hundred and sixty acres."

"Numbers mean nothing to me," Joseph said, shaking his head. He looked at John Crane. "Can you tell me how big such a piece of land would be?"

"It'd be one fourth of a square mile," John said. "Each side would measure four hundred and forty yards."

"Show me."

"Let me do it," Tall Bird said.

Picking up three surveyors' stakes from a basketfull gathered by the youngsters and brought to the camp for fuel, he walked the required number of paces in an easterly direction, thrust a stake into the ground, paced an equal distance to the north, planted another stake, then walked west, placed another, and finally came back to the spot from which he had started.

"If I counted right, the land inside the stakes is about one hundred and sixty acres."

Chief Joseph smiled, shook his head, and moved his right hand down and out in a throwing-away gesture. "If that is all the land a white man needs, it is of no consequence. We will make no trouble over his taking such a small piece when so much more is left for us."

If only half a dozen settlers had moved into the Wallowa, and if those who came had respected the rights of the Chief Joseph band as A. C. Smith and his friends had done, there would have been no problems. But by the summer of 1872, a total of sixty white settlers had come into the country and taken up claims. When the Nez Perces returned from their winter villages and found the whites there, Chief Joseph again protested mildly, saying that his people did not object to the whites hunting and fishing in the valley but the whites must not build cabins, bring in herds, or cut hay. In reply, A. C. Smith again pointed out that the Nez Perce tribal leaders had signed a treaty ceding the region to the federal government, which had declared it open for settlement.

"But I want to do what's fair and right," he told Joseph. "I'll be happy to go to Lapwai and talk to the agent and chiefs there. If you agree, I'll join you in writing a letter to Washington, requesting that some person in authority be sent out to settle the differences between us."

"That sounds good to me. Let us do it."

In response to the councils and letters, Agent John Monteith visited the Wallowa country in late August, 1872. After talking to the Indians and the white settlers, he wrote his appraisal of the situation to regional and national officials in the Bureau of Indian Affairs.

"It is a great pity that the valley was ever opened to settlement," he concluded. "It is so high and cold that they can raise nothing but the hardiest of vegetables. One man told me that the wheat was frozen after it was in the milk. It is fine grass country and raising stock is all that can be done to any advantage. It is the only fishery the Nez Perces have and they go there from all directions."

After meeting in Lapwai with Monteith and the nontreaty Nez Perces March 27, 1873, Oregon Superintendent of Indian Affairs T. D. Odeneal made a report to Washington, D.C. that was favorable to Chief Joseph's cause. As a result, the government decided on a reasonable compromise under which part of the Wallowa country would be set aside as an Indian reservation, with the government to appraise and pay for whatever improvements white settlers had made within its boundaries, and the rest of the country to be opened for settlement.

Although militia units were being formed in many eastern Oregon communities as protection against possible Indian uprisings, John Crane was pleased to note that the leaders of the group being organized in the Wallowa country made it clear that they had no bloodthirsty intentions. On May 17, they requested that the *Sentinel* publish the notice:

> Whereas, there have been reports circulated to the effect that we, the citizens of the Wallowa Valley, propose organizing for the purpose of committing criminal onslaught against peaceable Indians
>
> Therefore be it
>
> Resolved by the Wallowa Volunteers, that we only propose protection to ourselves against the depredations of unfriendly Indians —and then WAR TO THE KNIFE.

A day later another Wallowa resident wrote:

"As regards the contemplated Indian troubles, I know nothing but hearsay, which is worth less than nothing. I do not think there is much danger of the Indians committing any depredation, notwithstanding all that the Indian agents and superintendents can do to urge the Indians to break out. It is my honest opinion that a majority of the Indian agents steal the goods that the government justly allows red men and then encourages the Indians to murder the settlers."

Though the editor of the *Sentinel* was urging from the safety of his office sixty-five miles away that the citizens of Wallowa drive Joseph and his band from the face of the earth, Superintendent Odeneal, with Monteith's concurrence, calmly recommended to the Secretary of Interior:

"That a proper description of said valley be obtained for the purpose of an executive order setting apart this valley for the exclusive use of said Indians, and that white settlers be advised that they are prohibited from entering or settling in said valley."

In response to this sensible solution, the editor of the *Sentinel* shrieked in print:

"Those of the people who have not heard the news in some other place giving the Wallowa Valley to the Indians, will almost be struck dumb with the intelligence that such was the case. There have been many perfidious officials in Oregon, but the man Odeneal, Superintendent of Indian Affairs, stinks in the nostrils of every decent man east of the Cascades for the dirty part he has acted in robbing the settlers of the Wallowa of their homes.

"We now propose that the whites be put on a reservation and closely guarded so that they may inflict no damage on the noble red men!"

After reading the article to Tall Bird, John Crane said thoughtfully, "You know, putting his kind of white man on a reservation under close guard isn't a bad idea. Trouble is, who would be agent for a pack of mad dogs like them . . . ?"

4

In late March, 1873, Tall Bird's wife *Ha-ne-sa La-tes*—"Flower Gatherer"—died of a chronic lung ailment that had grown steadily worse during the winter. Since she was sixty-five years old and had given him four fine children, she had lived a rich, full life. He knew he should not grieve for her long but should lavish his attention and love on the children and grandchildren that were left him.

The oldest son *Teg-Teg*—"Cricket"—was now forty-six years old, married to a niece of Chief Timothy and living in the Alpowa area, where he ran a general store catering to both Indians and whites, and raised horses and cattle. A Christian, he had adopted the white name Frank Nichols.

The oldest daughter *Pis-Ku*—"Cabbage"—now forty-four, was married to a Christianized Nez Perce from the Lapwai band who had taken the white name Joshua Worth. Her husband and their family were try-

ing to eke out a living on twenty acres of allotted land, which they had
fenced to protect their milk cows, hogs, chickens, vegetable garden, and
fields of wheat and corn.

The youngest son *Peo-peo Kuz-kuz*—"Swift Bird"—now forty-one,
who had married a girl from the Kooskia band, lived on the South Fork
of the Clearwater near the extreme eastern border of the reservation, for
that was the home of his blood brother, Chief Looking Glass, who every
other year led hunting forays across the Bitter Root Mountains onto the
buffalo plains, where now and then they engaged in exciting skirmishes
with the Blackfeet. Like the other *Nimipu* families living in the area,
Swift Bird planted a garden, kept hogs, chickens, and a milk cow, but
was not nearly as "settled" an Indian as the Lapwai Nez Perces. Given
the slightest indication from Looking Glass that the time had come to
head for the buffalo country, he would turn the stay-at-home chores
over to his wife and children, jump on his horse and go. As for becoming a Christian, he ridiculed the word.

The youngest daughter *Peo-peo Uenpise*—"Singing Bird"—now
thirty-three, still lived with the Wallowa band, having married a strong
but crippled man named *Gagaz Aluin*—"Lame Brown Bear." Born with
a club left foot that had never developed normally, Lame Brown Bear
walked with an awkward gait, but he more than made up for this physical handicap by the extraordinary strength in his upper body and arms,
and by becoming one of the best riders and horse-breeders in the tribe.
Though he was amiable enough and treated her and their three children
well, Singing Bird often laughingly accused him of being more in love
with his horses than he was with his family.

So far as Lame Brown Bear was concerned, the way the Chief Joseph
band lived, which permitted him to move his large herd of fine horses
from the grass of the low country in winter to the grass of the high
country in summer, was the finest mode of life he could imagine.

To Tall Bird, who was still in good health save for the aches, pains,
and joint stiffness to be expected by a sixty-seven year old man, it was
pleasant to have his children living in so many different places in
Nimipu country, for it gave him an excuse to travel whenever he got the
urge, without the bother of taking along any more baggage than could
be carried on a spare horse. But of all the relatives he visited for short or
long stays, his favorites were Singing Bird and John Crane.

Whether pitched in a pleasant meadow on the lower slopes of the
high Wallowas in summer, or down in the deep, sheltered canyon of the
lower Imnaha in winter, Singing Bird's lodge was always a happy place,
full of laughter, joyous cries of playing children, and good smells of

cooking food. With Lame Brown Bear usually training, grooming, or breaking horses, Tall Bird took great enjoyment in seeing the patience and skill with which his son-in-law developed the talents of the animals so that they would bring the best price when the time came to sell them.

Though the agreement between Tall Bird and John Crane to be partners in the ranching enterprise was unspoken, they both accepted it as an accomplished fact. Because of the increasing number of white settlers that had moved into the valley, they had devised and registered a brand—*MJC* (Mark and John Crane)—with which they marked their horses and cattle, then like the other Indian and white ranchers, let the animals roam free on the abundant wild grass. In late spring, after the cows had dropped their calves and the mares their foals, Indians and whites joined forces in an area-wide roundup, following which the animals were sorted, cut, earmarked, branded, and then turned loose again to graze over their home range. Before winter came, the white ranchers would go to work with their riding mowers and hayrakes, cutting and stacking enough hay to carry their livestock through the winter months when snow covered the land, supplemented by grain they had grown and harvested. Before first snowfall, the Nez Perces would drive their stock down to the lower valleys; John would help Tall Bird accomplish that chore, then return to the cabin on their claim to spend the months during which the valley was isolated from the outside world.

Despite biased ravings by newspaper editors and correspondents, peace prevailed between the white settlers and the Nez Perces in the Wallowa country. In mid-June 1873, an appraising commission composed of Jasper Matheny, W. P. Berry, and Thomas H. Cox arrived from Salem, Oregon, and spent several weeks in the region, guided by A. C. Smith and John Crane. When they had finished their work, John told Tall Bird the results.

"They found eighty-seven white settlers and two incorporated companies, the Wallowa Road and Bridge Company and the Prairie Creek Ditch Company. The total improvements amount to $68,000, they say, which is far more than they expected."

"Will the federal government pay that much money to buy out the settlers?"

"To my way of thinking, that's a cheap price for permanent peace in Wallowa. The last Indian war in the Pacific Northwest cost six million dollars, I've been told. If the settlement goes through according to the recommendations made by the commissioners, the country will be divided in half, one portion of it being designated as a reservation for the

Wallowa Nez Perces, the other being opened for settlement by the whites."

"Where will the line be drawn?"

"Chief Joseph and A. C. Smith have suggested a north-south line running from the lower Grande Ronde River near the Oregon-Washington border to the upper Lostine in the mountains. What his people want, Joseph says, is the higher country along the headwaters of the Lostine, Wallowa Lake, the Imnaha, the Chesnimnus, Joseph Creek, and the broken country toward the Big Canyon of the Snake. What the whites want, Smith says, is the lower country to the west, which is flatter, more open, and gives them control of the bridges and roads to the Grande Ronde Valley and the Oregon Trail. If the line is drawn that way, with the white settlers being paid for what few cabins and improvements they're being asked to give up, it will be fair for all concerned."

As matters turned out, it was not the expense of establishing a reservation and extinguishing the citizens' claims that caused difficulty. It was the sheer stupidity of bureaucrats far removed from the area, who were not aware that the terms "upper" and "lower" in the Wallowa country referred to altitude and the direction water flowed, not to the way a map was hung on the wall.

What the commissioners intended to do was divide the Wallowa region so that the Nez Perces would have a place to hunt, pitch their tepees, and graze their horses and cattle six months out of the year, while the whites took claims and created permanent settlements in the rest of the area. The country most coveted by the Indians was the high, or upper country, along the headwaters of the numerous streams flowing down out of the mountains, including Wallowa Lake. What the white settlers wanted were the broad, open, well-grassed valleys which lay along the lower reaches of the river.

Apparently the bureaucrats who examined a map of the Wallowa country knew that north was "up," south was "down"—and that was *all* they knew. So when they drew the line awarding one part of the country to the Indians and the other part to the whites, they drew it from east to west instead of from north to south, with the final result being that the lands granted were exactly the reverse of what they should have been.

"Good God!" John Crane exploded when A. C. Smith brought him the news of what had happened. "How can they be so stupid?"

"They must work awful hard at it," Smith said in disgust. "Let's hope they straighten it out."

The decision had been made and the executive order signed even before the appraising commission completed its work, John learned, with a warning sent to Wallowa that no surveys or settlements were to be permitted on lands set aside for the reservation. Despite A. C. Smith's hope that the bureaucratic error could be corrected, reversing the decision once it had been fed into the governmental process proved to be as impossible as checking an avalanche with a broom.

Despite the verbal and written ravings being uttered and published outside the area, nothing of importance happened to change the peaceful relationship between the Nez Perces and the white inhabitants of the Wallowa country during the following twelve months. Since 1874 was an election year, candidates for office made glowing promises to "open the Willowa Valley for settlement," though they could not even spell its name properly, let alone define its boundaries or delineate which were to be white or Indian lands. Agent Monteith continued to put pressure on Chief Joseph to choose a spot in the Wallowa country as a year-round residence for his people. Joseph continued to resist that pressure, quite sensibly preferring to spend the six colder months in the mild climate of the lower Grande Ronde or Imnaha, the six warmer months in the delightfully cool high country adjacent to Wallowa Lake.

Writing to the Indian Bureau in Washington, D.C., Monteith indicated that his patience with Joseph was wearing thin:

> About one year ago the Wallowa Valley was given back to him and his band. I told him at that time that unless he and his people were willing to take their farms in said valley and settle down and go to work, I was of the opinion that they would not be allowed to keep the valley.
>
> Still, no heed has been given to my advice in this respect. They have spent part of the time in the valley and the balance on the Snake River or roaming over the country.
>
> The only thing that can be done with these Indians is to compel them to remain in one place or the other. To accomplish this, force will be necessary.

Though Monteith and the reservation Indians certainly knew better, it was a common misconception among the whites living in the area that the federal government was supporting the Indians with regular handouts of food, clothing, and money. John Crane knew such was not the case. What precious few dollars were spent by the government usually went to white contractors to build fences, mills, schools, and other improvements, with now and then a meager issue of blankets and clothes.

Thus, the only thing the Wallowa Nez Perces could hope to gain from settling down and living on a designated reservation year round was the eventual building of a few fences, barns, and houses, and perhaps a church and a school if and when funds were appropriated for these purposes. But since their skin tepees were portable and their livestock could be moved from the high country to the low country with the seasons, why bother with "settling" anywhere? Chief Joseph felt the same way Sitting Bull did, and quoted the great Sioux medicine man, who had said, "God made me an Indian. But he did not make me a reservation Indian."

When Chief Joseph was asked by the commissioners if he would not like a missionary sent to Wallowa and a church built there for his people, he politely declined the offer.

"They will teach us to quarrel about God," he said, "as the Catholics and Protestants do on the Nez Perce Reservation. We may quarrel with men sometimes about things on this earth, but we never quarrel about God."

After conferring with the military commander of the district, Monteith requested that contingents of troops be stationed during the summer of 1874 both at Weippe Prairie, where many Nez Perce families went to dig camas, and in the Wallowa country, where the Umatilla Confederation tribes as well as the Nez Perces went to gather salmon and redfish. Staying from early summer until the Indians left the high country in mid-October, the troops served the dual purpose of reassuring the whites and protecting the Indians from the sale of liquor.

"With the exception of two cases, I found that all the settlers I visited were on friendly terms with the Indians and have had no trouble," wrote Lieutenant Thomas Garvey. "The two cases referred to were Mr. McNall and Mr. Brown, who complained that the Indians allowed their horses to trespass and graze their land. McNall caught up some of the Indians' stallions and altered them in retaliation. He claims he done this to prevent his mares from breeding with such inferior stock as the Indian ponies. Neither of these men have their places fenced."

"So far as I could discover from the most careful attention, there is no cause to apprehend any present difficulty with these Indians," another officer wrote. "The settlers generally appear to wish to deal justly by the Indians, and I have heard a majority of the former express the opinion that while that course is pursued they have no fear of hostile acts on the part of the latter."

However, he did warn prophetically, "Should Government decide against locating an Indian reservation there, and order the Indians to leave or remain away, I respectfully suggest that timely and deliberate preparations should be made to reinforce that order, and protect the white inhabitants from the rage which probably might inspire the Indians under disappointment in being deprived of what they highly value and apparently consider as justly theirs."

Meanwhile, John Crane heard with concern, back in Washington, D.C., the government was changing its mind again. Unable to carry out the executive order issued in 1873 to establish a modest-sized reserve for the Nez Perces in the Wallowa country, pay a paltry $68,000 for the settlers' claims, and open the rest of the region for settlement, Congress gave in to pressure from Oregon politicians. On June 10, 1875, the earlier order was revoked by President Grant, the plan to establish a reservation was cancelled, and the entire area was opened to settlement.

"What happens now?" Tall Bird asked John Crane in complete bewilderment. "Where will we be permitted to live?"

"God knows, brother," John answered wearily. "And I suspect even He is confused."

5

But Agent John Monteith was not confused, for now the way was clear to bring the nontreaty Nez Perces under his control. When he heard about the reopening order, he immediately requested that troops be sent into the valley in case of conflict between the whites and the Indians, who usually arrived in late July. In response, two companies of cavalry under Captain S. G. Whipple were dispatched from Fort Walla Walla, reaching the Wallowa July 29. Though Chief Joseph and the main body of Nez Perces had not yet arrived, Captain Whipple reported that *Ollokot,* Joseph's younger brother, had visited the valley late in June.

"He appeared very friendly. Joseph is reported as saying his people were aware the valley was not to be reserved for the use of the Indians; that the white settlers would remain and others come, but that the

Indians would resort here as formerly and for the same purpose. This may be taken as an indication of amicable intentions on the part of the Indians."

When Chief Joseph and forty-five lodges of his band arrived in mid-August, he held a conference with Captain Whipple, requesting the presence of Tall Bird and John Crane to interpret for him. Captain Whipple spoke first.

"My troops and I are present as friends of both Indians and whites. As long as the Indians do right, the settlers say they do not object to the Indians being in the valley. They ask only that the Indians observe the laws and do no violence to persons and property."

"We have always observed the laws," Chief Joseph answered patiently. "We have never committed acts of violence against persons or property. We never will."

"I am pleased to hear that."

"We were bitterly disappointed to hear that the Wallowa was thrown open to settlement by the whites after it had been understood for so long that at least a portion of it would be set aside as a reservation for us."

"That decision was made in Washington, D.C. I cannot reverse it."

"This I understand. Under the circumstances, all we can do is share it with the white people, promising to do our best to live with them in peace and harmony."

"I am sure the whites feel the same way."

But the situation was not the same, John knew, for before it had been the white settlers who were interlopers on land given by federal treaty to the Indians. Since the reversal of the executive order, it was the Nez Perces who were trespassers on land given to the whites. Where before, sharing had been a matter of tolerance by the Indians, now it was a matter of tolerance by the whites. He feared the difference would be substantial.

According to the newspapers, pressures were growing in government circles to settle the Indian problems in the West once and for all by putting the tribes on strictly defined reservations and keeping them there—by force, if necessary. Led by such powerful chiefs as Red Cloud, Crazy Horse, and Sitting Bull, the Sioux were refusing to stay penned in and were threatening to go to war if the white men invaded their sacred Black Hills in violation of the treaty made with them in 1868. When Colonel Custer did mount a Black Hills Expedition during the summer of 1874, followed by a flood of white prospectors seeking gold, the Sioux began preparing for what threatened to be the most massive rebellion of Plains Indians against their military oppressors in the nation's history.

Following the news stories, John was concerned, for in the last letter he had received from his son, Major Luke Crane wrote he was still stationed at Fort Lincoln. Though his primary duty was overseeing the planning and building of roads, bridges, and fortifications, he was still burning to see action in the field with his good friend Custer.

Oddly enough, just a couple of summers ago, Looking Glass, Swift Bird, and a contingent of two hundred Nez Perce warriors had joined forces with the Crows to stalk, attack, and defeat the Sioux in the Yellowstone country in a brilliant campaign. It had been so successful, in fact, that at its conclusion the Crow chiefs gave Looking Glass a highly valued redstone pipe and a medicine pouch, swearing by the most sacred oath:

"While the waters run, the grass grows, and the sun shines, the Crows will be brothers to the Nez Perces. If ever you need our help, simply send the message: 'We still have the peace pipe.' When we hear that, we will come and help you wherever you may be."

Pleasing as that victory was to Looking Glass, Swift Bird, and the two hundred Nez Perce warriors they had led into battle, it made Agent Monteith even firmer in his conviction that the wild, independent elements of the tribe must be more rigidly controlled. Thus, he brought pressure to bear in every way he knew how in order to persuade the military to round up the Wallowa band and bring it to the Lapwai Reservation. But to his surprise and exasperation the new commander of the Department of the Columbia, General Oliver Otis Howard, did not appear to feel that firmness or haste were in order.

Now the sixth-ranking general in the Army, a devout Christian, and an experienced politician after having headed the Freedmen's Bureau in the South during the Reconstruction years, General Howard had lost his right arm in the Battle of Fair Oaks during the Civil War. The Nez Perces called him *A-tim Ki-wnim*—"Arm Cut." Receiving Captain Whipple's report at his headquarters in Portland, he read it with approval, then was quick to take credit for peace and make a judgment that would prove to be as mistaken as many of his later ones:

"The troubles at Lapwai and at the Wallowa Valley have not thus far resulted in bloodshed, but it has been prevented by great carefulness and prevision on the part of Government agents.

"I think it is a great mistake to take from Joseph and his band of Nez Perce Indians that valley. The white people really do not want it. They wish to be bought out. I think gradually this valley will be abandoned by the white people, and possibly Congress can be induced to let these really peaceable Indians have this valley for their own."

But in late June, 1876, real trouble did arise between whites and Indians following a dispute over strayed horses. Acquainted with the people involved as he was, John Crane found it ironic that a white man known to be a good friend of the Nez Perces was forced by circumstances to defend another white man known to be their bitter enemy.

A. B. Findley, whose ranch was not far from Indian Town, was an honest, conscientious, sensitive man, well liked and respected by the Indians who knew him, as well as by his white neighbors. One of those neighbors was Wells McNall, who was quick-tempered and had an intense dislike for Indians.

On June 20, 1876, Findley discovered that three of his horses were missing. Wells McNall, who was helping him with the summer work, rode with him in an attempt to track them down. Since white settlers shod their horses while the Nez Perces did not, distinguishing hoofprints was no problem. The trail led north, over the low height of land separating the drainage of the Wallowa River from that of the Chesnimnus. On June 23, the two men followed that trail into the camp of a small group of Nez Perces who were hunting deer in the Whiskey Creek area.

Though neither the missing horses nor the Indians were in the camp, it was apparent that the members of the hunting party had not gone far, for their rifles were leaning against a tree; they had presumably been placed there to relieve the hunters of weight while they took packhorses to pick up several deer they had just killed nearby. Wanting to question the Indians about the missing horses and not sure what their attitude would be, the two white men decided to take possession of the rifles until they had consulted with the red men.

When five Nez Perce hunters returned to camp with their laden packhorses, they were surprised and alarmed to find their rifles in possession of the whites. One of them, a strong, muscular, proud man named *Wil-lot-yah,* demanded belligerently:

"Why you take our guns?"

"We want to ask you some questions," Findley said patiently. "Three of my horses are missing. Their tracks led here—"

"Goddamn, I didn't steal no horses! Give me back my gun."

"Mind your mouth, you greasy bastard!" McNall snarled. "Them tracks we followed was as plain as day. They led right toward your camp, where we lost 'em when they got mixed up with the tracks of your horses. We want to know what you done with 'em."

"Nothing, I tell you! We didn't steal them and we done nothing wrong! Give me back my gun!"

"Go to hell! We want to know what you done with them horses."

Angrily, *Wil-lot-yah* moved forward, lunging toward his rifle, which Wells McNall had leaned against the trunk of a tree, shielded behind his body. Both men seized the gun, wrestling for its control. Hoping to stop the struggle before either of them got hurt, Findley raised a large-caliber buffalo gun he was carrying and pointed it at them.

"Stop it! Hear me—stop it!"

Getting his finger through the trigger guard of the Indian's rifle, McNall fired the weapon. Singed along the calf and foot, *Wil-lot-yah* let out a howl of rage and redoubled his efforts to wrest the rifle out of his adversary's hand. A small, wiry man, and outweighed by thirty pounds, McNall felt himself being overpowered. In desperation, he shouted:

"He's going to kill me, Fin! For God's sake, shoot him!"

In a reflexive action which he did not even realize he was taking, Findley pulled the trigger. Struck squarely in the chest by the huge ball, the Nez Perce hunter was killed instantly. Stunned by what had happened, the four other Indians turned on their heels and fled.

"My God!" Findley muttered hoarsely, staring down at the body at his feet. "What have I done?"

"You shot a red son-of-a-bitch who was about to kill me!" McNall exclaimed. He looked nervously around. "We'd better get out of here and tell our people what happened. When Joseph hears about this, he's bound to go on the warpath."

But for a time at least, the Wallowa Nez Perces took no hostile action. Since the main body of Indians had not yet arrived in the valley, the "massing of the settlers," as Judge Brainard reported it to Governor Grover, consisted only in a few of them spending the night at the Mc-Nall cabin, then riding down to the Indian camp next day to see what had happened. The Indians had gone, taking the body of the impetuous young hunter, *Wil-lot-yah*, with them for burial near their winter village. Ironically, two of the missing horses turned up near the Findley ranch a couple of days later. Adding to the irony was the fact that A. B. Findley, a deeply religious man, was so stricken by what he had done that he offered to give himself up to the Nez Perces for trial and punishment under their laws, though his white neighbors would not permit this.

The whites censured him not for the killing itself but for the fact his act might incite the angry Indians to take revenge upon their households. Greatest irony of all was that the Nez Perces, knowing Findley to be a good man and their friend, placed no blame on him for the killing, putting the fault where it rightfully belonged—on Wells Mc-Nall, who had seized the rifle of the young Nez Perce, grappled with him, cursed him, fired the first shot, and then called for Findley to shoot him.

Because contingents of troops had been sent into the Wallowa country during the two previous summers to make sure peace prevailed, the white residents had every reason to expect a quick response from the military to the word that blood had been shed. But by the time news of the killing reached Fort Walla Walla and the Department of the Columbia headquarters in Portland, it was June 27, 1876. By then reports had come to Chicago, and were being spread to all corners of the country by the national news services, of a disaster so stunning that it shocked the nation.

"Good God!" John Crane exclaimed to Tall Bird when he heard it. "There's been a major battle between the Army and the Sioux on the Little Big Horn. According to first accounts, Colonel George Custer and several hundred of his men have been killed."

"This is the white war chief who was your son's friend?"

"Yes. They were classmates at West Point and fought together during the Civil War."

"Was your son with him in this battle?"

"I don't know. In the last letter I had from him a month ago, he said the Army was planning a three-pronged campaign against the Sioux that would end their resistance forever. General Crook was moving against them from the south, General Terry from the northwest, with Colonel Custer and a regiment of cavalry hitting them from the east. Knowing how Custer operates, he said, he was sure that his troops would initiate the action—which he didn't expect to last long. Apparently it didn't. According to first reports, the soldiers were slaughtered in a matter of hours."

"But you do not know if your son was among them?"

"All I know, brother, is that he wanted to ride with Custer. Normally, an officer in the Corps of Engineers spends his time building things. But he's trained to fight, too. If Luke got his own way, he was with Custer. I can only hope he was ordered to serve elsewhere . . ."

6

From that day on, the right of Indians to live off the reservation as free men would find few champions in the American military, press, and public. But in the Wallowa country, apprehension of trouble from the Nez Perces soon wore off. In August, the first boat ever built for the express purpose of seining redfish in Wallowa Lake was launched by a man named John McCall. It was reported that fish by the thousands were appearing in the lake. Having found a way to deplete in a single season a food resource that had nourished the Indians since time immemorial, John McCall and his friends gleefully boasted that they were using a seine eighteen feet deep and one hundred and fifty feet long, literally hauling in redfish by the wagonload.

"Somebody ought to stop the greedy bastard," John Crane muttered.

"When Joseph and *Ollokot* return, somebody probably will," Tall Bird said. "Have you heard any news about your son?"

"Yes, he's safe. He was with General Terry aboard the steamer, *Far West.* And damned unhappy about it because the high brass kept pestering him to find ways and means to move boats up rivers with so little water in them they wouldn't float a duck. He says bitter things about Major Reno and Captain Benteen, who were supposed to support Custer's charge on the Sioux village but didn't."

"If there were six thousand Sioux in that village, as the reports said, Custer was foolish to make his charge. When defending their homes and families, the Sioux are deadly fighters."

"Probably there weren't that many Sioux warriors," John said, shaking his head. "But there's no question Custer's charge was rash. The point is, Luke says, the Sioux have no future as a free people. Either they submit to white rule and a restricted life on the reservation, or the Army will exterminate them. Luke says he wants to be in on the final kill."

"Hearing this makes me sad. All my life I have felt that the ways of peace are best . . ."

When bands of Nez Perces began arriving in the valley that summer they were not as friendly as they had been in previous years. Instead of visiting the white settlers as before, they set up targets and did a lot of riding back and forth on their war horses, hanging under their necks and shooting at a full run, a show-off stunt they had learned from the Sioux which no warrior who cared about accuracy and the conservation of ammunition would dream of using in battle. At night they frequently held war dances.

Toward the end of August, Chief Joseph arrived. By then Findley had become so conscience-stricken over what he had done that he swore he would never shoot the needle gun again—and he never did. Shortly after making camp in Indian Town, Chief Joseph came to the Findley ranch for a visit one late afternoon. Preparing the evening meal, Mrs. Findley happened to look out the open door toward the children who were playing in the yard. She saw an Indian approach on a spotted horse, halt, and dismount. Alarmed, she hurried out into the yard, then stopped as she saw the children run to the Indian, throw their arms around his legs, and greet him with laughter.

"Well, I do declare!" she exclaimed, smiling. "How are you, Joseph?"

"Your children grow big and strong. You must feed them good."

"They eat like starving bears. How is your family?"

"Healthy and hungry, too. Is your husband home?"

"No, but he will be soon. Can you stay for supper?"

"That would please me."

"Then I'll go in and finish getting it ready."

"Good. I'll stay out here and talk to the children."

"If they pester you too much, just yell. They can be an awful nuisance."

Chief Joseph laughed good-humoredly. "Not to me, Mrs. Findley. My village is full of children. They don't bother me at all."

When her husband came home and found Chief Joseph there, he was nervous at first, Mrs. Findley noticed, but the Nez Perce leader's calm manner and quiet dignity soon put him at ease. When supper was over he looked at her and said, "Take the children outside, please. Joseph and I must talk."

"Come, children. We'll go for a walk."

After a silence, Findley said, "You heard what happened?"

"Yes. Now I want to hear it from you."

As simply, honestly, and frankly as he knew how, Findley told him about discovering the three horses missing, asking Wells McNall to help track them down, and following their trail to the hunters' camp. He related taking possession of the Indians' rifles so that no violence could occur when they were questioned about the horses; how the act had been misunderstood by *Wil-lot-yah;* the struggle that had ensued; how he had tried to stop it; and how he had shot the Nez Perce without really meaning to do so. At that point, Joseph raised a hand and stopped him.

"Did McNall curse *Wil-lot-yah?*"

"Yes. As I recall, he did."

"He asked the Spirit Gods to make you shoot him?"

"He begged *me* to shoot him, best I can remember. Without meaning to, I did. So I'm the one responsible for the killing."

Brooding for some moments upon what he had been told, Chief Joseph at last shook his head. "You speak with a straight tongue, for this is the way the hunters who were there have told the story to me. In my view, you are not to blame. The white man Wells McNall is the real murderer."

During the weeks that followed, John Crane heard, Joseph traveled extensively over the valley, talking to white men and Indians in his quiet, patient way as he gathered evidence he would eventually present in whatever court of justice might consent to hear the case. But when he got word of the massive redfish-seining being undertaken by John McCall and his friends in Wallowa Lake, he lost his temper. Riding with *Ollokot* and half a dozen Nez Perce braves to the north shore of the lake, where McCall and two white helpers were scoop-shoveling redfish from the boat into a wagon, he spoke angrily.

"Why are you stealing our fish?"

"What do you mean, your fish? I caught 'em."

"Do you mean to eat them all?"

"Hell, no! I'm gonna sell 'em."

"You are taking food out of my people's mouths."

"Ain't that too damn bad!"

"You must stop."

"Who's gonna make me?"

According to the way John Crane heard the story, Chief Joseph moved toward McCall, reaching out for the scoop shovel in the white man's hand. McCall put a hand against Joseph's chest, pushing him away. Outraged by the affront to his older brother's dignity, *Ollokot* growled like a wounded bear, ripped the shovel out of McCall's hand, then used it to knock him down. The two other white men started to come to McCall's defense, but, as the Nez Perce braves in the party unlimbered their war clubs and surged forward, had second thoughts and backed away.

"As I heard it," Tall Bird told John Crane, "Joseph told the three white men that they were welcome to fish as the *Nimipu* did, so long as they took only their fair share. But they refused to listen to reason. So Joseph let *Ollokot* settle the argument his way."

"Which was—?"

"To sink the boat, cut the net into little pieces, give the fish that had been caught to Indian families, and tell the white men they must leave the Wallowa and never return." Tall Bird smiled. "They were given an escort, in case they had trouble finding the road. I do not believe they will return."

Having completed his gathering of facts, Joseph consulted with his tribal leaders and then decided upon a course of action. On the first of September, Nez Perce couriers visited the home of every white settler in the valley and politely informed them that they were to attend a council next day at Indian Town. The presence of A. B. Findley and Wells McNall was specifically requested.

Since the number of Nez Perces was far greater than that of the whites, the settlers knew that resistance would be useless. Meeting at the McNall cabin, they decided to send Tom Veasey and Jim Davis— two white men whom the Indians liked and trusted—to parley in advance and test the temper of the Indians. The Nez Perces held the two men hostage, sending word to the settlers at the McNall cabin that they were all to come to the Indian village at once.

Seventeen whites did go to the council, though they left Findley and Wells McNall behind.

The talks lasted all day. At their conclusion, Joseph issued an ultimatum. Unless the settlers left the valley by the end of the week, they would be driven out by force. After agreeing to meet next day at the McNall cabin, the settlers were permitted to leave.

While the other men returned to their families scattered over the valley, the Findleys and McNalls gathered at the McNall cabin. Thrusting as many rifle barrels as they could find through chinks in the cabin walls, they made a pretense of being prepared to fight. But when sixty Nez Perce warriors rode up next morning, the whites decided to talk rather than shoot. In an act of sheer bravado, Ed McNall, an older brother of Wells, went out in the yard as the Indians approached, sat down on a stump, filled and lit his pipe. Tall Bird, who had been with the party, told John Crane, who had stayed home, what happened then.

"Wil-lot-yah's daughter, who was with us, walked up to the cabin door and demanded to see the man who had killed her father. Findley came to the door, opened it, and spoke to her, saying he was sorry for what he had done. He said he was willing to give himself up to the Indians and stand trial. But his people would not let him leave the cabin."

After an angry exchange of words, the Indians again warned the settlers that they must leave the valley, wheeled their horses around, and rode away. Deciding that military help was needed, Ed McNall saddled a horse as soon as darkness fell and set out for Fort Walla Walla, a hundred miles away.

The reception given him there by Colonel Otis was cool. In fact, when Otis wrote Judge Brainard next day seeking more information, he made the caustic comment: "It is known here that McNall is not thoroughly reliable."

Feeling that he would get no help from the regular Army, Ed McNall rode back to the Grande Ronde Valley and appealed for volunteers to assist the Wallowa settlers in rounding up their livestock and hauling their goods to safety. Twenty-two men responded. Meanwhile, a pair of young men engaged in carrying messages back and forth very nearly started a war with their foolish boasts.

"Their names are Gerard Cochran and Al King," Tall Bird told John Crane. "You may remember them working with the white ranchers at last spring's roundup."

"Yeah, vaguely. A pair of cocky youngsters, as I recall, maybe not too bright."

"They certainly did a dumb thing, brother. Coming back from the Grande Ronde Valley yesterday, they met a Umatilla Indian on the road and told him that the volunteers who are supposed to help the settlers move their cattle really are coming to fight the Indians 'if they get too gay.' "

" 'If Joseph does not behave,' one of them said, 'all the Indians will be killed. I, myself, will kill Joseph, scalp him, and tan his hide for a bridle.' "

"Jesus Christ! Did Joseph hear that?"

"He did—and he's very angry. In Indian Town, I hear, *Ollokot* and a hundred braves are stripping and painting for war. When they find out where the two young men are staying, *Ollokot* says, they mean to go there, drag them out, and see what they've got to say for themselves."

"That could mean trouble."

"I know. Joseph has asked Tom Veasey to go with the war party this evening when it rides over to the ranch where he thinks the two young men are staying. He wants us to go, too."

Though the information regarding the presence of Gerard Cochran and Al King at the ranch of a white settler, Max Johnson, proved to be accurate, the two young men were not visible when the war party arrived. Realizing that the Indians were in no mood to accept lies, the settler's wife, Bertha Johnson, wasted no time giving the Indians the information they wanted.

"That young rascal, Gerard Cochran, is hiding under a haystack in the barn. T'other one, Al King, run into the house and crawled under my bed."

"Bring them out," Joseph said, his face stony. "I want to ask them some questions."

While Max Johnson headed for the barn and Bertha Johnson went into the house, Joseph's dark, burning eyes swept over the faces of the half dozen white men who were standing in ill-concealed fright in front of the cabin. "Why did you send to Grande Ronde for white men to fight us?"

"We were scared," a settler answered. "We called for help because we thought you were going to fight us."

"You were wrong. We do not want to fight you. All we want is for you to leave our country."

"But if *you* want to fight," *Ollokot* declared belligerently, with grunts and *ah-taat*s of approval issuing menacingly from the throats of the painted warriors surrounding him, "we will give you all the fighting you want. When your friends come from Grande Ronde, we will find a piece of open ground where there is room for a big battle. When you are ready, give us a signal and the battle will begin."

"Oh, Lord, we don't want a battle!" exclaimed Tom Cochran, the father of one of the boastful young men. "That damn-fool kid of mine done too much talking, that's all!"

"He sure did!" Max Johnson growled, dragging Gerard Cochran, who was white-faced and trembling, through the milling mass of Indians to face Chief Joseph. "Now we'll let him talk some more, if he feels like it."

In the doorway of the cabin, Bertha Johnson had one hand on the right arm of an equally pale, shaking Al King, while her other hand gripped his right ear. In a desperate effort to stay inside the cabin, he had placed his left arm and left foot against the door jamb, where for the moment he stuck.

"Let go, you addle-brained fool!" she cried, twisting vigorously on the ear. "We wouldn't be having all this trouble if you had kept your big mouth shut and not bragged so much! Let go, I say!"

With a high-pitched squeal of anguish, the youngster ceased resisting and let himself be dragged out into the yard. Walking toward him, Chief Joseph, who was carrying a deadly looking two-foot-long war club in his right hand, placed its head in the palm of his left hand, then moved it up and down several times in front of the young man's face, as if debating whether to shove its handle against his throat or raise it high, swing it, and cleave his skull. Motioning to the Umatilla Indian who had relayed the threats, he spoke in harsh, guttural Nez Perce.

"Look at this man and tell me the truth. Is he the one who said he would kill me, scalp me, and tan my hide for a bridle?"

"Yes. He is the one."

Seeming to feel that his questions would sound more threatening if translated by a white man, Chief Joseph beckoned to John Crane, who moved forward. "Ask him the same question in English."

"He wants to know," John said coldly, "if you said you would kill him, scalp him, and tan his hide for a bridle?"

"Oh, no!" the youngster moaned. "I never said nothin' like that!"

"You lie!" the Umatilla Indian grunted, slapping Al King sharply in the face. "I speak and understand English good. That is exactly what you said!"

"I was just blowin' wind and didn't mean it at all! Honest to God, I didn't!"

"Tell him," Joseph said, again in Nez Perce, "if he is ready to start killing, scalping, and skinning me, here I am. If he is not ready to start on me, tell him I am ready to start on him."

Doing his best to keep his face straight and his voice stern, John translated. His knees turning to rubber, the youngster sagged and would have fallen had not Herbert King, his father, stepped forward and held him up.

"It was only a foolish boast, John, like any damn-fool kid might make. For God's sake, let's not start a war over it."

"He came close to doing just that."

"He's sorry for what he said. And so am I. Tell Joseph I'm moving out of the country at once—and taking him with me."

"We'll leave, too," Gerard Cochran's father promised. "Last thing in the world we want is trouble."

"Good!" Joseph grunted, without waiting for a translation. "My horse would not like a white-skin bridle anyway."

Thus, once again the good judgment and good will of Joseph and the Nez Perces prevented a violent response under great provocation. In early September, the Indians moved their campground to the shores of Wallowa Lake. On September 10, a company of cavalry under the command of Lieutenant A. G. Forse arrived in the valley. Shortly thereafter Lieutenant Forse met with Joseph, *Ollokot,* and other Nez Perce leaders and had a friendly discussion of current problems.

Following Forse's assurance that Findley and McNall would be tried for the killing of *Wil-lot-yah,* Joseph agreed to send two witnesses to Union, Oregon, to testify when the case came to trial. Forse then told him:

"You must keep your Indians out of the western part of the valley. So long as they are in the Wallowa country, they must remain where they are camped, near the lake."

"They will do so."

"Keep your stallions and horses away from those of the settlers. When your people need to go to stores and trading posts for supplies, they may do so. But the less contact they have with the whites, the fewer causes for conflict there will be."

"We agree to that, also. To show you that our hearts are good, my warriors will empty their guns of the bullets put in them when we thought we would have to defend ourselves from the volunteers."

Forming all the warriors in the band in a single, spread-out rank, Chief Joseph gave a signal. Raising their rifles to point at the sky, they fired in unison. Chief Joseph made the sign for peace; Lieutenant Forse saluted him; then they shook hands and parted.

In letters written after his return to Fort Walla Walla, Forse expressed the opinion that if he and his troops had not arrived when they did, there would have been bloodshed. He expressed confidence that Chief Joseph would keep his word. He noted that the settlers who had left the Wallowa Valley when the trouble began had returned. He urged that the matter of "right to this valley" be settled soon.

Agent John Monteith, General O. O. Howard, and other white officials had long been urging the same thing. In early November the slow-grinding wheels of government, which had left the fate of the region and the nontreaty Nez Perces in limbo for years, finally took measures to settle the question once and for all.

Meeting in Lapwai, a five-member commission appointed to study, debate, and solve the problem, reached a conclusion and made a recommendation to the Secretary of the Interior.

7

Because of the controversy over the ownership of the Wallowa country, Major Henry Clay Wood, assistant adjutant general of the Military Department of the Columbia, had been asked to make a careful study of the Treaties of 1855 and 1863 and amendments modifying them. In July, 1876 he turned in his report to General Howard, who passed it on to the Secretary of War with his endorsement. Major Wood's conclusions were:

"The non-treaty Nez Perces cannot in law be regarded as bound by the treaty of 1863; and in so far as it attempts to deprive them of a right to occupancy of any land its provisions are null and void."

Speaking of President Grant's 1875 action revoking the 1873 executive order which had established a reserve for Chief Joseph's band in the Wallowa country, Wood wrote bluntly:

"If not a crime, it was a blunder. In intercourse with the Indian it is not wise to speak with a forked tongue."

When John Crane told him about the report, Tall Bird was pleased. "Does this mean the Wallowa will be given back to us? Does this settle the question of ownership?"

"I doubt it, brother. But it should give the commissioners good legal reasons to make a decision in your favor."

"Who are the commissioners?"

According to what he had read, John said, two of the commissioners knew the Indians and the region, and three did not. Brigadier General O. O. Howard and Major H. C. Wood, who were both stationed in Portland, were familiar with the area and its problems. Members William Stickney of Washington, D.C., A. C. Barstow of Providence, Rhode Island, and the commission chairman, D. H. Jerome of Saginaw, Michigan, were not. Reading the expressed purpose of the commission —"to visit these Indians, with the view to secure their permanent settlement on the reservation, their early entrance on a civilized life, and to adjust the difficulties existing between them and the settlers"—John was troubled, for it sounded as if a decision to limit the freedom of the Chief Joseph band had already been made.

Indeed, such proved to be the case, John discovered when he and Tall Bird went with Joseph to Lapwai for the first meeting with the commissioners in November, 1876. Despite the fact that three members of the commission were not acquainted with the region in question, they attempted to convince Joseph that the Wallowa country was not suitable as a permanent home for his band because of a number of reasons:

"The coldness of the climate . . ."

"It is embraced within the limits of the State of Oregon which cannot be induced to cede jurisdiction . . ."

"In case of conflict between the Indians and the white settlers, the President might not be able to defend the Indians . . ."

To these not very solid arguments, Joseph replied:

"The earth is my mother. I cannot consent to leave the land that bore me. I ask nothing of the President. I am able to take care of myself."

Though Oregon's Governor Grover was not present at the council, a specious comment he had made three years ago was repeated:

"Joseph's band do not desire Wallowa Valley for a reservation and for a home. This small band wish the possession of this large section of Oregon simply for room to gratify a wild, roaming disposition and not for a home."

Chief Joseph's answer was as clear and eloquent now as it had been then:

"I have been talking to the whites for many years about the land in question, and it is strange that they cannot understand me. The country they claim belonged to my father, and when he died it was given to me and my people, and I will not leave it until I am compelled to."

As other councils had, this one broke up with no real meeting of minds, for neither side had listened to the other. Convinced that his band still owned the Wallowa, that no government edict could take the country from them, Chief Joseph and his party left Lapwai and went home. On their part, the commissioners made their decision and filed their report without bothering to let the Wallowa Nez Perces know their conclusions, which were:

1. That the Dreamer medicine men be confined to their agencies, since their influence on the nontreaty Indians is pernicious;

2. That a military post be established in the Wallowa Valley at once;

3. That unless in a reasonable time Joseph consents to be removed,

he should be forcibly taken with his people and given lands on the reservation;

4. That if members of his band overrun property belonging to the whites, or commit depredations, or disturb the peace by threats of hostility, then sufficient force should be employed to bring them into subjection.

Hearing about the report, Tall Bird was bewildered. "What is this nonsense about Dreamer medicine men?" he asked John Crane. "The Dreamers have no followers in the Wallowa band."

"I know they don't, brother. But as a good Presbyterian, John Monteith feels that any wild Indian who won't cut his hair, give up his horse, move onto the reservation and become a farmer is an uncivilizing influence. He's heard about the Dreamer Prophet Smohalla, who claims he died, spent a year in the Spirit Land, then came back to earth with a new religion. He's afraid the Dreamer faith will steal some of his converts."

"But it isn't a religion at all. It's a simple, harmless dream that if the Indians will put their trust in the Earth Mother and go back to living as they did in the old days before the white man came, all will be well."

"With the white man going back to where he came from?"

"Yes. That is part of their dream."

"And with all the animals and Indians that have died returning to life and reappearing on earth?"

"That, too. They feel if they have faith all the dead wild game and their dead friends will return. It is like the white man's belief in heaven. Only their heaven will come to earth."

John shook his head. "Not if Monteith can help it. To him, the Dreamer faith is sacrilege."

Though once again it had been the white authorities, not the Indians, who spoke of the use of force to achieve their ends, Major Wood, to his credit, refused to sign the report. Instead he made a minority recommendation that "until Joseph commits some overt act of hostility, force should not be used to put him upon any reservation."

Wasting no time, now that a course of action had been outlined, the Department of Interior decided early in January, 1877 to remove the Joseph band onto the Lapwai Reservation—by compulsion, if necessary. An order to that effect was issued to Agent Monteith. Given the authority he had long desired, Monteith sent a delegation of Reservation Nez Perces to Joseph's winter village in the lower Grande Ronde

Valley, asking him to move willingly and soon—or suffer the consequences.

Since Lawyer's death a year ago, Reuben had been head chief for the treaty Nez Perces. He was Joseph's brother-in-law. It was he who led the delegation. Going with him was his son, James Reuben; *Whisktasket*, Joseph's father-in-law; and Captain John, a Nez Perce chief long friendly to the whites. Despite these blood ties and the well-reasoned arguments of his relatives, Joseph refused to move to the reservation.

"The interpreters at the council must not have translated accurately," he said. "The commissioners must have misunderstood me."

But the misunderstandings lay at a far deeper level than inadequate translation, John Crane knew. When the delegation returned to Lapwai and reported to Monteith, the agent wrote grimly:

"I think from Joseph's actions, he will not come on the reserve until compelled to. He has said as much to the Indians who have moved on the reserve, calling them cowards, etc., that he would be lowering himself in his own estimation, as well as that of his immediate followers, did he not make some show of resistance. By making such resistance, he could say to the other Indians, 'I was overpowered, and did not come of my own choice,' in case he is forced on the reserve."

After making the sensible recommendation that the Joseph band be permitted to spend four to six weeks each summer fishing in the Imnaha country, where there were no roads or settlers, Monteith then threw good sense to the winds, writing J. Q. Smith, Commissioner of Indian Affairs, February 9, 1877:

"I have given Joseph until April 1, 1877, to come on the reserve peaceably. They can come one time just as well as another, having nothing to hinder them in moving."

To John Crane, Monteith's statement was a clear indication that he knew little and cared less about the life-style of the nontreaty Indians. Most of their wealth was portable, true, but moving took time and could be done only in the proper season. Thousands of their horses and cattle were grazing now over the grassy flats and sheltered draws of the lower country; soon they would drop foals and calves. After a winter on the range and with offspring to nurse, the mares and cows would have neither the strength nor disposition to be rounded up and forced into a rigorous drive, which their young could not possibly survive.

Winter still lay on the land; snowdrifts covered the trails to the high country; no tracts of land had been set aside for the Joseph band on the Lapwai Reservation; no supplies of food, clothing and fuel awaited them there.

March, April, and May were root-gathering months. June was the month for moving livestock out of the lower valleys toward higher pasture. July and August were months for camas-gathering and fish-catching and curing. September and October were hunting months when the family laid in a supply of deer and elk meat and made pemmican for the winter food larder. By mid-October horses and cattle would be in good condition. Rivers such as the Snake, Salmon, and Clearwater would be at their lowest stage and could be easily crossed. Enough time would have elapsed to have selected homesites on the Lapwai Reservation and to have prepared the nontreaty Nez Perces emotionally for the soul-wrenching process of removing them permanently from their ancestral homeland. If the move had to be made, November 1 would have been a reasonable deadline. April 1 was ridiculous.

Though Chief Joseph and the leaders of the other nontreaty bands had successfully ignored Agent Monteith's moving date, they did agree to meet in council with General Howard at Lapwai May 3, 1877. Knowing how important these talks would be, the chiefs of the five dissident bands held a conference a few weeks earlier in which they decided upon the strategy they would pursue. Tall Bird reported their decisions to John Crane.

"Looking Glass will speak for the Kooskia band, White Bird for the Salmon River, *Hush-hush Cute* for the Asotin, *Too-hool-hool-zote* for the Snake River, and Joseph for the Wallowa. The chiefs agree that *Too-hool-hool-zote* should be the principal spokesman, for he is the firmest of all the leaders and will take the strongest stand."

"He's a Dreamer, I hear. That won't set well with Monteith and Howard."

"We are not going to the council to please them. We are going to save our homelands. But if *Too-hool-hool-zote* speaks too strong, the chiefs will let White Bird, who is older, talk more gently, though he will still make the whites think we might go to war. If the voice of a younger chief who has proved his ability in conflict with the Sioux is needed, Looking Glass will speak."

"What role will Joseph play?"

"As the most eloquent of all the chiefs, he will remain in the background until a final voice of wisdom is needed to make the ultimate bargain. In the end, it will be he who says yes or no."

"Well, I wish you luck, brother. You're going to need it."

Because Chief Joseph asked him to attend the council as a friend and interpreter, John Crane went to Lapwai with the party of Wallowa Nez Perces, which numbered fifty. From the beginning it was evident that

General Howard had made up his mind to force the five nontreaty bands to move onto the Reservation, whether they wanted to or not. It was also clear that he meant to put up with no nonsense from dissidents, for, after threatening to arrest and punish two "old Dreamers for being saucy and quarrelsome," he was reported to have told Monteith curtly:

"Severity of manner in dealing with savages is believed by many of the Indians' friends to be always uncalled for and decidedly wrong. It may be so, but the manner of dealing must depend upon the peculiarities of the people with whom you have to deal."

Agent Monteith piously agreed. Exactly which tenet of Howard's avowed Christianity allowed him to base his "uncalled for and decidedly wrong" behavior on "the peculiarities" of the people he was dealing with, he did not bother to state. But then, John Crane supposed, as a devout Christian and the army general in charge of the Department of the Columbia, he was not required to explain his actions to any lesser beings than God and the Secretary of War.

On the fourth day of the council, which had been opened with a prayer by a Christianized treaty Nez Perce named Alpowa Jim, the growing hostility between General Howard and the Indians' principal spokesman, *Too-hool-hool-zote,* exploded.

"We do not want to interfere with your religion," Howard said testily. "But you must talk about practicable things. Twenty times over you repeat that the earth is your mother. Let us hear it no more, but come to the business at once."

"What is the business?"

"Do you intend coming on the reservation peacefully? Or shall I put you there with my soldiers?"

"You threaten us with guns and soldiers?"

"Yes, I do. I have brought enough men and guns with me to enforce my order."

"What person pretends to divide the land?" *Too-hool-hool-zote* asked angrily. "Who says where he will put me on it?"

"I am that man. I give you thirty days to move."

"You have brought a rifle to a peace council. Do you mean but thirty suns for gathering our stock?"

"Yes. That is exactly what I mean."

"We will not do it. We will fight."

Though Howard, Monteith, and some of the white army officers present later claimed that the Indians turned hostile, growled angrily, and had a gun, knife, or tomahawk under every blanket, thus forcing General Howard to take the action he did in order to prevent a massacre, the only reaction John Crane observed was a stunned dismay on the faces of the Indians, followed by audible expressions of shock. As *Too-hool-hool-zote* moved forward a step, Howard leaped to his feet and pointed at him.

"Captain Perry!"

"Sir!"

"Arrest that Indian and throw him in the guardhouse!"

"Yes, sir! Corporal of the guard! Use whatever force is required!"

Under other circumstances, John Crane mused sardonically, the use of force by a corporal and a couple of privates would not have sufficed to subdue and imprison the tough old Dreamer chief, *Too-hool-hool-zote.* Among members of his band, his strength was legendary.

"He once shouldered and carried two full-grown black-tailed buck deer he had killed down out of the mountains to his lodge," Tall Bird had told John. "No other man has ever done that. Another time, when he went on a drunk and became bothersome, some of his friends thought to quiet him by throwing him down and tying him up. Eight men took hold of him but could not get him down, and were obliged to let him go."

But now, for some reason, he made no resistance, quietly submitting to the indignity of being arrested by the corporal's guard, led away, and confined in the Fort Lapwai guardhouse.

The charade of a friendly discussion between the whites and the non-treaty Nez Perces was over. The truth was, John Crane learned, it had been a farce from the very beginning. Even on the day the council began, Agent Monteith had handed General Howard an official letter, which read:

"I would respectfully request that you assist me in the removal of Joseph's and other roving bands of Nez Perce Indians and to locate them upon proper lands within the boundaries of the Nez Perce Reservation by the use of such troops as you may deem necessary."

To the leaders of the free-roaming bands, there were no options left but to give in or fight. With Chief *Too-hool-hool-zote* imprisoned and the rifles of the soldiers aimed at their hearts, White Bird, Looking Glass, *Hush-hush Cute,* and Joseph accepted the inevitable. After making a brief tour of the reserve escorted by General Howard and Agent Monteith, they selected the lands onto which they would presently move their livestock, lodges, and all their earthly possessions. Returning to Fort Lapwai, they respectfully requested that *Too-hool-hool-zote* be released. When freed, he, too, accepted the fact that he must move onto the reservation.

The date was May 14, 1877. The nontreaty bands were given exactly thirty days to collect their animals and material possessions and become what God had not made them to be—reservation Indians for the rest of their mortal days on this earth.

Chief Joseph made one final attempt to delay the move, protesting:

"Our stock is scattered and the Snake River is very high. Let us wait till fall, then the river will be low. We want time to hunt up our stock and gather supplies for the winter."

But General Howard would not be swayed from the course he had chosen, replying:

"If you let the time run over one day, the soldiers will be there to drive you on the reservation, and cattle outside the reservation at that time will fall into the hands of the white men . . ."

PART TWO

WAR AND A KIND OF PEACE
1877–1879

1

The task confronting the Wallowa Nez Perces—rounding up all their livestock and moving all their people and possessions a hundred miles in a month's time—was impossible, John Crane felt. The extent of country over which their horses and cattle ranged comprised a million acres of extremely rugged terrain. Male adult members of the band available to ride in the roundup numbered no more than sixty—barely an adequate crew for a summer-long gathering of livestock scattered over the area, and certainly not capable of finding and driving thousands of winter-thin, spooky animals from their wilderness range to the Lapwai Reservation in only one month's time.

Because snowmelt in the high country supplied the major portion of water for the region's rivers, the Wallowa, Imnaha, Grande Ronde, Snake, and Salmon all became raging torrents between mid-May and mid-June, dangerous to strong, mature horses and cattle forced to breast the rapid currents, and sure death to the weak and young. Knowing that any Indian livestock left behind would fall into their hands, white settlers in the area were certainly not going to assist the Nez Perces in flushing out strays.

In order to make sure that the Joseph band complied with his directive to move onto the Lapwai Reservation, General Howard sent Captain S. G. Whipple with a command of five officers, ninety-seven enlisted men, and a Gatling gun into the Wallowa country. Marching his troops north to the Grande Ronde over rugged, mountainous, broken country, Whipple took three days to ride only fifty miles.

Though none of the Nez Perces complained about the weather for the next few weeks, Captain Whipple certainly did:

"During the entire month, the weather has been most unpropitious for field operations, there having been long rain storms—with some snow—or frequent hard showers. The ground was made very soft by the excess of moisture which rendered travel very difficult, the horses sinking at nearly every step to the fetlocks, and much of the way to a greater depth. Particularly this was the case from the camp to the Lewiston crossing of the Grande Ronde. From the Wallowa Valley to the last named point there is no other road than an Indian trail upon which no labor has ever been done and over which no wheeled vehicle has been, and as a great portion of the distance is heavily timbered and swampy, taking the Gatling gun through proved laborious."

At this same time, in the same weather, and over even more difficult terrain, John Crane, Tall Bird, and sixty Nez Perce men were laboriously combing the hills and hollows to round up whatever horses and cattle they could find in the short time allotted them, while back in their villages the women, children, and old people packed, pulled down the tepees, and prepared to move. Incredibly, by the end of May the Indians had rounded up what John guessed to be around six thousand head of livestock, and were loose-herding the animals on the new spring grass of the lower Imnaha Valley.

Running in full early-summer flood, the Snake in the depths of the Big Canyon was a monstrous river. Varying in width from several hundred yards to as little as sixty-two feet, it carried a tremendous volume of water through the mile-deep gorge, its current moving with such force that no animal or human pulled into its whirlpools, falls, and rapids could possibly survive. Usually the river did not frighten the Nez Perces, John knew, for they had been crossing it from time immemorial and knew how to overcome its hazards. But never before, Tall Bird told him, had they tried to cross the Snake with their livestock and families here at Big Eddy when it was running so high.

Though they had no wooden boats or rafts, the Nez Perces quickly converted the skin coverings of their tepees into round, watertight bundles that served well for crossing the river. Watching the preparations, John marveled at the skill with which the Indians worked. While the large herds of horses and cattle were held beyond the ridge on the flats of the lower Imnaha, the long, narrow gravel bar on the west bank of the Snake was covered with spread-out tepee skins which, after being loaded with goods and belongings, were made into rounded bales, with the skins tightly roped so that the goods would be protected from the water. On top of the bundles, which were buoyant and would support considerable weight for a time, sat the women, children, and old men too feeble to swim, seizing whatever hold they could find. Tying tow-ropes to each bale, two strong young men mounted their best-swimming horses stripped to their breechclouts, dragged their burden into the water, and then set out for the far shore.

All involved made a game of it, the young swimmers howling in mock anguish as the icy water engulfed them, shouting insults at one another, while the women screamed instructions, the children squealed with glee, and the old men moaned in complaint, a few of them chanting personal death-songs as bundles on which they were riding tilted and they feared that their time had come. But the game could turn deadly serious, John knew, for more skill was required of the leading swimmers than simply pointing the noses of their horses at the far bank and putting them into the water.

"We learned long ago that the *Ki-moo-e-nim* is too strong a river to fight," Tall Bird told John, as they followed the progress of the towed bales with their precious human burdens across the channel. "We use its power to help us go where we want to go. Here at Big Eddy, so much water flows down the river and the channel is so narrow that some of the water is forced to circle, moving across from this side to the other, flowing upstream for a short ways, then turning back toward this shore to join the main current, and again heading downriver. The trick for the swimmers towing the bundles is to keep the heads and bodies of their horses angled into the current in such a manner that the force of the water will push them across the channel rather than downstream."

"As it would if they tried to swim directly across," John said, nodding. "But if horse and rider don't know what they're doing, they can panic and drown."

"It happens, yes. But these men and horses have swum many rivers."

Miraculously, by the end of the long day every man, woman, and child in the Wallowa band had been transported safely from the Oregon to the Idaho side of the river, without a single person being lost. But next day, when the huge herd of horses and cattle was driven across the ridge, down to the long gravel bar, and then forced into the surging current, the loss of life by drowning, turning back, and bolting out of control was considerable, for with so many wild, spooky animals to handle there was no way they could be led across one by one.

Bunching the stock into mixed herds of horses and cattle numbering five hundred or so, which was all they could handle at one time, with several strong-swimming Nez Perces on river-wise horses riding point and leading the herd into the river, the animals were stampeded by shouts and waved blankets between twin lines of mounted flankers whose duty was to keep the stock moving in the right direction. Once into the icy water, there was little the herders could do to control the swimming beasts. So long as they kept their noses angled slightly upstream, stayed afloat, and followed the leaders, the force of the eddying current quickly pushed them across the river and into the shallows near the far shore. But when a colt or a calf that had never before swum in such adverse conditions bleated in panic, swallowed water, and instinctively tried to turn back toward the safety of the solid ground it had just left, its mother turned, too. Once a mill formed and the swimming animals lost the aid of the cross-channel current, they were doomed, for downstream from the eddy churned rapids and whirlpools too powerful to overcome.

By late afternoon, the last of the horses and cattle had been forced into the water, with the survivors joining the stock being herded up the canyon trail rising from the Idaho side of the Snake. Tall Bird's son-in-law, Lame Brown Bear, who had crossed and recrossed the river many times during the past two days as he towed bundles and led herds, limped across the gravel bar leading a pair of horses. Respectfully, he stood in silence while John Crane made one last attempt to reason with his brother.

"For God's sake, Tall Bird, you're too old to swim the river."

"It won't be me swimming, it will be the horse. Lame Brown Bear says it's half sturgeon."

"That water's ice-cold, brother. It'll freeze your balls off."

"Much older men than I already have crossed with the Joseph band. My people plan to gather at *Te-pah-le-wam* for one final ceremony as free *Nimipu*. I want to be with them."

John understood that. "Have it your way," he said, extending his hand. "Come home when you can."

Helping Tall Bird up to the back of a sturdy gray horse, Lame Brown Bear tossed him the single rein, mounted his own horse, then gave John a smile. "Do not worry, brother. I will not let him drown. If I did, Singing Bird would never forgive me."

Watching them cross the river with no difficulty, John answered their salute as they turned to wave at him from the far side, then wheeled his horse around and headed for home. As he crossed the ridge, faint shouts of triumph reached his ears from the heights above. Looking up, he could see several mounted white men standing in their stirrups, circling their hats in the air, celebrating the departure forever of a race that had lived free in the Wallowa for ten thousand years. Best he could make out, they would be two or three hundred yards away. Absently touching the recently purchased '73 Winchester in the saddle scabbard under his leg, he found himself wishing one of the scaly bastards up yonder would take a potshot at him, giving him an excuse to try out the rifle's range and accuracy.

But much to his disgust, none of the scaly bastards did . . .

2

Long a traditional meeting place for the Nez Perces, *Te-pah-le-wam*—
"Split Rocks" or "Deep Cuts"—was a large, open flat, lying deep in the
canyon of the Salmon River, with plenty of room on which to graze
livestock, pitch tepees, race horses, have parades, and stage mock war
games. Nearby, a small body of water, Tolo Lake, was convenient for
people and animals. With the southern border of the Lapwai Reservation only a day's easy travel away and with a week still remaining
before the June 14 deadline, the five bands of Nez Perces considered by
General Howard and Agent John Monteith to be "unsettled," went into
camp and prepared to spend the brief time of freedom left them mourning a way of life they would live no more and speculating upon what
appeared to be a very bleak future.

In total numbers, they comprised only one fifth of the Nez Perce
tribe, Tall Bird knew. The largest band, the Wallowa, numbered around
sixty adult males of warrior age, though few had ever done any fighting.
Joseph certainly could not be regarded as a war chief, for he had made
only one trip to the buffalo country as an adult and had never been in a
battle. He was primarily a man of peace, determined to avoid bloodshed
at any cost, as his final acceptance of leaving his beloved Wallowa
homeland had proved.

If physical acts of bravery and valor were to be required, his younger
brother *Ollokot*—"Frog"—was far better equipped to perform them
than he. Several years younger, standing six feet, two inches in moccasins, with a jovial, mischievous manner but a glint in his eye that hinted
at the sleeping fighter within him, *Ollokot* was respected by all the band
as the leading warrior among the Wallowas. Yet he accepted Joseph's
decisions as chief.

Second in size was the White Bird band, which numbered around
fifty men of warrior age. Called *Peo-peo Hih-hih* by the *Nimipu*, White
Bird was in his seventies, the oldest of the nontreaty chiefs. Standing a
little under six feet, he bore himself with great dignity and commanded

attention wherever present. Being a medicine man and boasting a long line of noted warrior ancestors, his influence was considerable. Though mild of temper and speech, his sojourns in the buffalo country and his experience in warfare assured him of being given an honored place in all councils. The homeland of his people lay along the Salmon and nearby White Bird Canyon.

The third band of nontreaty Nez Perces was headed by Chief Looking Glass. Numbering no more than forty men of warrior age, a small portion of the Kooskia band's domain lay within the reservation while the larger part, over which the band felt free to roam, extended eastward toward the crest of the Bitter Root Mountains. Since they were not being forced to move, their presence at *Te-pah-le-wam* was an expression of sympathy for the Chief Joseph band and a manifestation of loss for the Wallowa, which was a place all *Nimipu* loved.

Leading the fourth band, which numbered around thirty men, was the strongman of the tribe, the tough, indomitable old Dreamer, *Too-hool-hool-zote,* whom General Howard had contemptuously dubbed the "cross-grained growler" before losing patience with him and throwing him in the guardhouse. Because of his strength of character and reputation as a war chief, he was always listened to in council, Tall Bird knew. But as he had proved at Lapwai, rather than involve his people in a war they could not win, he would suffer personal indignity and follow the path of peace. The domain of his band lay along the lower Salmon River and its confluence with the Snake.

Last of the nontreaty Nez Perces assembled near Tolo Lake was the once proud, now fragmented remnant of the Palouse band, a mere sixteen warriors, led by Chief *Hah-tal-e-kin,* who lived with one group near Palouse Falls, and by *Hush-hush Cute*—"Naked Head," who lived with another, known as the *Wa-wai-wai* band, fifty miles up the Snake River. Like *Too-hool-hool-zote, Hush-hush Cute* was a proponent of the Dreamer faith—and thus a target for General Howard's dislike and contempt.

In all, the Nez Perces camped in White Bird's territory on June 12, 1877—two days before the deadline for their moving onto the Lapwai Reservation—numbered about six hundred souls. Of these, most were women and children. Because this was an important event in the long history of the *Nimipu,* which must be noted, remembered, and passed on verbally to generations yet to come, Tall Bird knew that *Howlis Wonpoon*—"War Singer"—was exercising great care and judgment in learning the names of the people present and the details of what they did.

A stooped, wrinkled, mild-mannered member of the White Bird band, War Singer was in his late sixties and known throughout the tribe for his remarkable memory. For time beyond recall, members of his family had observed and listened to happenings important in tribal history, so that they could be remembered and passed on. Though the "war singer," as such a tribal historian was called, could not be present to personally observe everything that happened, it was long-standing custom among the *Nimipu* that when a war party returned from a battle, when a hunting expedition came back from the buffalo country, or when a traveler to a distant land rejoined his people after seeing or doing unusual things, these individuals would have long talks with the war singer so that the happenings would always be remembered.

As a final salute to a way of life they would lead no more, War Singer related, the Nez Perces camping at *Te-pah-le-wam* staged a parade June 13, the day before they were to move onto the plots of land selected for them within the boundaries of the Lapwai Reservation.

Riding double at the rear of the column on a single horse were two young men of the White Bird band, *Wah-litits*—"Shore Crossing"—and *Sarp-sis Ilp-ilp*—"Red Moccasin Tops." Known to be fine, upstanding young men of good family and character, they were first cousins—or, in Indian parlance, "brothers."

Wah-litits was mounted in front. While passing through the camp, his horse accidentally stepped on a spread-out canvas covered with *kouse* roots drying in the sun. Seeing this, an older man, *Hey-oom Mox-mox*—"Yellow Grizzly Bear"—shouted angrily at the young rider.

"See what you do! Playing brave, you ride over my woman's hard-worked food! If you so brave, why you not go kill the white man who killed your father?"

A few years earlier, War Singer explained, *Wah-litits*'s father, Eagle Robe, had owned and farmed a piece of land near Slate Creek in the lower Salmon River country. With his permission a white man named Larry Ott settled nearby. Though at first promising not to trespass on Eagle Robe's garden spot, Ott gradually took more and more land, until finally one day he built a fence that excluded the Nez Perce from his own property. Eagle Robe protested, an argument ensued, and suddenly without provocation Larry Ott grabbed a gun and shot the Indian.

Not wanting to start a war, Eagle Robe, as he lay dying, told his son, who at that time was still a boy: "Do nothing to the white man for what he has done to me. Let him live his life."

Growing to manhood, *Wah-litits* had respected his father's command. But now, stung by the taunt and burning with resentment at being forced by the whites to give up his freedom and leave his home, he said to Yellow Grizzly Bear, "You will be sorry for your words."

When the parade was over, *Wah-litits* went home and cried, according to War Singer. Then he sought his "brother," *Sarp-sis Ilp-ilp,* and told him he had decided to avenge his father's death and show that he was a man by killing Larry Ott. Would his brother join him? *Sarp-sis Ilp-ilp* said that he would. The revenge-seeking Indians left the village early the next morning, heading for Larry Ott's cabin. Accompanying them was a seventeen-year-old nephew, *Wet-yet-mas Wah-yakt*—"Swan Necklace"—whom *Wah-litits* ordered to come along as a "horseholder," without divulging the purpose of his mission.

Whether the white man had taken alarm and fled or just happened not to be at home was not clear, War Singer said. By one account, Larry Ott had become so frightened at the presence of the large encampment of Nez Perces in the neighborhood that he had disguised himself as a Chinese, joined a group of Orientals mining near Florence, and thus escaped discovery and death. In any event he was not home when the aroused young Nez Perces reached his cabin. But they had no trouble finding other white men who, in their minds, deserved to die.

The first was a settler named Richard Devine.

A crotchety, elderly man living alone on the Salmon River eight miles above the mouth of Slate Creek, Devine was known to have killed a crippled Nez Perce woman, *Da-koop-pin* for an offense no greater than her removing one of his horses that had strayed into her garden. More recently, he had set his vicious dogs on Indians passing by his place and had threatened them with his rifle.

But this time neither his dogs nor his rifle protected him. Invading his cabin without warning, *Wah-litits* and *Sarp-sis Ilp-ilp* took the gun away from Devine before he could use it, killed him with it, helped themselves to a supply of cartridges and a horse, then rode in search of other victims.

The second man killed was a rancher named Henry Elfers. He, too, had a reputation for abusing Indians.

Returning to the vicinity of the *Te-pah-le-wam* camp, the two warrior Indians stopped some distance away, sending young Swan Necklace into the village to tell the people what they had done. They did this for two reasons, War Singer said: first, to show that theirs had been an act of personal vengeance, for which the White Bird band as a whole was not responsible; second, to invite individual warriors who felt as they did to join them in further acts of retribution against the whites—again, without involving the entire White Bird band. Next morning they were joined by sixteen young Nez Perces who were burning with a spirit of revenge.

When the first attacks took place, Joseph and *Ollokot* were some miles away, killing beef cattle south of the Salmon River. Tall Bird was with the party, which included several women to do the butchering and a number of horses to carry the meat back to camp. After spending several days in the area, the party had a dozen horses loaded with meat as it neared the home village. Seeing a rider approaching at a dead run, *Ollokot* said to Joseph, "Look, it is Two Moons. He is in a hurry. He must have news."

"War has broke out!" Two Moons shouted, reining his horse to a halt. "Three white men killed yesterday!"

"Come, brother," Joseph said. "We must see about this." As he and *Ollokot* started to ride to the camp with Two Moons, Joseph spoke to Tall Bird. "You will stay with the women and help them take the meat to the village?"

"Yes. I will stay and help them."

By the time Tall Bird reached the camp with the women and the laden horses, it was a turmoil of activity, with lodges being struck, horses packed, and almost all of the *Nimipu* present preparing to desert the area and seek refuge in their home villages. Chief Joseph and *Ollokot* were riding among them, imploring them not to move.

"We are not at war with the whites," Joseph said. "What has happened was done by a few rash young men. They will be held responsible for the killings."

"The Army will come," White Bird answered. "When it does, I want my people to be in their home village, where we can defend ourselves if we have to."

"Yes, I know the Army will come. But let us stay here together, ready to greet the white men with friendship. The Cut-Arm Chief is a reasonable man. We can make some kind of peace with him."

But the two brothers could make no one listen. Panicked by what had happened, all the Nez Perces except Joseph and *Ollokot* were determined to leave *Te-pah-le-wam* at once, as if the physical act of deserting the spot would separate them from the terrible event that had been instigated there and the awful consequences it was sure to bring. Talking it over with his son, Swift Bird, Tall Bird learned that Chief Looking Glass had declared firmly:

"If war comes, it is White Bird's war, not mine. I am taking my people back to our village at Kooskia. There, we will keep the peace, no matter what happens elsewhere."

Deciding that their bands, too, should break away from the people and place where the first bloodshed had occurred, *Hush-hush Cute* and *Hah-tal-e-kin*, with their Palouse band, and *Too-hool-hool-zote*, with his lower Salmon River band, chose to join Looking Glass and his people in their Kooskia village, which was well removed from White Bird's territory yet was within the boundaries of the reservation, offering whatever protection that location might afford.

Since the Wallowa band had agreed to take allotted plots of land in the Lapwai area and had many blood ties there, most of these families chose to move with White Bird and his people to the village he called home. Since his daughter, Singing Bird, was going there with her family, while his son, Swift Bird, was going to Kooskia with his family, Tall Bird was torn as to where he himself should go.

"Come stay with us for a while," Swift Bird urged. "Joseph says that when the Cut-Arm Chief comes, he will offer to make peace if White Bird will surrender the young men who committed the murders. But this will take time. Until peace is made and the Wallowa Nez Perces are settled on the reservation, Singing Bird will find it difficult to make a home for you. In the Kooskia village, my family already has a home, with a fine garden, a cow, chickens, and pigs, and plenty to eat."

Tall Bird shook his head. "I am worried over what Joseph and *Ollokot* are saying. Do you really believe the Cut-Arm Chief will talk peace? Or will he simply send his soldiers to make war?"

"Looking Glass is worried, too. He has heard talk that Joseph and *Ollokot* plan to desert their people, slip away in the dark of night, go to Lapwai and surrender on any terms they can get, leaving the rest to fight on their own."

"This is foolish talk! There is no war yet. Why should they not talk peace?"

"I only tell you what people say. But you would be wise, Father, to come home with me."

In the end, Tall Bird agreed that this was the thing to do. By the middle of the next morning, only two tepees remained on the well-worn flat of *Te-pah-le-wam*, those of Joseph and *Ollokot*. Had it not been for the fact that his wife was expecting to give birth to a baby any moment now, Chief Joseph probably would have acquiesced to the wishes of his people and joined their move to the lower reaches of White Bird Canyon, which lay a half day's travel to the east. But as Tall Bird told him goodbye, he still appeared to be hopeful that the rash actions of the young men would not set off a war.

"The Cut-Arm Chief knows my heart," he said calmly. "I know his. We both are honorable men who have chosen to follow the path of peace. There will be no war . . ."

3

Peacefully inclined as he was, Chief Joseph did not know how inflammatory news of Indians murdering settlers could be in the white world, whose system of communication had become incredibly rapid. As word of the killings was carried first to the nearby towns of Mount Idaho and Grangeville, then to Fort Lapwai, and thence to Fort Walla Walla and the country at large, the minor uprising was magnified into a full-scale war even before a single soldier became involved.

In all, during the three days of bloodletting, the reported number of white victims killed by the Nez Perces in the Salmon River and Mount Idaho area ranged from fourteen to twenty-two, according to whose figures were accepted as accurate. General Howard gave the lower figure; a local resident named Arthur Chapman the higher.

From what Tall Bird knew about Chapman, the man was not to be trusted, even though he had married a Umatilla woman, spoke the Nez Perce language fluently, and was on friendly terms with Looking Glass. Like other white men living on the border of the reservation, he raised horses and cattle, did some trading, and always had a supply of whiskey on hand, which he was not against selling to white or Indian buyers. For a time he had operated a ferry across the Salmon River near the mouth of White Bird Canyon, from which experience his white friends had facetiously dubbed him "Admiral," which they later abbreviated to "Ad."

When the uprising broke out, he was living on Cottonwood Creek, eight miles southeast of Grangeville, near the trail traveled by the Looking Glass band on its way from *Te-pah-le-wam* to their Kooskia village. Though Swift Bird told his father that Arthur Chapman was disliked because he was suspected of stealing and selling Nez Perce cattle to Chinese miners at Florence, he apparently had dealt honestly enough with Looking Glass during horse-trading deals. As the owner of four hundred horses and a valued potential buyer, he was, in the view of Looking Glass, entitled to be told what had happened. Accompanied by his brother, *Tu-cal-las-a-sena,* Looking Glass personally carried the warning to him.

"The young men of White Bird's band are killing whites," Looking Glass said. "Already, seven white men are dead. You must leave your ranch and go to Mount Idaho."

"Well, if war has really broke out, I reckon you're right. I'll tell my woman to start packing."

"No! There is no time to pack. Get on your horse and go!"

Reaching the small settlement of Mount Idaho, Ad Chapman, as the local expert on Indian and military matters, had no difficulty convincing the townspeople and outlying settlers what must be done. First a messenger was dispatched to Fort Lapwai, sixty-five miles to the northwest, with word of what had happened. Second, a council was held, its chief subject being what the local whites could do to defend themselves. In short order, it was decided that a company of volunteers must be organized. By unanimous vote, Ad Chapman was elected its captain.

Next morning, Chapman again met with Looking Glass and his brother, who gave him the latest news of the continuing killings on the Salmon River.

"But my band is not at war," Looking Glass insisted. "We will go back to our village at Kooskia and remain at peace, no matter what happens in White Bird's country."

"We'd ought to tell General Howard there's been more killings," Chapman said. "But I doubt if a white messenger will risk riding to Fort Lapwai, just now. Would your brother go?"

"Yes. He will carry whatever message you wish to send the Cut-Arm Chief. When you write that message, be sure and say what I have told you—that this is White Bird's war, not mine, and that my people will take no part in it."

"Sure. I'll tell him that."

Since General Howard had just arrived at Fort Lapwai to make sure that the nontreaty Nez Perces were moving onto the reservation by June 14, there was no need for the post's commandant, Captain David Perry, who held the brevet rank of Colonel, to waste any time requesting orders from his superior. Feeling he must send relief to the white settlers, and convinced that at least five hundred hostiles were already committed to war, Howard gave no thought to negotiating peace. Available for duty at Fort Lapwai were only two companies of cavalry; just under one hundred men. Certainly he was not going to risk a major engagement with such odds against him.

"I do not intend to feed the enemy with driblets," he told Perry. "All I expect you to do is keep the hostiles engaged and contained until reinforcements can be brought up."

Those reinforcements would include Captain Whipple's two companies now stationed in the Wallowa country, a contingent of infantry summoned from Fort Walla Walla, and however many more troops might be drawn from other parts of General Howard's district. Though the pack train being assembled at Lewiston had not returned to Fort Lapwai by evening, June 15, Captain Perry, whose men had been issued five days' rations and forty rounds of ammunition apiece, asked permission of General Howard to leave without waiting for the support group. Confident in the officer's ability and judgment, Howard granted the request. As the column prepared to depart in the warm, early summer dusk, Perry saluted and said:

"Goodbye, General!"

"Goodbye, Colonel. You must not get whipped."

"There is no danger of that, sir."

After the soldiers had disappeared into the growing darkness, General Howard retired to his quarters, where for the next several nights and days he fretted in deep concern for his officers and men. But he was confident enough to write in one of his official dispatches:

"Think they will make short work of it."

Custer had thought that, too . . .

4

The stark reality of the terse account written by Sergeant John P. Schorr, Company F, Twenty-first Cavalry, gave a truer picture of the first encounter between the federal troops and the Nez Perces than later reports written by officers.

We left Fort Lapwai about 8 P.M. on the 15th, and rode all that night with a short rest to get a bite to eat for man and horse. We then again took up the march and on 16th June we saw the many depredations committed by the Indians such as killing of horses, and robbing prairie schooners and burning down ranches. I guess the Red Devils were pretty well filled up with firewater.

Noon on the 16th found us at Cottonwood. Here we had another short rest, then off again for Mount Idaho, arrived there about 10 P.M., and with about four hours rest we were in the saddle again.

At 2 A.M. we were rousted out of what little sleep we could catch in the saddle when a halt without dismounting was ordered. We were near entering White Bird Canyon to make a surprise attack on the Indians at daybreak. But let me state right here, we were to have the surprise of our lives . . .

In view of the odds Captain Perry thought were facing him, a surprise attack was not a part of his strategy. True, pressures had been put on him that were hard to resist. Late the previous afternoon, a group of citizens led by Ad Chapman had ridden out to meet the soldiers. Being unacquainted with the terrain, Perry asked Chapman to come along as a guide and to supply him with as many citizen volunteers as he could muster. Chapman promised "twenty-five or thirty" men. But when the group showed up it numbered only eleven.

"Where are the others?" Perry asked.

"Hell, Captain, you know how settlers are. Some are talkers an' some are fighters. These men are fighters."

"Before we commit ourselves to a battle, I'd like to know exactly what we're up against. Can you tell me where the hostiles are camped?"

"White Bird's village is down at the bottom of the canyon, just this side of the Salmon. Least, that's where it was a few days ago. Once them cowardly bucks of his'n heard soldiers was comin', a lot of 'em cut an' run, takin' their stolen stock with 'em. Unless we attack 'em at first light, they'll be scattered to hell and gone."

"You don't think they'll put up much of a defense?"

"No, I don't, Captain. I'm real well acquainted with them White Bird Nez Perces. A bunch of cowardly scoundrels, that's what they are. Give us volunteers enough rifles, we could whip 'em easy by ourselves."

Though Captain Perry was too cautious a commander to accept a civilian's assessment of the situation at face value, he realized that if he let the Indians escape without making an effort to overtake them, he would be severely criticized by the local settlers. Deciding to lay the matter before his officers, he summoned Captain Trimble and Lieutenants Parnell and Theller to a conference.

"According to the best information Ad Chapman has gathered, the hostiles are camped in a large village at the lower end of White Bird Canyon. Unless headed off and prevented from crossing the Salmon, they will disperse the moment they sight our soldiers, he feels, taking the stock they have stolen and the murderers who have killed the settlers with them."

"Which means we attack or let them get away?" Captain Trimble said.

"It would seem so, yes."

"What are the chances for surprising them?"

"Good, Chapman says. Since I haven't seen the terrain myself, I'm reluctant to order an attack until we learn what we're up against. As I understand it, after we top the crest at the head of the Canyon, there's a steep drop of several thousand feet in a distance of three or four miles. If we go as far as the crest by midnight or so, we can wait there for daylight—which at this time of year will come a little after two o'clock in the morning."

"Which is when we attack?" Lieutenant Theller asked.

"Which is when we advance cautiously, with scouting parties ahead and proper reconnaissance taken to make sure we know what we're getting into. Despite what's been said about the poor fighting ability of the Indians, I do not intend to take chances."

"Oh, hell, the bastards will run when the bullets start to fly!" Chapman grunted. "You can take my word for that!"

After discussing the situation briefly with the other two officers, Captain Trimble said, "Sir, we are in agreement. We think an attempt should be made to bring the hostiles to bay as quickly as possible."

With his staff's approval, Captain Perry gave the order to ride in total silence to the head of White Bird Canyon.

The force waiting now in the predawn darkness consisted of ninety-nine officers and men of the United States Army, most of whom because of budgetary restraints had fired only a few shots in practice and none in battle; eleven citizen volunteers with no training or discipline whatsoever; and half a dozen Lapwai Nez Perces who had come along as scouts and interpreters and carried no arms.

In just thirty hours, the command had traveled more than seventy miles over steep, muddy, timbered terrain. With both man and beast bone-weary, the unseasoned troops, untrained mounts, and undisciplined volunteers sat waiting for first light, when they could go riding down the steep, rocky slope of a deep canyon in what they hoped would be a surprise advance against a foe on his home grounds whose position and strength were not well known.

If ever there were a formula for military disaster, it had been perfectly mixed here.

To compound the problem, there had never been the slightest chance of surprising the Indians, War Singer said later, for the keenest ears and eyes in the Nez Perce tribe were stationed in hiding at the head of the canyon, listening and watching for the appearance of the troops which they long had known would come.

The sharp senses belonged to *Its-kimze-kin*—"Feet and Hand Cut Off"—who despite his handicap was the finest rider and the best scout in the White Bird band.

What his origin had been and how he had lost both feet and one hand, even War Singer did not know, though he was inclined to believe that the small-statured, incredibly nimble Indian had lived for a time as a slave among the Yakimas, where Chief *Kamiakin* had inflicted the harsh punishment on him that had cost him two feet and a hand.

"As a slave, he had become a sly, cunning thief," War Singer said. "To cure him of this bad habit, *Kamiakin* had his hands and feet shackled with traps and ordered that he be left naked outdoors on a cold winter night. When daylight came, his feet and one hand were so badly frozen they had to be cut off. Feeling he had been punished enough, *Kamiakin* gave him his freedom. In time, he came to us. Afoot, he is not much of a man. On a horse as a scout, no man is better than he."

As the mounted soldiers sat waiting on their horses watching the stars begin to pale, the bloodcurdling cry of a coyote split the darkness —a cry Sergeant Schorr knew was made by no animal.

"At that sudden nerve-shattering howl I felt my hair standing up, well knowing its import. There was no repetition, no answering echo. Just that one eerie, prophetic, death-laden cry that could not be misinterpreted."

Immediately following the cry, the muffled thud of unshod hoofs was briefly heard, then silence again fell over the vastness of the canyon.

By the time *Its-kimze-kin* rode into the village at the base of the canyon several miles to the south, all the warriors able to be up and about were stirring. In council last night, White Bird and Joseph, who had moved into the village, had agreed that a final effort toward peace must be made. *Ollokot* moved quietly among the young men, who were painted and stripped for battle, checking their weapons for the last time, and trying not to trip over the inert bodies of warriors who had drunk too much stolen whiskey to be in condition to fight.

"We will not fire the first shot," *Ollokot* said urgently. "We will ride to meet the soldiers carrying a white flag of truce. If they will listen, we will talk."

Selected to lead the commission of six Nez Perces who would be carrying the white flag, was a Nez Perce named *Wet-ti-wet-ti How-lis*— "Vicious Weasel"—a man of good reputation among both his own people and the whites, known to the whites as John Boyd. As daylight grew and he led the truce party out of the village and up the dusty slope toward the approaching soldiers, he waved the white flag he was carrying and cried:

"Remember what the chiefs have told us. We will not fire unless fired upon."

Viewing the ruggedness of the terrain below him from the head of the canyon in the growing light, Captain Perry grew apprehensive. Motioning Ad Chapman to his side, he waved a hand at the slope below.

"That's rocky, broken ground, a killer for horses. We can't manueuver much there."

"It gets better lower down, Captain. After a mile or so, the valley opens out and gets smooth. We'll have plenty of room to fight there."

"Let's hope we don't have to fight. Lieutenant Theller!"

"Sir!"

"Take your trumpeter, a couple of Nez Perce scouts, and a detail of eight men and proceed as advance guard. The main column will follow. Don't get more than one hundred yards ahead."

"Yes, sir."

"Shouldn't me and the volunteers go with 'em, Captain, 'case they run into trouble?" Ad Chapman asked.

"Very well. But you're to obey Lieutenant Theller's orders, understand? The moment you make contact with the hostiles, he will halt the detail, deploy his men in defensive positions, and immediately send word back to me by messenger or bugle call that a confrontation is imminent. Under no circumstances, are you to initiate action."

"Gotcha, Captain! I ain't no greenhorn when it comes to fighin' Injuns."

Accompanying the detail was a young, happy-go-lucky, likeable trumpeter, Private John M. Jones, whose only notable feat since enlisting in the Army was having gotten drunk five weeks ago and being thrown in the Fort Lapwai guardhouse with the tough old cross-grained growler, *Too-hool-hool-zote*. Despite barriers of language, age, and race, the two men had become such good friends during their incarceration that upon his release Trumpeter Jones had boasted:

"If war ever comes, boys, I'll be safe. My old buddy *Too-hool* promised he'd tell the Indians not to shoot *me.*"

Because of the dust, din, and confusion of a cavalry-Indian encounter, the services of a trumpeter to relay officers' orders to troops scattered over wide distances were extremely important. Each of the two companies in Captain Perry's command had a bugler; each man, by regulation, carried a bugle and a spare.

Riding a short distance ahead of Lieutenant Theller's detachment were the two Nez Perce scouts, Abraham Brooks and Frank Husush. When they sighted the six Nez Perces carrying the white flag, they stopped and motioned to Lieutenant Theller, one of them crying:

"Men from the village! They carry a white flag! They want to talk!"

At the head of the volunteers, a short distance to the left, Ad Chapman shouted, "Talk, hell! I'll give the greasy bastards somethin' to listen to!"

Spurring his horse forward until he sighted the group of nearing Indians, which had ridden behind and now emerged from the shelter of an outcropping of rock, he threw his rifle to his shoulder and fired. When the first shot took no effect, he fired again—missing this time, too.

Because Ad Chapman was wearing the wide-brimmed white hat he always wore, the White Bird Nez Perces recognized him instantly, realized that with him leading the volunteers there would no longer be a chance to talk, and committed themselves to battle. As the warriors came swarming out of the village and up the slope, Lieutenant Theller deployed his men in defensive positions, ordering Trumpeter Jones to blow the call that would bring the main force forward. Two Moons, who was with the charging Indians, later told War Singer what happened.

"I joined with the others, among them Yellow Wolf and my partner, *Ots-tot-poo*—'Fire Body'—an old-like man. There was a gun report to the north and soon, right away, we saw a man wearing a broad, white hat and riding a white horse coming fast. He was on high, flat land along a rock-tipped ridge lying just west of us. That rider was Chapman, a known bad man. When he saw us he fired across at us but his shot was lost.

"Several, maybe, twenty, soldiers followed close after Chapman. There was a bugler and when the party all stopped, this bugler rode a little ahead of them. He began calling orders on his trumpet. *Ots-tot-poo* said to me, 'You now watch! I will make a good shot and kill that bugler!'

"He did make the long-distance shot, and dead dropped the bugler from his horse. Chapman and his soldiers whirled and rode rapidly away from there."

Contrary to statements made by General Howard and widely quoted by the press, only fifty-five Indians took part in the battle. Chief Joseph was not among them, War Singer said, nor was he in command. Fighting on their own ground, the Nez Perces did not require any grand strategy devised by a "Red Napoleon"—which the reporters declared Chief Joseph to be. The *Nimipu* simply fought in the Indian way—exposing themselves as little as possible, making every shot count, inflicting as much damage on the enemy as they could, while receiving very little damage themselves.

For generations they had been horse Indians. They rode only their best-trained horses when they made meat in the buffalo country, and they rode these same horses when they went into battle. Few of the mounts of the cavalrymen had ever heard shots fired from their backs, let alone heard bullets whistling toward them. It was inevitable that they should go wild with fear, pitching and bolting. When cavalrymen went into action, the standard tactic was to dismount and fight on foot, with one man holding his own and three other mounts in some sheltered spot. With his hands full controlling four terror-stricken animals, he could do no fighting—which reduced the firepower of his troop by one fourth.

The Nez Perces, on the other hand, had so accustomed their horses to the sound of gunfire, War Singer said, that "a *Nimipu* pony will stand and eat grass while its warrior owner fights."

Though one company of cavalrymen did dismount and fight on foot, the other for some obscure reason was permitted to shoot from the backs of their horses, with the result that their fire was wildly inaccurate. The often-repeated story that the Nez Perces stampeded a band of wild horses toward the soldiers in order to frighten the cavalry horses was not true, War Singer said. Aboard each of those apparently riderless animals was a daring, athletic Indian, clinging like a burr to the far side, holding on with a moccasined toe hooked across the horse's back and a hand grasping a hunk of mane, guiding the animal with a length of braided rawhide looped around its lower jaw.

No Indian in his right mind ever attempted to shoot a rifle at an enemy while performing this stunt, War Singer said. With ammunition scarce and expensive, the Nez Perce fighting men wanted every shot to count.

"When a warrior wanted to fire, he rolled off the horse to the ground, took deliberate aim, shot, and then mounted again, the horse remaining patient and quiet beside him."

Despite Captain Perry's efforts to rally his troops and make a stand, he could not organize a defensive line that would hold. Following the first charge by the Indians, the citizen volunteers turned their horses around and headed for home—with Ad Chapman and his broad-brimmed white hat leading the way. Because they and Lieutenant Theller's detail were being counted on by Captain Perry to hold the high ground to the left, that flank was now exposed. From the vacated height the Indians poured a murderous fire into the rest of the command.

Nobody had thought to retrieve Trumpeter Jones's bugle. Desperately needing a means of communicating with his officers and men, Captain Perry managed to locate Captain Trimble's trumpeter. Unfortunately he had lost his bugle. There was a spare around someplace, but no one could find it.

"A cavalry command on a battlefield without a trumpeter," Captain Perry later said wryly, "is like a ship at sea without a helm."

In the din of battle, Perry's voice could carry no more than a few yards. Hand signals which he intended to mean "Hold up and make a stand on that ridge a hundred yards to the rear" or "Retreat slowly, with half of your men moving in deliberate fashion while the other half covers for them" were read to mean "Every man for himself" or "We've lost the fight—run like hell." Time and again, Perry claimed, Ad Chapman prevented a regrouping in a defensible position by shouting, "There's a better place further on!", leaving the disorganized, stunned, exhausted soldiers behind to be shot or clubbed to death by the Indians.

It was not until he had reached the Henry Johnson ranch, four miles north of the head of White Bird Canyon, that Captain Perry was able to halt his fleeing men and take a defensive position on a high point of land. By then he was so deep in shock that he had lost track of time. After looking at his watch, he said to Lieutenant Parnell:

"It's seven o'clock, isn't it?"

"Yes, sir."

"Good! In an hour, it will be turning dark. We should be able to defend this position until then."

"Captain, it's seven o'clock in the *morning,* not in the evening!"

"Is it, really?"

"The men have only ten rounds of ammunition apiece left. But they're too tired to go any further."

In contrast to Ad Chapman, who had initiated the battle by firing at the peace envoys, then turned tail and fled, three of the young Indian warriors who had started the uprising showed a bravery long remembered by their people. Two Moons told War Singer:

"I, Two Moons, saw *Sarp-sis Ilp-ilp, Wah-litits,* and *Tip-yah-lah-nah Kaps-kaps,* all wearing full-length red blanket coats and two of them on fine-looking grey horses, come riding side by side at the head of the charge. These warriors came through that wild charge and mixing up the soldiers untouched by the hail of enemy bullets. After this battle, these three men were known as the 'Three Red Coats.' "

Incredibly, the only casualties suffered by the Nez Perces in the battle were three men slightly wounded. Troop losses were thirty-four men killed and two wounded. As Captain Perry wrote in his report to General Howard, in proportion to the number of soldiers involved, the disaster was equal in magnitude to the Custer Massacre just a year earlier.

Like that disaster, news of it stunned the Army and the nation . . .

5

Estimating the number of hostiles arrayed against him at the Battle of White Bird Canyon to be 125, Captain Perry warned General Howard that it would take "at least 500 men to whip them." Apparently displeased with this admission that four professional soldiers equalled only one untrained Indian, General Howard immediately upped his subordinate's estimate of the forces pitted against him to "at least five hundred Indians bearing arms."

Even before the battle, Howard had ordered all available troops stationed at posts throughout Washington and Oregon to come to Fort Lapwai. Now he extended the summons to military installations as distant as Sitka, Alaska, San Francisco, and Atlanta, Georgia. This time he would lead the troops himself. Within a week he had assembled a force of four hundred fighting men and a hundred scouts and packers. Equipped for a lengthy campaign, he led the command out of Fort Lapwai on June 22, leaving Captain Perry and the remnants of two companies behind to stand guard at the post.

In white settlements all over the interior Pacific Northwest, panic spread with the rapidity of a forest fire driven before a roaring wind. When word reached the Wallowa country that Joseph's band of Nez Perces had taken part in a battle against the soldiers and that General Howard was crediting him with being the master strategist who had instigated and was now leading his people in the war, few of the white settlers stopped to recall the gentle, intelligent, peace-inclined Indian who long had been their friend, who had never gone to war, and had sworn he never would. Overnight in their minds he became a cruel, vicious, diabolical wild Indian capable of the vilest deeds . . .

Because the Kooskia village on the South Fork of the Clearwater lay a day's travel northeast of the site of the battle, trouble with the whites was not expected there. With the agency headquarters and the military post at Lapwai just a day's travel to the northwest, and with both Indians and whites riding frequently between the settlements and the Indian camps, Tall Bird had no difficulty learning what was going on in matters concerning his relatives and friends.

When he heard that Singing Bird's husband, Lame Brown Bear, had played an active role in the battle and accounted for himself very well, he shook his head and said sadly:

"This is a bad thing. I wish he had not fought."

"What is bad about defending one's home and family?" Swift Bird demanded. "He would have been a poor kind of man if he had not done so. I am proud of him."

"It is not bad that he had the courage to fight, my son. What is bad is that he had to fight. Now that blood has been shed, peace will not be made easily."

"The way the whites are talking, no peace will be made with the Indians who took part in the battle. If they surrender, they will be sentenced to death without a trial and will be hanged."

"This I do not believe. Chief Joseph says the Cut-Arm Chief is a just man."

"The same thing was said about Colonel Wright, Father, when I fought on the side of the whites against my brothers twenty years ago. But it was a lie. The justice he gave the Palouse and Yakima warriors was at the end of a rope. I saw it happen."

"We must hope things will be better this time. The *Nimipu* cannot win a war against the whites. We must make peace and trust to their mercy."

"For the sake of my sister, Singing Bird, for Lame Brown Bear, and for all the innocent people in White Bird's village, I hope peace comes, Father. Looking Glass hopes so, too. But he fears bloodshed . . ."

Feeling that he should offer his help in negotiating peace, Tall Bird left the village of the Looking Glass band after a few days, rode to Lapwai, and conferred with his oldest daughter's Christianized husband, Joshua Worth, regarding what could be done. He was surprised at the bitterness of his son-in-law's response.

"What can be done? After White Bird and Joseph lost control of their young men, let them get drunk, kill white men, rape their women, steal their livestock, burn their cabins, and bring on a war none of us wanted—after all this, you ask me what can be done? They can pay for their crimes! That's what can be done!"

"You condemn your own people for defending themselves when the soldiers attacked them?"

"I condemn them for starting a war that may ruin us all. Already there is talk among the whites of taking away what little land we were given by the treaties. Even though only a small portion of our tribe murdered the settlers and killed soldiers, we all will suffer."

Among the Reservation Nez Perces, which comprised four fifths of the Nez Perce tribe, there was little sympathy expressed for the White Bird and Joseph bands, Tall Bird discovered, regardless of what secret feelings the settled Indians had toward their wild brothers. A number of them were even serving as scouts and skirmishers with the large, well-armed command now moving toward White Bird Canyon in a determined effort to crush the hostiles. Accepting the fact that there was nothing he could do to help Singing Bird and her family until the present crisis was resolved, Tall Bird remained at Lapwai, anxiously waiting for news, passing on what he learned in letters written to his brother, John Crane, in the Wallowa country.

For General Howard and his command, the campaign was not going well, despite his careful planning. Reaching the White Bird Canyon battleground, Howard detailed squads to the grisly task of burying the dead, then moved on to the site of the Nez Perce camp near the juncture of White Bird Creek with the Salmon River. There his worst fears were confirmed. The Indians were gone, leaving behind clear signs that they had crossed the turbulent Salmon and were now on the loose in the wild, rugged country to the south and west. Much as he and his troops dreaded the swift, deep, rapids-filled river, it must be crossed if the Nez Perces were to be caught and forced into battle. Preparations for the crossing were begun.

Meanwhile, the victorious White Bird and Joseph bands had been joined the day after the battle by two renowned and experienced warriors, Rainbow and Five Wounds, who had just returned from the buffalo country. In a council of tribal leaders it was decided to cross the Salmon, move down it a short distance, and there await the coming of the soldiers. As Joseph's band had done three weeks earlier in crossing the far more dangerous Snake, this crossing was made with no fuss or bother and no loss of goods or lives.

But behind them, the soldiers were having problems. One of these was the lack of information about the Indians. The main question troubling Howard was whether the entire band of hostiles was camped on the far side of the river or had left just a small group behind while the main body went elsewhere. If the Joseph band, for example, decided to return to the Wallowa country, that could mean serious trouble to the settlers, for Captain Whipple and his troops were no longer there to protect them.

Finally Howard decided to cross his entire command. Lieutenant Harry L. Bailey, Company B, Twenty-first Infantry, wrote on June 30:

"Have just crossed the swift and dangerous Salmon River in a skiff with four men and four oarsmen. The stream at this point is about 200 yards wide, with a plunging current. By a good deal of labor and loss of time, a large rope had been stretched across. This morning a number of horses and mules were made to swim the river and a famous swim they made of it. Some of them were turned over and over, and others carried away down the stream, but I think all got over."

Crossing the five hundred men, two Gatling guns, a small piece of field artillery, all their horses, arms, and supplies took the whole of one day. Meanwhile, the main body of Nez Perces, which was camped not far away, loaded up and moved some twenty miles down the Salmon to what was called Craig's Ferry. Next morning they recrossed the river there, leaving the soldiers with nothing to combat but the country and the elements.

It took Howard and his troops forty-eight hours to travel the same distance the Indians had traversed in half a day.

"The 5th of July brought us to Craig's Ferry," Howard wrote in exasperation, "where it became evident that all the Indians had passed back and taken the trail toward Cottonwood, sixteen miles distant. At first I hoped by a proper crossing to join Perry, but, having no boats, a raft had been constructed from the timber of a cabin near the ferry."

General Howard neglected to mention that the cabin belonged to a friendly Nez Perce Indian named Luke Billy, who had gone to work for the Army as a scout. Watching the soldiers tear down his house and use its timbers to make a clumsy, unwieldy raft, he was puzzled, wondering why the white men were going to all that trouble when a buffalo hide stretched over a frame of willows would have served the purpose just as well.

"Our first attempt on the morning of the 6th to cross the river, here a perfect torrent, lost us our raft," Howard reported mournfully, "which tumbled down the rapids at a swift rate, with all on board, for three or four miles."

The home Luke Billy watched vanish downriver had been a substantial one, War Singer related with malicious glee, for its timbers were a foot thick and forty feet long.

"The Cut-Arm Chief told him to turn in a claim for its value, which he did," War Singer said. "Twenty-three years later he was still trying to collect from the government for its loss."

Unable to cross the Salmon at this point, Howard ordered a retrograde march upriver, made the crossing near the mouth of White Bird Creek, and then retraced his route to Grangeville, which he reached July 8. In the two weeks since his force had left Fort Lapwai he had accomplished exactly nothing . . .

Meanwhile, acting under Howard's orders, one of his subordinate officers precipitated a confrontation that turned a peaceful band of Nez Perces into deadly foes. After giving news of the outbreak to Ad Chapman, Looking Glass and his people had returned to their village on the South Fork of the Clearwater, fifty miles northeast of the White Bird Canyon area. There, they had since lived quietly, uneasily hearing news of the war but taking no part in it.

But while preparing to cross the Salmon the first time, General Howard had received a dispatch which disturbed him.

"The evening of June 29th positive information is obtained that Looking Glass, who, with his people, had stood aloof from the hostiles, had been furnishing reinforcements to them of at least twenty warriors, and that he proposed to join them in person, on the first favorable opportunity. With a view of preventing the completion of this treachery, I sent Captain Whipple to surprise and capture the chief and all that belonged to him."

Never mind that Looking Glass had as yet committed no hostile act. Never mind that the Kooskia village where he and his people lived was within the boundaries of the reservation. All were to be "surprised and captured."

"As soon as Chief Looking Glass and the Indians camped with him have been taken prisoner," Howard told Captain Whipple, "you're to turn them over for safekeeping to the Mount Idaho Volunteers. In that way, they'll be immobilized."

"I'm to capture their horses too, sir?"

"Especially their horses, Captain. They must be set afoot."

How safe the Indians would have been in the custody of Ad Chapman and the Mount Idaho Volunteers may well have been questioned, War Singer said. At any rate, as the event was related to him, Captain Whipple and his command reached the village early Sunday morning, July 1. According to *Peo-peo Thol-ekt*—"Band of Geese"—who was in the chief's tepee at the time, Looking Glass told him to go out and meet the soldiers.

"Tell them to leave us alone. We are living here peacefully and want no trouble."

Peo-peo Thol-ekt mounted his horse and rode out to talk to the soldiers. He told War Singer:

"One man greeted me friendly in Nez Perce. I gave him my chief's message that we wanted no trouble and therefore had I come from my people. But those soldiers would not listen. They seemed drinking. They came near killing me. I understood little English. One said to me, 'You Looking Glass?' He jabbed me with his gun muzzle. He did not hit easy! The first man told him, 'Hold on! This not Looking Glass! Only one of his boys.' "

Ordered by the soldiers to go back to the village and tell Looking Glass that he must come and talk with them, *Peo-peo Thol-ekt* did so. But having seen the whites mistreat his messenger, the chief was suspicious and refused to go. After more confused parleying and threats by the whites, someone fired a shot. And the battle—if such it should be called—began.

"An opportunity was given Looking Glass to surrender," Captain Whipple reported, "which he at first promised to accept, but afterwards defiantly refused, and the result was that several Indians were killed, the camp with a large amount of supplies destroyed, and seven hundred and twenty-five ponies captured and driven to Mount Idaho."

If by "several Indians killed," War Singer later said with contempt, Whipple meant the Nez Perce wife of Peter Pliater and the baby strapped to her back, then his fatality list was accurate, for they were the only Nez Perces who lost their lives during the encounter. They drowned when the mother's horse was pulled under as she was crossing the Clearwater in an attempt to escape the hail of bullets ripping through the tepees. Not surprisingly, the outcome of the attack was negative.

"Of course this stirred up a new hornet's nest," Howard lamented, "and did not get Looking Glass and his treacherous companions into custody."

With his village looted and burned, his horses taken, and his peaceful intentions scorned, Chief Looking Glass wasted no time joining forces with the hostiles. *Too-hool-hool-zote, Hah-tal-e-kin,* and *Hush-hush Cute* went with him. Meeting White Bird, Joseph, *Ollokot* and the other nontreaty leaders near Cottonwood on Camas Prairie, Looking Glass expressed his changed feelings in a bitter speech:

"Two days ago my camp was attacked by the soldiers. I tried to surrender in every way I could. My horses, lodges, and everything I had was taken away from me by the soldiers we had done so much for. Now, my people, as long as I live I will never make peace with the treacherous Americans. I am ready for war."

"So am I," Swift Bird said passionately, after embracing his beloved sister, Singing Bird, who had always been so cheerful and happy but had now forgotten how to sing or smile. Shaking the hand of his brother-in-law, Lame Brown Bear, his dark eyes burned with hate. "You killed two bluecoats in the battle, I hear, which makes me very proud. Now, I, too, am ready to fight and kill to save our people . . ."

6

Following the attack on the Looking Glass village, Captain Whipple and his men moved to Cottonwood, some thirteen miles northwest of Grangeville. The captain was unaware of the fact that by now, July 5, General Howard and his troops had crossed to the south side of the Salmon and were converting a cabin into a raft at Craig's Ferry. Nor did he know that the main body of Nez Perces had recrossed the river at the same point and were heading in his direction. He therefore sent a pair of white scouts out looking for the hostiles. The two citizen volunteers, William Foster and Charles Blewett, found some Indians, all right. In fact, they blundered directly into the path of the main body of angry Nez Perce warriors.

Before he could turn his horse around, Blewett was shot out of the saddle by an Indian named Red Spy. Foster managed to escape, returning to Captain Whipple's command on a horse nearly killed by hard riding. Wanting more information about the number and identity of the hostiles, Whipple detailed Lieutenant S. M. Rains and ten soldiers to go to the place of the encounter, with William Foster as their guide. Unfortunately for these twelve men, they met the Indians just as the Nez Perce warriors were preparing to mount a surprise attack on the entire Whipple command. *He-mene Mox-mox*—"Yellow Wolf"—a twenty-two-year-old nephew of Chief Joseph who became a respected fighter during the long campaign, later told War Singer his version of the encounter:

"In the draw I saw my friends gathered together. When I got where I could see them better, they made a left swerve. I looked in this new direction, and saw a blanket waving, a signal of war. I ran my horse that way and, reaching a small hump, I saw about twelve soldiers.

"There was shooting, and one soldier fell from his horse. Then another went down a little way from us. Soon a third fell, and another and another, not far apart, went to the ground. Some distance on, a man—maybe wounded—got down from his horse and was killed. I will not hide anything. That part of the fight was not long. Those six soldiers did not get up.

"The remaining six soldiers ran their horses up a hill, maybe one-half mile. Then they jumped off and lay among the rocks and began shooting. Those soldiers were trapped. They had no show. When they began shooting, it was just like their calling, 'Come on! Come on!' A calling to death."

Surrounded by an overwhelming force of nontreaty Nez Perces—whose supply of arms had been augmented by sixty-three excellent Springfield rifles lost by the troopers during the Battle of White Bird Canyon—Lieutenant Rains and his detail were wiped out to the last man. As yet, the only damage the soldiers had been able to inflict on the Indians was the destruction of one of their villages, the capture of some of their horses, and the accidental drowning of a mother and child.

Twenty miles to the southeast, in Mount Idaho, Captain D. B. Randall organized a company of sixteen armed citizens and led them toward Cottonwood, where he planned to join forces with the soldiers. This was on the morning of July 5, the day the two scouts, Lieutenant Rains, and his detail were killed. It was also the day Luke Billy saw his cabin vanish down the Salmon.

Meanwhile, on July 4, Captain Perry had left Fort Lapwai with a pack train of ammunition and supplies, lightly escorted, bound for Cottonwood, where he expected to meet Howard's command. Instead, he was surprised to run into Captain Whipple, who told him what had happened. As senior officer, Perry took command.

Made cautious by the recent defeats, he put the soldiers to work digging entrenchments at Cottonwood so that they could better defend themselves in case of an attack by a large number of hostiles. While engaged in this task, he and his men saw a group of whites a mile or two away being attacked by Indians. This was Captain Randall's group of Mt. Idaho Volunteers. Again, Yellow Wolf related the encounter:

"Coming to the wagon road, we looked in the direction of the ferry. We saw them—about twenty armed horsemen. Not uniformed soldiers, but more like citizens.

"Then those men made for us. We were lined across their path. As they charged, we gave way—let them go through. We then struck after them, racing to flank both sides. The shooting became faster, and soon those whites stopped and dismounted. The fighting was from about half past ten o'clock to the middle of the afternoon. We did not know why the soldiers in their dugout rifle pits did not come to the fighting. We could see them where they were on higher ground. They seemed a little afraid."

Whether it was fear or caution that caused Captain Perry to be reluctant to commit any of his soldiers to the rescue of the civilians was debatable. Certainly his junior officer, Captain Whipple, believed that he was being overly timid. After observing the commotion for several minutes, Whipple spoke to Perry with great agitation:

"What's happening, sir?"

"The hostiles seem to have surrounded a group of civilians."

"Shouldn't we try to help them?"

"It's too late, I afraid. They're being cut to pieces."

"But, sir, they're still alive and resisting. With your permission, I'll lead a party to attempt a rescue."

"Permission denied, Captain!" Perry exclaimed nervously. "It's a ruse on the part of the hostiles aimed at getting us out of the entrenchments. If you try to help those people, the Indians will surround your party and wipe you out as they did Lieutenant Theller's detail at White Bird Canyon."

Disgusted as he was with what he regarded as cowardice on the part of his senior officer, Captain Whipple knew he dared not pursue the matter any further. But George Shearer, the leader of twenty volunteers who were serving with the command, had no compunctions against violating Captain Perry's orders. During the Civil War, Shearer had served as a captain in the Confederate Army, seeing considerable action against Union forces. Since coming to Idaho, he had been in the Territorial Legislature, was a respected citizen of the Grangeville area, and had been one of the first men to enlist in the militia headed by Ad Chapman. In fact, before the Battle of White Bird Canyon he had been second in command to Chapman, and, when the action began, had made a vain attempt to force the militia to dismount, fight on foot, and hold a position protecting the soldiers' left flank, leaving the scene only after the other civilians had broken and fled. Now, after watching the beleaguered citizens fight off the Indian attack for another half hour or so, he simply mounted his horse and cried to his friends:

"Come on, men! Let's give 'em a hand!"

By then, the charges of the Nez Perces had eased off. Whether shamed by the unauthorized rescue effort of the volunteers or deciding that no entrapment was planned by the hostiles, Captain Perry ordered a detachment of soldiers to follow and give relief to the Mount Idaho contingent. Yellow Wolf told War Singer that the *Nimipu* by that time had decided to break off the engagement anyway.

"The sun was halfway down in the afternoon sky, when, looking back, we saw soldiers coming, their big gun in the lead. The chiefs now called out, 'Let us quit for a while.'

"Hearing that order, we left the fighting, taking *Wees-cul-a-tat* with us. Three times wounded at the beginning of the fight, he lived until about dark. With two bad wounds, he could not hold his life. Not old, about middle-aged, he was the first warrior killed. We lost a good fighter."

Ironically, the white volunteer who shot the Indian was a young man named Charley Crooks, who had been raised among the Nez Perces and whose father was considered to be such a good friend that the Indians in an earlier fight had yelled at him that if he would take his father's horse and go home they would not harm him.

Casualties in the fight for the Mount Idaho Volunteers were three men wounded and two killed, the mortalities being Ben Evans and Captain D. B. Randall.

At this point in the war only one Nez Perce warrior had died in battle. Up to July 6, 1877, the whites had lost forty-six fighting men and twenty-two noncombatants . . .

7

After luring Howard's command across the Salmon and traveling twenty-five miles west to Craig's Ferry, the Wallowa band was well on its way toward its home country, if it wished to return there. But Joseph knew that a return to the Land of the Winding Waters was impossible now, so he went along with White Bird and *Too-hool-hool-zote* in the decision to recross the Salmon and head northeast across Camas Prairie.

"All this time we were counciling to determine what was best to do," Joseph later told Tall Bird. "Whether we should leave the region and move toward the Snake River country, or go to the buffalo plains and join Sitting Bull in the British Possessions. Some wanted to surrender to Howard, but they feared they would be shot or hung."

The Nez Perce chiefs knew that the famous Sioux leader, Sitting Bull, had fled to Canada with a number of his followers after their stunning victory over General George Armstrong Custer a year earlier. Safe for the time being because Canadian authorities refused to send him back to the United States against his will, he was a great hero to Indians north and south of the border, a symbol of embarrassment to the American Army, and a man whose presence worried Canadian officials.

Following the annihilation of Lieutenant Rains and his men, and the skirmish with Captain Randall's volunteers near Cottonwood, the nontreaty Nez Perces moved at a leisurely pace across Camas Prairie to the South Fork of the Clearwater, setting up camp a few miles upstream from its juncture with the Middle Fork. Persisting in his belief that Chief Joseph was commanding the hostiles, General Howard told one of the many newspaper reporters who were now covering the developing campaign:

"If Joseph will remain one day longer burning houses and bragging of his victories, I will be able to strike him a blow."

Never mind that Joseph was neither burning nor bragging, the publicity process that would cast him and Howard as strategically opposed leaders in the minds of the newspaper and magazine-reading American public had begun. Because of his national reputation, General Howard made news with every statement he issued. If he chose to simplify the Nez Perce War into a great contest between himself and a "Red Napoleon" named Chief Joseph, few reporters would object. This was front-page copy. Unfortunately, Joseph himself was giving no interviews, so Howard had to speak for him.

Under the guidance of Ad Chapman, Howard led a mixed force of cavalry, infantry, and artillery toward the spot where Chapman thought the hostiles would be camped. Thanks to Chapman's bad judgment, Howard and his troops missed the village by several miles, had to backtrack, and then found themselves in a poor position to attack. They attacked anyway—and the conflict was on.

For the better part of two days the Battle of the Clearwater continued in sporadic fashion, with neither side inclined to mount a serious charge. All the Indians wanted to do, War Singer said, was protect their village. Lying prone behind the rocks strewn over the bare slope across which the soldiers must charge, the Nez Perces could fight from excellent cover. On higher ground, cut off from water, with little natural cover, and on terrain where they could not use their howitzer and Gatling guns to good effect, the soldiers had to be content with long-range fire aimed in the general direction of mostly unseen targets. Even when the target was seen, the marksmanship of the troopers was extremely poor.

"At this era of our army we had had almost no target practice," Lieutenant Harry L. Bailey complained. "A number of us saw a poor old horse, probably wounded, standing for some hours out in my front, and I suppose several hundreds of bullet were fired at him without apparent effect. That was one of the lessons I had about our shooting when we had in our army three shots per man per month for target practice."

Most of the casualties were suffered early in the fight. Strung out in a line over two miles long and stumbling into the village by accident, Howard's command was never in a position to mount a concerted attack in force. Fewer than one hundred Nez Perces were able to turn back four times their number, with tough old *Too-hool-hool-zote* and twenty-four of his warriors acting as dismounted sharpshooters, first in one position, then in another, all along the defensive front.

During a lull in the fighting in midafternoon of the first day, Swift Bird, who had just returned to the line after checking to make sure his wife and children were still unharmed in their tepee, heard a voice calling in Nez Perce:

"*Peo-peo Amtiz! Gagaz Aluin!* Hear me, Swift Bird and Lame Brown Bear! I bring a message from your father!"

Moving to Swift Bird's side, Lame Brown Bear peered up the slope toward the scattered rocks several hundred yards away, behind which the soldiers were lying.

"Who is it that calls our names?" Lame Brown Bear asked.

"Some dog of a Christian *Nimipu,*" Swift Bird muttered contemptuously. "For a few dollars of blood money, he has sold his soul to the bluecoats and serves them as a scout. We will not answer."

"Your father is a man of peace," Looking Glass said, hunkering down beside them. "It will do no harm to hear his message." Cupping his hands around his mouth, Looking Glass shouted, "Tall Bird's sons are here! They are listening! What is the message he sends?"

"He wants them to stop fighting. He has talked to the Cut-Arm Chief, he says, who promises no harm will come to the *Nimipu* if they quit fighting and surrender now."

"We have heard that promise before! We know it to be a lie!"

"Tall Bird believes it. He wants the war to end."

"Who are you, to tell us this?"

"*Elas-kol-a-tat,* of the White Bird band. When I became a Christian and married, my wife and I moved to the agency headquarters at Lapwai."

"You are working as a scout for the Army?"

"Yes. But only to help end the war. I, too, want peace."

"Are you the son of *Wees-cul-a-tat?*"

"Yes. He is my father."

"Did you know he is dead? The soldiers killed him four days ago in a fight at Cottonwood."

For long moments, silence lay over the battlefield. Then a scream of anguish pierced the air, followed by the keening of a death-song. Startled by the sudden sound, nervous soldiers began firing a fusillade of shots, to which the Nez Perce warriors responded with a volley of their own. Rising from his place of concealment, *Elas-kol-a-tat* stood erect, took off the United States Army campaign hat that had been issued to him, slammed it to the ground, unbuttoned his uniform blouse, threw it down, and then started running blindly down the slope from the white to the Nez Perce line, heedless of the bullets being fired from both sides. Miraculously, he reached the shelter of the Indians without being struck.

"I was born a *Nimipu* and I will die a *Nimipu!*" he declared, seizing Looking Glass by the right hand. "As my father did, I will fight for my people!"

Torn by conflicting feelings, individual Indians switched allegiance the other way, too, War Singer said. "During the Clearwater fighting, *Alik-kees*—'Hair Cut Short'—a good fighter who was known to the whites as Alec Hays, decided to quit the war and did. Also, *Al-lah-kol-i-ken*—'Buck Antlers'—became scared on the first day, ran away, and joined the Christians."

Judging from the reluctance of both General Howard and the Indian leaders to commit their forces to a decisive battle, the line between being prudent and becoming scared and running away was hard to draw. Since the soldiers would not attack, the Indians saw no point in pressing the fight. One by one, warriors left their defensive positions, returned to the village, packed up, and prepared to travel. The evacuation began in the morning and continued until midafternoon in full view of the soldiers, with nothing done to stop it. Not until the village was empty of Indians did General Howard at last order a charge. Of this pointless attack, he bragged:

"For a few minutes there was a stubborn resistance at Joseph's barricades; then his whole line gave way."

Whether any Indian line remained to give way was questionable, for the main body of nontreaty Nez Perces was permitted to move downriver to the vicinity of Kamiah without molestation, while the soldiers occupied the site of the village and appropriated whatever goods and valuables had been left behind. Lieutenant Bailey wrote:

"It was a wonder to see the tons and tons of flour and other foods, and fine Indian goods, mostly burned. There was gold dust, jewelery, and fine silver tableware, some of which I judged dated from an early Hudson's Bay period. All this being brought to light, the packers and citizens helped themselves, while I tried to get a few souvenirs, but as fast as I got a little bundle, someone took it from me as I was looking after the troops."

Both Indian and white historians called the Battle of the Clearwater a draw, War Singer said, which seems fair enough, for neither side won a clear-cut victory or suffered a decisive defeat. White casualties were fifteen killed and twenty-seven wounded. By their own count, the Nez Perces had four killed and five wounded, though Howard set their losses much higher.

Badly in need of a piece of good news after the setbacks he had suffered, Howard raised no objection when Captain Keeler, who had been with the supply train, dispatched a wire:

"Have been with General Howard in the battle today, which he reports in detail. I consider this a most important success. Joseph is in full flight westward. Nothing can surpass the vigor of General Howard's movements and action."

"The Indians fought as well as any troops I ever saw," Howard reported to his superior, George Irvin McDowell, "and so did ours, not one man failing in duty."

Though the public might admire a general who praised his enemy and his troops, it did not like a loser. At the moment Howard needed a win, as was noted in a return telegram from General McDowell:

"These dispatches came most opportunely, for your enemies had raised a great clamor against you, which, the press reported, had not been without its effect in Washington. They have been silenced, but I think they (like Joseph's band) have been scotched—not killed—and will rise again if they have a chance."

How prophetic those words were would soon be seen . . .

8

In the Kamiah area, the Middle Fork of the Clearwater flowed in a northwesterly direction, so Captain Keeler's dispatch stating that the Indians were "in full flight westward" was partially correct. But it was not the intention of the nontreaty bands, which now numbered two hundred and fifty fighting men, plus four hundred or so women, children, and old people, to go downriver to Lapwai and the heart of the reservation. There, they knew, in addition to the hostility of four fifths of the tribe, they would face arrest, trial for their crimes, and possibly death. Their only hope for freedom lay in the mountain wilderness north and east of the Clearwater. Again they prepared for the crossing of a swift, turbulent river, with a practiced skill that made it look easy.

"You have asked me how we crossed the Salmon and other deep, swift streams with our families and goods," Yellow Wolf later responded to a question from a sympathetic white friend. "I will tell you all, how done. Owning that country, the Nez Perces knew all such streams. Crossed them often without difficulty.

"We had plenty of buffalo robes. With them we made hide boats. In making such a boat, the hide, hair-side up, was spread on the ground. Across the hide were laid green willow or other limber poles about the thickness of your thumb. The hide and poles were bent up and lashed to other bent poles forming a long circled rim. The rim was on outside. That was all. Such boats carried big loads, and children and old people rode on top of the packs. No paddles used. Boats were hauled by ponies guided by men. Two, maybe three or four, ponies to a boat. Two men swam at the sides to steady it."

Not being pressed by the soldiers, the Indians made camp for the night on the left bank of the river. The next morning they put together boats and began ferrying their people and goods to the far shore.

"While this was doing, we saw the soldiers riding down the distant hill toward us," Yellow Wolf said. "We found hiding and waited for the soldiers. When they reached the riverbank, we fired across at them. We thought we killed one."

If the soldiers did not know by now that the Nez Perces were excellent marksmen, they were slow learners. But General Howard certainly was exercising caution. Instead of attempting to cross the river here in the face of deadly hostile fire, he decided to go down the Clearwater half a day's march to Dunwell's Ferry, where the crossing could be made in peace and safety. Describing the march downriver as an attempt at strategy, he reported:

"There was a junction of trails beyond Joseph fifteen or twenty miles. Could I but get there! Perhaps I could by going back a little, then down the river and across; quick, indeed, if at all, and secret! But their eyes were too sharp for the success of this maneuver, for I had not proceeded more than six miles before the Indians began to break camp, and to retreat in good earnest, along the Lolo Trail toward Montana and the east."

Chief Joseph was given credit for having delayed pursuit and fooling Howard by conducting a lengthy *"wa-wa"* across the river with the general, in which he proposed surrendering if proper terms were offered. With all action by the military suspended until the Indians had gotten out of danger, Joseph then was supposed to have laughed at Howard, turned his bare bottom toward him, and slapped a buttock in derision as a farewell gesture.

It did not happen quite that way. Apparently Howard was given the impression that some of the Indians might surrender, which did cause him to delay in giving marching orders. But it was not Joseph who gave Howard the reverse salute. It was a young warrior named *Tsa-ya Tee-ma-nah*—"No Heart"—a relative of Yellow Wolf. In response, a soldier fired a shot, which missed as usual, and the warrior hopped on his horse and rode away laughing.

By July 15, the nontreaty bands had traveled thirty miles in a north-easterly direction to the ancient tribal camas-gathering and camping grounds, Weippe Prairie. There they paused to hold a meeting in which they would decide what to do. Participating in the council were Chief Joseph, White Bird, Looking Glass, *Too-hool-hool-zote,* and *Hah-tal-e-kin.* Also present were the renowned warriors, Rainbow and Five Wounds, who, having recently returned from the buffalo country, could give the council reliable information regarding enemies and allies there.

A number of possibilities were discussed. They could cross the Bitter Root Mountains by the Lolo Trail, go north through the land of the Flatheads to Canada, or they could turn south into the land of the Shoshones, from whence they could double back into the Salmon and Snake River country. For a time, White Bird and Joseph favored the latter alternative.

But the Flatheads and their nearby neighbors, the Blackfeet, might not be friendly. The safer course might be to go south up the Bitter Root Valley to the headwaters of the North Fork of the Salmon, swing east through the Big Hole country, Camas Meadows, and Yellowstone Park, then follow Stinking Water or Clark's Fork east into the country of the Crows.

"Why must we run away from the land where we were born?" Chief Joseph demanded passionately. "What are we fighting for?"

"Freedom to live as men," Swift Bird answered. "We will not be penned up like sheep or hogs."

"We fight to defend our families," Looking Glass said. "We did not attack the bluecoats. They attacked us."

"It is good to know what you are fighting for," Joseph said solemnly, nodding his head in agreement. "Before the war began, some of you said that I was afraid of the whites. Now I say to you, stay here with me and you shall have plenty 871 of fighting. We will put our women behind us in these mountains, and die in our own land fighting for them. I would rather do that than run I know not where."

"When Five Wounds and I left the Crows," Rainbow said, "they were talking about going on the warpath against the whites. I say we should go to their country and join them."

"This is true," Five Wounds agreed. "As soon as they learn we have started the war, they will back us up."

"Ha!" Two Moons snorted skeptically, with the veteran warrior *Wot-tol-en*—"Hair Combed Over Eyes"—nodding vigorous agreement, "who can trust a Crow? They are born liars and thieves!"

"That is not true!" Looking Glass said passionately. "Since the war party I led fought on their side against the Sioux five years ago, they have been our strongest allies. As long as we keep the peace pipe they gave us, they will be our friends."

"I hope this is true," White Bird murmured, shaking his head. "But I find it hard to believe."

"Listen to me, my chiefs!" Looking Glass exclaimed. "The Crows are the same as my brothers! If you go there with me you will be safe!"

Though *Wot-tol-en* and Two Moons still mistrusted the Crows, a group of Nez Perces recently returned from the buffalo country had left a number of good horses with their Flathead cousins in the lower Bitter Root Valley. Why not go there and count on the Flatheads for help?

The final decision of the council was to take Lolo Trail to the buffalo country, under the leadership of Looking Glass. On the morning of July 16, camp was broken and the exodus of six hundred and fifty nontreaty Nez Perces from their ancestral homelands began. Since their tepee poles had been left behind in the village deserted on the South Fork of the Clearwater—and would have been an extra burden for their horses to drag along on that steep, narrow, rugged trail—shelter for the next few weeks would be only what they could improvise each night.

Contrary to reports by some fanciful writers, they took no beef cattle with them. They did take horses, though, lots of them—one for every man, woman, and child old enough to ride, plus from two to three thousand spare animals. As they always had, they used them unmercifully, for in their traditional way of life only the strongest animals survived. As rear guard, Looking Glass detailed five young warriors to stay behind at Weippe Prairie.

"You will remain at the camping ground for three suns, watching for enemy scouts and troops," he told them. "If none are seen during that time, you are to come on and overtake us. But if enemies should be sighted, two of you will ride ahead with news of the danger, so that we can prepare to hold the troops back on the trail and the people can escape to a place of safety."

The Lolo Trail could easily be blocked by a few warriors. It was narrow and steep and wound through a heavy growth of trees, and would force the pursuing soldiers to move up the rocky path in single file. This gave rise to the imaginative tale that the retreating Nez Perces sawed through the bases of tall trees, greased the saw marks so they would not show, and left the trees standing on their stumps, to be pushed over once the troops had moved into the trap. This would form a log corral within which the soldiers could then be butchered by the Indians.

"It did not happen," War Singer said with a laugh, when told the story. "In the first place, the *Nimipu* had no saws, only axes. In the second place, they did not know how—as, indeed, no one ever has known how—to pull such a gravity-defying stunt. In the third place, they discouraged pursuit in a far easier, more conventional way—with rifle shots fired from ambush."

General Howard, whose command was following cautiously, sent a dozen Christian Nez Perce scouts, led by Captain John and James Reuben, ahead of the main body of troops with orders to pursue the hostiles for "two marches" and find out what direction they were headed. The scouts managed to make contact with the rear guard of the Nez Perces in only half a day. They were then ordered to ride still further ahead to investigate the increasingly fresh signs.

Shortly after the scouts disappeared into the timber, the sound of gunfire was heard. Major Mason, far to the rear with the regulars, responded by ordering the mule-packed howitzer unloaded and prepared for action. What he intended to shoot at was not clear—but his troops found a target. When a detachment of volunteers came galloping back to inform the regulars that hostilities were under way, the soldiers got so excited they started shooting—at the volunteers. As usual, they missed.

When Captain John, James Reuben, and the scouts came riding back, a Nez Perce known as John Levi, or "Sheared Wolf," was lost. He was found a while later, lying in the grass with forty-five bullet holes in his body. According to War Singer, he got what he deserved, for the nontreaty Indians had on several occasions captured Indians who were scouting for Howard, warned them to cease and desist, and then let them go.

"We knew you had taken up arms against us," he had been told after being captured for the second time, "but for relations' sake we let you go. You promised us before that you would remain at home and not help Howard to destroy us. Every word you promised us has proved to be a lie. We will let you go again, but we want you to understand that the next time we capture you acting under Howard, we will kill you at once."

This time, as Sheared Wolf lay wounded on the ground, he begged the member of the rear guard, *Watz-am-yas,* who was standing over him, "Spare my life! I am badly wounded and have news to tell you!"

"We have spared your life too often," *Watz-am-yas* replied. "You can tell us your news after you get to the happy hunting grounds."

With that, he put a bullet through the scout's head.

Rugged though the trail was, the Nez Perces were so accustomed to traveling it that Yellow Wolf passed over its difficulties with a mere four-word phrase in the middle of a sentence: "For about six days, coming through the mountains, we saw no more fighting."

But to General Howard, the going was incredibly difficult.

"The trail ahead being obstructed by fallen trees of all sizes and descriptions, uprooted by the winds and matted together in every possible troublesome way, a company of forty 'pioneers' with axes, was organized and sent to open the trail, wherever possible. It is true that the Indians had gone over this trail ahead of the troops but they had jammed their ponies through, over and under the rocks, around, over and under logs and fallen trees and through the densest undergrowth, and left blood to mark their path, with abandoned animals with broken legs or stretched dead on the trail."

Over this kind of terrain, Howard considered sixteen miles a day excellent progress for the troops. When asked why the soldiers had so much trouble traversing country that the Nez Perces considered ordinary, Howard repeated the comment of his guide, Ad Chapman, who said, ungrammatically, "No man living can get so much out of a horse, like an Indian can."

Furthermore, Howard added:

"Had we, for three days, along the Lolo Trail, followed closely the hostiles' unmerciful example, we would not have had ten mules left on their feet to carry our sugar, coffee, and hard-bread."

Leaving General Howard and his troops struggling up the trail far behind them, the Nez Perces topped Lolo Pass, paused to camp for a time near a marshy meadow on the eastern slope of the Bitter Root Mountains, then moved at a leisurely pace toward the broad, peaceful valley occupied by their "cousins," the Flatheads, and by the white merchants and ranchers with whom they had long traded for goods and horses on friendly terms during their trips to and from the buffalo country.

In the view of the tribal leaders, remaining behind in the Nez Perce country would have meant a long and bloody war. Leaving their homeland meant choosing the path of peace, for they could not imagine that the soldiers would follow them very far.

But the soldiers were following them, though very slowly. Furthermore, having received word that "hostiles" were about to "invade" the Bitter Root Valley, a thin blue line of thirty regulars was preparing to block the way—backed by two hundred brave volunteers and a number of Flathead Indians, who might be persuaded to turn traitor to their own kind if the prospect of loot in the form of goods and horses was great enough.

To show how much in earnest they were, the soldiers were doing a thing unknown to the Nez Perces in their style of warfare. They were felling trees to blockade the mouth of Lolo Canyon. Did they actually think that a few downed trees would stop the Indians? Wanting to find out, Looking Glass, Joseph, and the other tribal leaders raised a white flag and rode down to the barricade to have a talk with the bluecoat in charge of the defense . . .

9

The note John Crane received from Tall Bird was brief and starkly urgent in its appeal:

> Brother, can you come to Lapwai at once, with good mountain horses and camping gear for two, prepared for a long, tough trip? My children are fleeing their homeland to go they know not where. Cousins are killing cousins. An army of white soldiers is gathering to pursue and murder the nontreaty Nez Perces without offering them peace or mercy. When I talk to the white leaders, they do not listen because they think I am a wild Indian ignorant of law and justice. Because you are white, known to and respected by them,

perhaps they would listen to you. Please come and help me, brother. The fate of my family and my people is at stake.

Asking A. C. Smith and a few sympathetic neighbors to keep an eye on his cabin and livestock in case he was gone for the rest of the summer—which he feared he would be—John made the two-day ride to the reservation, wincing at the way his muscles and joints ached and throbbed after long hours in the saddle, even though he rode daily and was in good shape for a man his age. But this jaunt would be like a Sunday ride in the park, he suspected, compared to the trip Tall Bird had in mind.

"Looking Glass leads the people now," Tall Bird told John in his daughter's lodge near the agency headquarters. "Since his village was attacked without cause, he is so bitter that he considers no course but war, no matter how badly the people suffer."

"Your son, Swift Bird, agrees with him, I suppose?"

"To my son, Looking Glass is a great war chief, who can do no wrong. Where Looking Glass leads, he will follow."

"You think they're headed for the Bitter Root Valley?"

"That is the word the scouts bring back, yes. Looking Glass wants to go on east to the land of the Crows, who he says are his brothers. Some of the chiefs want to go north to Canada, where they think the Sioux will make them welcome. Still others say that once they cross the Bitter Root Mountains the war will be over, for they have no quarrel with the white settlers there. They think the Cut-Arm Chief will not follow them."

"They're wrong, brother. From what I've heard, General Howard keeps the telegraph wires humming, bringing in federal troops from all over the country. There's a new post a few miles north of the eastern foot of Lolo Pass, I'm told. He'll likely fetch troops from there."

"I know. But Looking Glass is a stubborn man, who thinks no idea is any good unless he thought of it first himself. His idea now is freedom or death. If he cannot lead his people to a land where they can live free, he will make them fight until they all are killed."

"What can we do about that?"

"The Nez Perce scouts working for the Cut-Arm Chief all live on the reservation, so are not trusted by the nontreaty Indians. Even though men like Captain John and Old George have sons or daughters with the hostiles, while James Reuben is related to Joseph and is called head chief, they cannot get close enough to the hostiles to make them listen to peace talk. But if you and I can approach them, I believe they will talk to us."

"Why would they trust us and not the others?"

"Because they know that all my life I have never injured a living person. Because they know that you are my brother and the best white friend they have. Because *Moki Hih-hih*, our father, came to the Nez Perce country seventy-two years ago with the great chief, William Clark, who made a promise of friendship between your people and mine that has never been broken until now. If the hostiles will talk to anyone, they will talk with us."

"You may be right," John said thoughtfully. "But General Howard's army is between them and us. How do we deal with that problem?"

"Your son is a white soldier chief, you have told me many times, who went to the same war school General Howard did, led troops in the Civil War, as Howard did, and is known by him. So when you ask a favor from General Howard, he will listen to you with more respect than he would to me."

"I'm not sure General Howard respects anybody but God, the Secretary of War, and the reporters covering his campaign," John said dryly. "But maybe I can get him to listen. What do you want me to ask him?"

"For a paper stating on what terms he will make peace. If he will write down an offer that his country will honor, we will take it to Looking Glass, Joseph, and the other leaders and try to get them to accept it. Then this terrible war can be brought to an end."

Shaking his head, John stared into the fire smoldering in the center of the lodge, silent for a long while as he considered the immensity of the task Tall Bird had proposed. The conflict had long since outgrown local limits. With over eighty white soldiers and civilians already killed, federal troops and a famous general humiliated by defeat in battle after battle, hordes of allegedly bloodthirsty Indians overrunning the country, a swarm of sensation-hungry reporters covering the campaign for the national press, and the victory over Custer by the Sioux just a year ago still fresh in the memory of the Army and the public, bringing this war to a peaceful end by means of a simple paper written by General Howard and agreed to by the nontreaty chiefs was an extremely remote possibility.

Still, John admitted, it might be worth trying. He gave Tall Bird a wry smile.

"I'll say this much for you, brother. You don't think small."

"You'll do it, then?"

"As well as I can. But we'll have a few problems."

"This I know."

"In the first place, neither of us are as young as we used to be. Following the Army and the hostiles across Lolo Trail won't be a picnic."

"Many of the grandfathers and grandmothers who are with my people are older than we are. Since they were forced to leave their tepee poles in the village they deserted on the Clearwater, they will have no shelter until they get far enough ahead of the soldiers to take the time to stop and cut more. What they must suffer, we can endure."

"Well, at least the weather is decent. Maybe when we catch up with Howard we can persuade him to hold back his troops, let the hostiles make camp in the Bitter Root Valley, then call a peace conference so that the leaders can discuss terms. As a beginning, maybe they'll agree that the women, children, and old people should be declared noncombatants and permitted to come back under escort to the reservation, where they can get better care."

"No, brother, the women, children, and old people would never consent to that," Tall Bird said, shaking his head. "If peace is made, it must be made for all at the same time."

To the *Nimipu,* Tall Bird explained, this kind of war was different from what they traditionally had known. When his people had made war against another Indian tribe in time past, the time, place, and manner of the campaign was discussed by a council of chiefs, a leader was chosen, and a certain number of warriors were designated to go with the party. In such warfare, the women, children, and old people always stayed home. While skirmishes with the enemy might be violent and bloody, they were usually brief, governed by the sensible rule that it was better to make an enemy respect you by a brisk, quickly broken-off attack than to demonstrate a foolish courage by a rash charge from which you could not disengage without grave risk to your life. Thus mortalities were usually light.

Even when on long sojourns with their families in the buffalo country, the *Nimipu* seldom fought great battles with the Blackfeet or Shoshones. By unspoken agreement, all the tribes making meat there knew that a skirmish between roving bands of hunters was a hit-and-run affair, not to be taken too seriously. But an attack by a band of warriors upon a group of women dressing and drying meat in a camp whose tepees housed their children and parents was taken very seriously, for when hostiles chose to make war upon women, children, and old people, all the members of the offending tribe could expect swift, terrible vengeance to be taken against their own families.

"Three times now the soldiers have attacked the villages of our people," Tall Bird said grimly, "making no distinction between warriors and those who cannot fight. Because of this, my people feel that the soldiers cannot be trusted. When peace is declared, it must be for all. Look what happened to *Temme Ilp-ilp* when he tried to surrender."

Normally living in the Kamiah area, the band of which *Temme Ilp-ilp*—"Red Heart"—was chief was returning from a lengthy sojourn in the buffalo country when it met the fleeing nontreaty Nez Perces on Weippe Prairie. Numbering seventeen warriors and twenty-eight women and children, the members of the band had known nothing of the war until now. Talking it over with Looking Glass, Joseph, and White Bird, Chief Red Heart decided that he and his band would have nothing to do with the conflict. Instead, they headed for their home village on the reservation and what they thought would be a life of peace.

But when the Red Heart band met General Howard and the soldiers their reception was not at all what they expected. Instead of being treated kindly for having chosen the path of peace, they were treated as hostiles who had surrendered after being defeated in battle.

"These peaceable, innocent people were seized and taken to Kamiah," Tall Bird said bitterly, "where their horses, saddles, and other belongings were confiscated as booty of war. Under a guard of cavalry, they then were marched over sixty miles on foot through the dust and heat to Fort Lapwai. The Cut-Arm Chief even bragged about what he had done."

Indeed he had, for at last he could report that he had taken a substantial number of prisoners—never mind how. And prisoners they would remain for the duration of the war. Twenty-three adult men, nine adult women, and one three-year old boy were held under military guard at Fort Lapwai, then moved by wagon to Lewiston and by boat downriver to Fort Vancouver. Watched over by the post's band, for the next nine months they would be seen as evidence of the bloodthirsty hostiles General Howard had taken out of action . . .

10

When Looking Glass saw the log barricade with which the soldiers were attempting to block Lolo Canyon, he laughed and said contemptuously:

"If the officer wishes to build corrals for the Nez Perces, he may. But they will not hold us back. We are not horses."

Truth was, Captain Charles C. Rawn knew the task facing him was bleak. Though the defensive forces available to him were equal in number to those of the "invading" Nez Perces, they lacked two vital motives that welded the hostiles into a formidable fighting force: first, a cause for which they were prepared to fight to the death; second, the desperation of battle-hardened exiles with nothing to lose but their freedom.

In command of Company L, Seventh Infantry, and just recently posted to newly built Fort Missoula a few miles to the north, Captain Rawn had assembled his forces as hastily as he could after receiving orders to intercept and delay the hostiles by all possible means. What was possible was not known, for the disparate elements of his command had never been tested as individual units under fire, let alone as a force working together.

Because erecting a stockade would serve to protect their own bodies, the thirty regulars could be depended upon to work like beaver and fight like demons, for they knew they would stand no chance if they tried to run. The fifty Flatheads were something else. To insure their support, vague promises had been made that they would not be confined to a reduced reservation; that the federal government would regard their assistance as a friendly act, for which they would reap a rich reward in goodwill; and that, if the hostiles surrendered, no one would object strenuously if the Flatheads helped themselves to Nez Perce horses and goods.

In order to make sure that no friendly Indians got shot, Captain Rawn ordered each Flathead warrior to tie a white cloth around his forehead. But he had strong doubts that the "whitehead" Flatheads would remain loyal if bullets started to fly.

As for the two hundred volunteers, their motives ranged from whiskey courage through the attitude that "an Indian fight ought to be a lot of fun" to the more serious-minded mood of ranchers and merchants willing to fight to protect their homes and businesses—if a fight could not be avoided.

Watching the group of Nez Perces approach the barricade carrying a white flag, Captain Rawn walked forward to meet them, both arms extended with palms open in a gesture of peace. In response, the Indians raised their right hands. Telling the half blood, Delaware Jim, who was acting as interpreter, to translate his words truly, Looking Glass said:

"We come in peace. Why are you trying to block our way?"

"My orders are to stop you by whatever means necessary."

"We are not at war with the people of the Bitter Root Valley. For many years, we have passed through the valley on our way to and from the buffalo country. We have left horses in the care of white rancher friends living in the valley. We have traded with white merchants, paying for what we bought in gold dust which they were glad to get. We have never cheated or harmed them. They have never cheated or harmed us. We regard them as friends."

"That well may be. But I have my orders. Lay down your arms and surrender."

"If we do," Chief Joseph asked quietly, "what terms will we be offered?"

"None. My orders are that your surrender must be unconditional. Again I tell you, lay down your arms."

Looking Glass shook his head, his eyes smoldering with anger. "If you want my arms so bad, you can start taking them. Before leaving Idaho, I made up my mind that we would talk with the white man only through our guns."

Assured by the peaceful manner of the Nez Perce leaders that there would be a great deal of talk between the hostiles and the soldiers before violence ensued, a number of curious white-banded Flatheads and uneasy volunteers moved forward to within hearing distance of the discussion. With Looking Glass, White Bird, Joseph, and *Hah-tal-e-kin* speaking for the bands they led through Delaware Jim in a masterful combination of diplomacy and the threat of force, the nontreaty leaders managed to convince the volunteers that their families would not be harmed nor their property stolen if they permitted the Nez Perces to cross the Bitter Root Valley in peace. In fact, Looking Glass said, his people were badly in need of flour, sugar, salt, bacon, ammunition, and other supplies, which they hoped to purchase from the local merchants and for which they would pay in gold dust or coin.

"Tell the storekeepers we hope they will be open for business tomorrow," Looking Glass said through Delaware Jim. "For we will be ready to buy."

"Well, if it comes to a choice 'tween fightin' and tradin'," exclaimed a merchant from the settlement of Stevensville, seventeen miles up the valley, "call me a chickenhearted lover of the free enterprise system! Captain, I'm gonna let you defend the country! I'm goin' home and open my store!"

Relieved by the prospect of peace and trade, most of the volunteers followed his example, speaking in friendly fashion to the Nez Perce leaders, asking them to tell their people to stop by the business establishments or ranches of their longtime white friends as they traveled south up the Bitter Root Valley. Observing this desertion from the bluecoat defense, the white-banded Flatheads began muttering uneasily among themselves. As they milled about uncertainly, Captain Rawn saw a short, stocky, elderly Indian armed with a repeating Winchester rifle ride into their midst, upbraiding them angrily.

"Zikauau! Uapalaksa! Zikamkal! Ueta Teminze!"

Spurring his horse first to one Flathead brave, then to another, he reached out and ripped away the white cloths tied around their foreheads and threw them to the ground. Sheepishly, other Flathead warriors tore off the cloths they were wearing and discarded them before he could get to them, then turned their horses around and slunk away.

"What was that all about?" Captain Rawn asked Delaware Jim, who, like the Nez Perce chiefs, was watching with a smile.

"He called these people cowards and dogs, unworthy of being trusted as men. Because they lack the courage to stand behind their blood kin and fight against the whites, he is rejecting them as his adopted people, he says, even though his wife is a Flathead and his children and grandchildren have Flathead blood in their veins. From now on, he says, he will live and fight to the death with his own tribe—the Nez Perce."

"He is Nez Perce, then?"

"Half Nez Perce, Captain. And half white. His father was one of the leaders of the Lewis and Clark party."

Watching the fierce-visaged old man ride over to Looking Glass, Joseph, White Bird, and *Hah-tal-e-kin,* vigorously shake their hands, strike his own chest then theirs, making gestures that were obviously pledges of eternal friendship, the captain noted that the stringy, unbraided hair of the Indian was a yellowish straw color, rather than black, while the lines of his face gave evidence of the white blood in his veins.

"Me Clark!" the old Indian was exclaiming to the chiefs. "*Tzi-kal-tza* —Flathead name. Me Clark! *Temme Nimipu!*"

"Clark!" Captain Rawn exclaimed. "Is he the man I've heard rumors about ever since I came to Montana? The old fellow whose mother was a Nez Perce woman and whose father was Captain William Clark?"

"He is the man."

"Good Lord! That would make him seventy years old!"

"That's right."

"What's he doing in Flathead country?"

"The best I can make out, his mother was a niece of Chief Broken Arm, who was an important Nez Perce chief in the Kamiah area. From the day he was born, he's known he was Captain Clark's son—and he's proud of it. After he married a Flathead woman, he came to live in the Bitter Root Valley. But now that the Nez Perces have gone to war, he's going back to his people, he says. He vows to fight with them till the end."

Deserted by the Flatheads and the volunteers, Captain Rawn knew he had no choice but to let the Nez Perces pass. In a desperate attempt to stall for time, he suggested to the Indian leaders that they meet again tomorrow to council. Willing to let him save whatever face he could, the chiefs agreed, but as soon as they went back and rejoined their people plans were set afoot to bypass the barricade early the next day.

Protected by a dozen warriors who stayed between the main body of Nez Perces and the breastworks below, the long column of women, children, old people, loose horses, and pack animals carrying camp supplies moved along the sides of the steep, tree-covered hills flanking the fort, beginning the movement with the first light of dawn, and continuing well into the morning. The voice of Looking Glass could be heard addressing his warriors:

"Don't shoot! Don't shoot! Let the white man shoot first."

Fortunately for the soldiers, they did not shoot. What they did not know was that, hidden behind rocks and fallen trees on the slope above them, Indian sharpshooters were in perfect position to pick them off— despite the barricade, whose wall on that side was too low to protect them. From that day on, the untested barrier would be known locally as "Fort Fizzle."

As the caravan moved out across the relatively flat, open floor of the valley, a group of volunteers who had swallowed a bit of liquid courage decided to demonstrate how brave they were by mounting a charge at the column of women and children. At once, Looking Glass signaled a band of warriors forward into a position between the whites and the head of the column. Seeing the warriors coming soured whiskey courage into well-watered vinegar in the veins of the volunteers. Admitting that he had turned tail and ridden as fast as he could go in the opposite direction, one of the volunteers later recalled sheepishly:

"I don't know what I did with my gun. Somehow I lost it. I remember using my hat to whip my horse to a faster pace. Although he was a fast runner, I thought that I never was on a slower mount. The Indians did not fire on us, nor did they appear to hasten in their gait. Perhaps they thought we were staging a free riding exhibition for their amusement . . ."

11

With Fort Fizzle behind them and a verbal peace treaty made with the white settlers, the leaders of the nontreaty bands held another council regarding the route to be taken. White Bird, *Too-hool-hool-zote*, Red Owl, Two Moons, and *Wot-tol-en* favored turning north, traveling down the Bitter Root Valley through the country of the Flatheads and then on to Canada. Looking Glass, Five Wounds, and Rainbow wanted to go south, up the Bitter Root Valley, then east through the Big Hole country, Camas Meadows, and Yellowstone Park to the land of their Crow allies.

Chief Joseph took no part in the council, declaring:

"I have no words! You know the country, I do not!"

Since Looking Glass had succeeded so well as a leader up to this point, his route was chosen.

Here the fleeing Indians were joined by six lodges of Nez Perces who had taken up more or less permanent residence in the Bitter Root Valley. They were also joined by the Yakima, *Ow-hi;* by a half-blood Delaware named Tom Hill; and by a small-statured, shrewd, part-blood Nez

Perce known variously as *Ki-nik-nik, Squal-sac,* Lean Elk, or Poker Joe.

With fondness and talent for cards and fast horses, Poker Joe had spent a good deal of time in the buffalo country. On his way back to Idaho with his family, he had been within six miles of Kamiah when he learned of hostilities.

"I did not want to go to war against the whites," he told Looking Glass, "but I did not want to be taken prisoner like Red Heart and his people. So I turned back toward the Bitter Root Valley, where I planned to live in peace until the war was over. By accident, I cut my leg badly with a knife. When the white people saw the bandage, they thought I was a hostile who had been wounded in the war, and would have nothing to do with me. So I might as well join you and go where you go."

"Good!" Looking Glass said. "My brothers, the Crows, will make you welcome."

At Stevensville, a small settlement on their route, the Nez Perces went into the stores of the white merchants and purchased whatever supplies they needed, scrupulously heeding the admonition of the chiefs that they mind their manners, paying the high prices asked in gold dust, coin, or horses. When some of the local citizens criticized the merchants for "trafficking with the enemy," the storekeepers made a vigorous, logical defense of their actions.

"Hell, what else could we do? If we hadn't sold 'em the stuff, they'd of took what they wanted without paying for it. Would you have helped us stop 'em? Not by a damn sight, you wouldn't! And business *is* business!"

Only on two occasions during the movement of the Indians up the valley were there instances of misbehavior on the part of the Nez Perces —and Looking Glass was quick to discipline those responsible. The first occurred when a young brave got drunk on whiskey foolishly given him by a white blacksmith. Looking Glass ordered the young man put under guard and escorted back to camp.

In the second occurrence, several unruly members of Chief *Too-hool-hool-zote*'s band raided the deserted home of a rancher named Myron Lockwood, packing off several hundred pounds of flour, bacon, and other supplies. When Looking Glass heard about it, he became very angry. Insisting that the tough old chief accompany him, he confronted the guilty Indians.

"Did you not hear the peace pact I made with the white settlers?" he demanded.

"I heard," *Too-hool-hool-zote* answered for them.

"Then you know that these men are thieves. You know that they must pay for the goods they stole."

"They will pay. I will see to that."

"How can we pay?" one of the Indians protested. "We have no money."

"Do you have horses?" Looking Glass asked.

"Yes. We have many horses."

"Good! You will take three good horses to the white man's ranch and put them in his corral. You will go into his barn, find his branding iron, build a fire, heat the iron, and put his brand on the horses. Do you think you can do that?"

While the guilty Indians stared sheepishly down at the ground, *Too-hool-hool-zote* nodded grimly. "It will be done, brother. Before this day is over, the white man will have three good Nez Perce horses bearing his brand in his corral."

The pace set by Looking Glass was an easy one, twelve to fifteen miles a day. "Why hurry?" he said. Peace had been made with the white settlers. The Cut-Arm Chief and his bluecoats were far behind in Idaho. Ahead lay a pleasant country with plenty of water, grass, and trees, where they could go into camp soon and cut tepee poles for their lodges before moving on toward the land of his brothers, the Crows. Why hurry?

But a few of the Nez Perces were having uneasy premonitions. One morning *Wah-litits,* one of the Red Coat warriors who had started the conflict, rode through camp calling loudly to his people, as was the custom when a person had seen a vision foretelling the future:

"My brothers, my sisters, I am telling you! In a dream last night I saw myself killed. I will be killed soon! I do not care. I am willing to die. But first, I will kill some soldiers."

Lone Bird, who was also known to be a brave fighter, had a similar vision. Riding through the camp, he proclaimed:

"My shaking heart tells me trouble and death will overtake us if we make no hurry through this land! I cannot smother, I cannot hide that which I see. I must speak what is revealed to me. Let us be gone to the buffalo country!"

Looking Glass still refused to move any faster. Reaching their traditional camping ground on the Big Hole River, the Nez Perces settled in for a stay of several days. The first night, *Wot-tol-en,* who had strong medicine powers, dreamed of soldiers. His dream so impressed a group of young Nez Perce warriors that they decided ten or twelve of them should select the fastest horses they could find, ride back down the

Bitter Root Valley on a scout, and see if a force of soldiers was on their trail. Going to an elderly Indian named Burning Coals, who had a number of good horses, two of the Nez Perce warriors told him what they wanted to do.

"We need fast horses. Will you loan us yours?"

"No," Burning Coals answered curtly. "I think too much of my horses to let them be ridden by a bunch of reckless young men. I will not loan you my horses."

When they sought help from Looking Glass, Swift Bird, and Lone Bull, they did not get it either. Whatever his fine qualities as a leader may have been, Looking Glass had one bad fault—he was against every idea not first thought of by himself.

"Scouting our back trail to see what the white soldiers are doing would be a waste of time," he said. "There will be no more fighting! War is quit."

Unfortunately, he was mistaken. War was suspended, not quit. Alerted by messages from General Howard and Captain Rawn, Colonel John Gibbon, with 15 officers, 146 men, and all the soldiers that Rawn could spare from his command had left Fort Missoula August 4 on the trail of the dawdling Nez Perces. Transporting the foot soldiers by wagon much of the way, the command made from twenty-five to thirty miles a day, traveling twice as fast as the Indians.

At Stevensville, a day's march south of Missoula, the Gibbon command was joined by thirty-five citizen volunteers—the very same white settlers who had been only too glad to agree to a verbal peace treaty a few days ago when they had been outnumbered and thought themselves threatened by Nez Perces.

Now, offered loot in the form of Nez Perce horses and goods if they helped the military, the good citizens had no compunction against unilaterally abrogating the treaty. So far as they were concerned, peace was quit now. At the first opportunity, war would be resumed against Nez Perce men, women, and children—hopefully by a surprise dawn attack when the possibility of resistance by the Indians would be negligible . . .

Catching up with General Howard and his 500-man force near the abandoned barricade at the lower end of Lolo Canyon, John Crane and Tall Bird were relieved to hear that a truce had already been made between the nontreaty Nez Perces and the white residents of the Bitter Root Valley. In discussing it with them, General Howard expressed mixed feelings.

"If the settlers and the Flatheads had backed him up, Captain Rawn could have forced the Nez Perces to surrender," Howard said. "But when they deserted him, he did the wise thing in not attacking Joseph and his hostiles with the small company of regulars under his direct command. At least bloodshed was averted for the time being."

"It's not Joseph who is acting as war chief," John Crane said quietly. "It's Looking Glass. Since his village was attacked, surrender is not in his vocabulary. He swears he'll fight to the death."

"I don't know what your sources of intelligence are, Mr. Crane," Howard said crisply. "But mine combine the knowledge of Christian Nez Perce Reservation chiefs with that of a white man who speaks their language and has lived among them for years. Therefore, I shall regard my intelligence as more reliable until proven otherwise."

"You're referring to James Reuben, Captain John, Old George, and Ad Chapman, I take it?"

"I am. Furthermore, I have met in council with Chief Joseph on several occasions and have talked with him at great length. There is not the slightest doubt in my mind that he is the leader of the hostiles."

Seeing nothing to be gained by arguing with the highly opinionated officer, John made an unobtrusive sign at Tall Bird, meaning "Leave it on the ground," shrugged, and spoke placatingly.

"Well, whoever is running things for the hostiles, a truce is working now. Tall Bird and I would like to help make a permanent peace."

"What can you do?"

"Tall Bird has a son and a daughter with the hostiles. He's related to Chief Joseph and has a reputation among the Nez Perces as a man of peace. Whatever offer you give him to take to them will be considered seriously."

"At this point I can only ask for their unconditional surrender. Can he get them to accept that?"

"I'm afraid not. My suggestion is that you offer them peace with amnesty for all except the young men who committed the murders that started the war. Anything less won't be listened to."

"You sound very sure of yourself, Mr. Crane."

"I've lived with the Nez Perces a lot longer than Ad Chapman has, General Howard. I think they respect me a lot more than they do him. A few years ago, I went to Washington with a delegation of chiefs when they signed amendments to the 1863 Treaty. For a while, I worked as a subagent at Lapwai. I know how the Nez Perce mind works."

"Your son, Major Luke Crane, is a West Point graduate, now serving as an officer with the Corps of Engineers, I believe you told me. He fought in the Civil War."

"Yes, sir. He and Custer were classmates and friends."

"Where is he now?"

"The last letter I had from him he was assigned to Fort Keogh, a new post in eastern Montana, overseeing work there. He moves around a lot."

"A fine officer, as I recall. Give him my regards the next time you write."

"I certainly will."

"Now, as to your suggestion that I offer Joseph and the hostiles peace with amnesty for all except the original murderers, Mr. Crane, that is easier said than done. Many white people have been killed. It would be difficult for me to justify making peace without punishing all the Indians who have rebelled against the government. In addition, it is a sound military principle that only a victory in battle puts the enemy in a proper frame of mind to accept peace."

"Less than a third of the hostiles are men of fighting age, General. The rest are women, children, and old people. Yet three times now your soldiers and the volunteers have attacked their villages, without making any distinction between warriors and noncombatants. Surely you don't have to win another battle against these poor people to bring about peace."

Before General Howard could answer, his adjutant, Lieutenant Charles Erskine Scott Wood, saluted casually and then approached, handing him several dispatches.

"These just arrived, sir."

"Thank you." After reading the dispatches, Howard smiled and said, "Excellent! Thank heaven for the telegraph wires!" He looked triumphantly at John Crane and Tall Bird. "The reinforcements I requested are being sent in from all directions. A few days ago, I passed on to General Sheridan a suggestion made by the agent in charge of the reservation at Fort Hall—that some of the Indians living there be enlisted as soldiers and scouts to take the field under my command against the hostiles. A force of fifty Bannocks has been organized, led by Chief Buffalo Horn. It will join us in the upper Bitter Root Valley in a few days."

"Good Lord!" John murmured. "The Bannocks and the Nez Perces have been enemies for generations! You can't set them against each other!"

"Furthermore, Chief Washakie of the Northern Shoshonis on the

Wind River Reservation says that if the government will give him enough horses and rifles, he can whip the Nez Perces in a single day!"

"Not the Shoshonis, too!"

"But the best news is that Colonel Gibbon, with a force of one hundred and fifty regulars and thirty-five volunteers, passed Stevensville two days ago. He is now near the head of the Bitter Root Valley and should be in a position to strike a decisive blow against the hostiles within a matter of hours. So far, it appears that the Indians have not detected his presence. He plans to attack at dawn . . ."

1 2

Lying just a few miles east of the Continental Divide at an elevation of 6,800 feet, the Big Hole area where the Nez Perces traditionally camped on their way to and from the buffalo country was called *Izh-kun-ziz-la-kik* by its aboriginal owners, the Flatheads, because its extensive meadows were honeycombed with the burrows of small picket-pin ground squirrels. Here in late summer, days were pleasantly warm and nights cool, grass was abundant for the horses, camas were available in the marshy areas, the clear mountain stream teemed with fish, firewood was readily at hand, and the slopes to the west were covered with lodgepole pine. Following their long, tiring weeks of flight, a few days of rest in this pleasant spot was a welcome prospect.

After tepee poles had been cut, peeled, and set up, eighty-nine lodges were pitched on the open flat in a V-shaped alignment. Still a rich tribe so far as possession went, the Nez Perces used treated hides as lodge covers, rather than canvas as did many of the poorer reservation Indians. Camped in the area were some 800 nontreaty Nez Perces, War Singer said, of which 125 were warriors.

Reaching the campsite the afternoon of August 7, refusing to scout the back trail because they were sure war was quit, Looking Glass and the other leaders relaxed. Hunting parties rode out in search of game. Some of the women dug and cooked camas, while others cut tepee poles. The boys fished, swam, and played games.

Behind them, Colonel Gibbon's command, which had been covering twice as much ground as the Nez Perces each day, reached the head of the Bitter Root Valley in late afternoon, August 7. A scouting party sent ahead located the Indian camp the morning of August 8, dispatched word back to Gibbon, then withdrew four or five miles, awaiting the arrival of the main force. Wanting to move quickly and quietly, Colonel Gibbon ordered that only two days' rations and one hundred rounds of ammunition be issued to each man. The wagons, the mountain howitzer, and extra supplies were left behind to be brought up later. He then moved out at 10 P.M. in a silent march through the night. Long before dawn, August 9, the command reached the Big Hole Basin. Here it halted on the timbered hills overlooking the sleeping village and waited for the coming of day. The force numbered 191 men.

"The *Nimipu* knew that white men were in the area," War Singer said, "for in their trip up the valley they often had seen whites on the trail. This gave them no concern, for they had made peace with these local people. It was only the Cut-Arm Chief who wanted to make war on them, they thought, and he was probably still far behind in Idaho."

The nephew of Chief White Bird, who was ten years old at the time, later vividly remembered the Big Hole encampment:

"We came to that place in the afternoon, toward evening. We stayed that night and next day. Evening came on again, and it was after sundown, not too late, lots of us children were playing. It was below the camp, toward the creek that we boys played the stick or bone game. It finally grew dark and we had a fire for light and warmth.

"Two men came there wrapped in gray blankets. They stood close, and we saw they were white men. Foolishly we said nothing to the older people about it. We ran away and came back to our playing.

"Just about this time I became tired. I went to bed and to sleep, resting until morning. Of course I was in the same tepee with my father and mother.

"Father got up early to go look after the horses. Another man was perhaps forty steps ahead of him, going for his horses. The soldiers shot him down. They did not try to capture him, but killed him first thing. Father saw the gun flash, heard the report and turned back to camp.

"Right away the troops began shooting. Bullets were like hail on the camp; on the tepees. The noise was like Gatling guns, as I have since heard them. The sound awoke me. I heard bullets ripping the tepee walls, pattering like raindrops.

"I did as my mother told me. Horses hitched overnight, ready to go for other horses, were all killed. I ran only a little ways when I came to a low place in the ground. I stopped and lay down. Several women were there, and Mother came fast after me.

"Mother picked me up, saying, 'Come, son, let us get away somewhere.' She took my right hand in her left and we ran. A bullet took off her middle finger, the end of her thumb, and shot off my thumb, as you see. The same bullet did it all. Mother pointed to the creek and said, 'Get down to the water! Then we may escape away!'

"I started and she told me to go up the creek to some bushes out in the stream. I noticed one woman digging in the bank so she could hide. We reached the bushes, and Mother sat down, her head only out of the water. I stood up, the water to my neck. Five of us were there, and two more came. One little girl was shot through the under part of her upper arm. She held the arm up from the cold water, it hurt so. It was a big bullet hole. I could see through it.

"It was not full light when we ran to the creek, but it grew light and the sun came up. An Indian, who had been shooting fast at the soldiers, was killed. The woman I saw digging was shot in the left breast. She pitched into the water and I saw her struggling. She floated by and mother caught and drew the body to her. She placed the dying woman's head on a sandbar just out of the water. She was soon dead. A fine-looking woman, and I remember the blood coloring the water."

Given the advantage of position, firepower, and surprise, the failure of Colonel Gibbon's force to overwhelm the Indian camp in short order was difficult to understand, War Singer said. Certainly no fault could be found in the way he planned the attack. Three units of his command were to charge down the hill, across the stream, and into the sleeping village simultaneously. A fourth unit was held back as a reserve force. It was understood by the soldiers and the citizen volunteers that they were to shoot at everything that moved and that no prisoners were to be taken, though specific orders to that effect were not given.

But in execution of the well-laid plan, several things went wrong. In the predawn darkness an elderly Nez Perce with failing eyesight was one of the five Indians leaving the village and going out to the horse herd to select mounts for the coming day. The four other men were afoot. They sensed that enemies lay hidden in the timber ahead, turned around, and hurried back to the village. But *Na-tal-e-kin,* the old man, was riding a horse because he knew its eyesight was better than his own. As the animal approached the hiding place of the soldiers, three citizen volunteers opened fire, killing the old man instantly.

"*Na-tal-e-kin* holds a place of honor in the memory of his people,"

War Singer said. "At the cost of his own life, he alerted the village to its danger."

Signal for the attack was to be the firing of three volleys, followed by a concerted, three-pronged charge. As in earlier battles, the presence of untrained men ruined the plan. In command of a mixed company of volunteers and regulars stationed opposite the northern end of the village, Lieutenant James H. Bradley had not yet gotten his men into position when the killing of *Na-tal-e-kin* by the citizen soldiers aroused the Indian camp. Though still back in the trees, Lieutenant Bradley ordered the three volleys fired, then led the charge down the slope, across the stream, and toward the hostile camp.

Only three men followed him. The rest of the company remained behind in the timber. Caught in the open by quick-reacting Nez Perce warriors, Lieutenant Bradley and a volunteer named Morrow were shot and killed. This left the company leaderless and freed the northern end of the village from pressure against it, permitting its warriors to go to the aid of the rest of the camp.

At first it appeared that the battle would be a short one, for in less than twenty minutes the center and right-flank forces overran the camp and were riddling the tepees with rifle shots. Following Colonel Gibbon's orders, the soldiers began setting fire to anything that would burn. Children were crying, women were screaming, warriors were seizing whatever weapons they could find and running out to fight the foe. Over the din, War Singer said, the strong voices of Looking Glass and White Bird could be heard as the chiefs rallied their people.

"Wah-litits! Sarp-sis Ilp-ilp! Um-til-ilp-con!" Looking Glass shouted at the three redcoat warriors. "This is a battle! Now is the time for you to show your courage and fight. You can kill right and left! I would rather see you killing than the rest of the warriors, for you commenced the war!"

Though over seventy years old, with his warrior days long behind him, Chief White Bird quickly responded to the attack.

"Why are we retreating?" he cried. "Since the world was made, brave men have fought for their women and children! Are we going to run to the mountains and let the whites kill our women and children before our eyes?"

Unbelievably, the tide of battle began to turn in favor of the Indians. As daylight grew and more and more warriors found and began to use weapons, the attackers began to suffer serious casualties. Receiving a thigh wound himself, Colonel Gibbon ordered the command to withdraw from the village and take a defensive position along the timbered slope on the far side of the Big Hole River.

The marksmanship of the Nez Perces amazed him. "Almost every time one of their rifles went off," he reported later, "one of our party was sure to fall."

In hand-to-hand combat, the Indians fought with the ferocious courage of people defending their families, their freedom, and all their earthly possessions. Grizzly Bear Youth, a Nez Perce warrior, related his personal experiences to War Singer:

"When I was following the soldiers, trying to kill as many as possible, a big, ugly volunteer turned around swearing and made for me. I suppose he had not time to load his needle gun, so he swung it over his head by the barrel and rushed at me to strike me over the head with the butt end. I did the same thing. We both struck and each received a blow on the head. The volunteer's gun cut a brand on my forehead that will be seen as long as I live.

"My blow on his head made him fall on his back. I jumped on him and tried to hold him down. The volunteer was a powerful man. He turned me over and got on top. He got his hand on my throat and commenced choking me. I was almost gone and had just strength left to make signs to a warrior, who was coming up, to shoot him. This was Red Owl's son, who ran up, put his needle gun to the volunteer's side and fired. The ball passed through him and killed him. But I had my arm around the waist of the man when the shot was fired and the ball after going through the man broke my arm."

After the Indian camp had rallied and driven the soldiers back into the timber, War Singer said, Two Moons heard that his friend, the noted warrior Rainbow, had been killed early in the battle. Going to where the body lay, he recalled what Rainbow had told him about his protective medicine:

"I have the promise given that in any battle I engage in after sunrise, I shall not be killed. I can there walk among my enemies. I can face the point of the gun. My body no thicker than a hair, the enemies can never hit me. But if I have any battle or fighting before the sunrise, I shall be killed."

Since the whites had attacked before dawn, Two Moons noted sadly, the protective medicine of Rainbow was not in effect. Five Wounds, Rainbow's close friend, wept when he saw the body.

"My brother has passed away," he lamented. "I too will now go, as did his father and my father die in the war years ago. They lay side by side where the battle was strongest. Now I shall lie down beside my brother warmate. He is no more, and I shall see that I follow him."

Shortly thereafter, Five Wounds made a lone suicidal charge against the entrenched soldiers, falling only a few steps away from where they were dug in.

"Another great warrior was gone," Two Moons said. "His mind no longer on the battle, his *Wy-a-kin* power had left him. There was nothing to protect him from enemy bullets."

The idea that friends close in life should be equally close in death was part of the Nez Perce warrior philosophy, War Singer said. *Wah-litits,* one of the young men who had started the war by avenging his father's murder, was asleep in his tepee when the soldiers attacked the village. Seizing his gun he ran outside, dropped behind a log, and began firing at the troopers in Captain Logan's company. Beside him, *Wah-litits's* wife was wounded. After killing at least one soldier, *Wah-litits* was shot and killed—probably by Captain Logan himself. The Indian warrior's wife picked up her dead husband's rifle and killed Captain Logan. Moments later, she herself was killed by the soldiers.

Hearing about the death of his brother, *Sarp-sis Ilp-ilp,* who had also participated in the Salmon River killings of the whites, made a rash charge at the troop entrenchments and was killed.

As in earlier battles, Chief Joseph took no active part in the fighting, War Singer said, yet he played an important role in saving his people from capture or death. Two Moons recalled meeting him shortly after the battle began. Carrying his wife's recently born baby in his arms, he cried to Two Moons, "Remember I have no gun for defending myself!"

"Skip for your life!" Two Moons replied. "Without a gun you can do nothing. Save the child!"

The fact that Chief Joseph was not a war leader at this time in no way diminished his stature as a man, War Singer pointed out. For the Nez Perces there were no noncombatants in this war. There were women, children, and old people to be looked after. Tepees must be struck, belongings packed, and the wounded cared for. If the two thousand horses owned by the five bands had been scattered or lost, the Indians would have had no recourse but to remain camped in the Big Hole Basin until more soldiers arrived, when they must surrender or die. Without horses, they could not travel.

While Looking Glass, Swift Bird, *Too-hool-hool-zote,* and *Ollokot* commanded a company of sixty sharpshooters which kept the dug-in soldiers pinned down, Joseph and White Bird oversaw the breaking up of camp. Indians too severely wounded to ride were strapped to travoises. By noon, lodges were struck, the horses were packed, and the main body of Nez Perces was on the move again, traveling now in a southeasterly direction along the base of the spur of mountains which formed the Continental Divide.

Meanwhile, Colonel Gibbon and the embattled soldiers were wondering what had happened to the twelve-pound mountain howitzer, the two thousand rounds of rifle ammunition, and the twenty-man escort which was supposed to join them in midmorning. Here, too, well-laid plans had gone awry. According to *Peo-peo Thol-ekt*—"Band of Geese":

"Passing the battle on the upper side, I rode up the creek. Hearing cannon shots, I whipped my horse till I came in sight of the cannon, standing fast to six mules. *Ke-talk-poos-min*—'Stripes Turned Down'— rushed forward, shot and killed the soldier loading the cannon, while *Te-met-ti-ki* shot and dropped the off-lead mules. The man taking care of the ammunition escaped, skipping for his life to shelter in the brush. *Ke-talk-poos-min* and *Te-met-ti-ki* both hurried to the mules and I took the cannon. I said to them, 'We will take it down near to the trenches and use it against the soldiers.' "

But *Peo-peo Thol-ekt*'s companions refused to let him use the mules. Unharnessing the animals, they took them away, along with the two thousand rounds of rifle ammunition. Left alone, *Peo-peo Thol-ekt* hitched his lone horse to the cannon, which was mounted on a two-wheeled carriage, and tried to drag it into position over the rough, timbered terrain.

"But it soon got stuck on a rock," he told War Singer. "I then unscrewed the wheels, taking them off the spindles. I took the gun from its resting place and rolled it down a steep bluff, where I buried it."

For the rest of that day, that night, and until just after dark the next day, the force of sixty Nez Perce sharpshooters kept the soldiers pinned down. Then, having given their people plenty of time to move out, and knowing that General Howard and the troops under his command would be reaching the scene shortly, the Indian warriors began to withdraw.

The Battle of Big Hole was over.

Losses for Colonel Gibbon's command had been heavy. Of its seventeen officers, fourteen had been killed or wounded. In all, the soldiers had lost thirty-one men killed and thirty-eight wounded.

On their part, War Singer said, the Nez Perces had lost between sixty and ninety Indians killed, with a number more wounded. Among the dead were Lame Brown Bear and two of his children, while Swift Bird had lost his wife and three of their children. Caring for his surviving eight-year-old son as well as for her own six-year-old daughter and four-year-old son was his sister, Singing Bird, whose song had long since died on her lips and in her heart.

Some of the greatest warriors in the tribe were dead. Faith in Looking Glass as a leader had been badly shaken, for it was he who had assured them the war was over. As they fled south in confusion, mourning their dead, they now looked to Lean Elk for leadership, and for a time he seemed uncertain as to what their future course of action should be.

Of one thing they could be sure, War Singer said. All white men were their enemies now. From this day on the whites they encountered would be neither trusted nor shown mercy . . .

13

It was *Jo-kais*—"Captain John"—and *Meop-ko-wit*—"Old George"—who gave Tall Bird the sad news about the death of the children of his son and daughter and the loss of Singing Bird's husband and Swift Bird's wife. Riding ahead of General Howard's command with an advance party of regulars and scouts, the two elderly Nez Perces had been among the first to reach the battlefield. After identifying the Indian dead, most of whom were unburied, and talking to survivors left behind because they were too badly wounded to be moved, the two Christian Indians relieved their first anxieties, finding out that their own daughters had not been killed; then, when Tall Bird and John Crane arrived with the main body of troops, they told them what they had found.

Unfortunately, Chief Buffalo Horn and fifty bloodthirsty, undisciplined Bannock warriors were also traveling with General Howard. Before he and the stunned officers realized what they were up to, they were combing the battleground for survivors, whom they killed and scalped without regard to sex or age, and were ghoulishly digging up and mutilating corpses which a few of the Nez Perces had managed to bury in shallow graves. When John Crane made a vigorous protest, he found most of the army officers unable—or unwilling—to stop it.

"It's the nature of wild Indians to scalp their enemy dead," Lieutenant George Bacon said with a shrug. "So long as we employ them as allies, we can't expect them to change their ways."

"By God, it's not Nez Perce nature to scalp women, children, and old people who are already dead or mortally wounded!" John raged. "These Bannocks are worse than animals!"

"I'm inclined to agree. But how can I stop it?"

"For one thing, you can ask General Howard to issue an order that if the Bannocks don't stop it, they'll be discharged and sent home."

"If I presumed to tell General Howard what orders he should issue, he'd take *my* scalp, Mr. Crane. In the present situation, the taking of trophies by Indian allies is the least of his concerns."

"If that's the case," John said coldly, "perhaps I should talk to some of the newspaper and magazine reporters who are tagging along with the command and tell them what you just said to me. I'll make sure they spell your name right."

Turning red and looking flustered, Lieutenant Bacon appealed to Howard's adjutant, who had approached in time to hear John Crane's last remark.

"Can you reason with him, Lieutenant Wood?"

"I'll try." Giving John a friendly smile, Lieutenant Wood said, "The outrageous behavior of the Bannocks will be stopped, Mr. Crane. You have my word for that. I have already told Chief Buffalo Horn that General Howard insists that it be stopped."

"Has he issued such an order?"

"If he did, Mr. Crane, that would give official recognition to the fact that the outrageous behavior took place. Which would be sure to come to the attention of the press. But if I can stop it with an informal request, no order will go into the record. Won't that suit you just as well?"

John laughed. Of all the regular army officers he had met, Lieutenant Charles Erskine Scott Wood impressed him the most favorably. In his mid-twenties, dark, handsome, and with a self-confidence that at first seemed close to arrogance, but was merely the poise of a man who knew his capabilities, he was just three years out of West Point. His hair, which was as curly as Luke Crane's had been at his age, partially covered his ears in a stylish cut which was just on the verge of violating regulations; his bushy, Custer-type mustache drooped over his lips in a dashing way. As aide-de-camp to the most religious, morally upright general in the American Army, he appeared at first glance to be something of a misfit. But the better John Crane came to know him, the more he appreciated how indispensable Lieutenant Wood's intelligence and diplomacy made him to the commanding officer.

"I'll accept it, Lieutenant. I know General Howard has bigger problems."

"Right now, he's wondering where Joseph will be leading the hostiles. You and Tall Bird know Joseph well. What's your opinion?"

"We think they'll stick to their original plan, going east through the Yellowstone country and the land of the Crows. If they aren't welcomed there, they'll head north for Canada."

"Some of the settlers say they may double back to the west through the Lemhi Valley to the Salmon River country. So does Ad Chapman."

"Some of the settlers are wrong. So is Ad Chapman—as usual."

Lieutenant Wood eyed him shrewdly. "You don't think much of Ad Chapman, I take it."

"In my opinion, Lieutenant, he's a crude, ignorant, greedy man, who's been wrong in every judgment he's made since he told Captain Perry what cowards the Nez Perces were before the Battle of White Bird Canyon. Why General Howard put him on the army payroll as an interpreter and scout is beyond me."

"Would you consider working for the Army?"

John shook his head. "Only if General Howard is willing to negotiate a peace on reasonable terms. But I'm afraid that's out of the question now."

True to his promise, Lieutenant Wood made sure that the Bannocks and his fellow officers got the word that no more mutilation of the Nez Perce dead would be tolerated. Before resuming pursuit of the hostiles, the better part of two days was spent nursing the wounded, digging, and marking graves for both white and Indian casualties. Later, John knew, the whites who had fallen in the battle would be disinterred and their remains moved for reburial in civilian cemeteries near their homes in the Bitter Root Valley or in military cemeteries as distant as Fort Lapwai, Fort Walla Walla, or Fort Vancouver. But for the Nez Perce dead, there would be no removal, no reburial, nor even lasting markers to denote the gravesites, for it was custom among the Nez Perces to bury those killed in battle where they fell, letting the unmarked graves revert to their natural state as soon as possible, trusting the Earth Mother to receive her own.

Though his heart bled for Tall Bird in his grief, John did not impose upon his privacy by offering to help him while Tall Bird, Captain John, Old George, and the squad of regulars Lieutenant Wood had assigned to the burial detail dug and filled the graves. But in late afternoon of the second day, when Tall Bird came to him and said he wanted to talk, John nodded and answered quietly.

"My ears and heart are open, brother."

"I see no peace for my people. They must escape or die."

"Did Captain John and Old George make contact with them?"

"Yes. Carrying a white flag and taking a risk of being shot by the rearguard warriors, they were met two hours' ride south of here yesterday noon by Swift Bird and *Ollokot. Ho-to-to*—'Lean Elk'—leads the hostiles now. He is not sure where they are going. But they are all sure that they cannot trust the white volunteers or the soldiers. If they surrender, they think they will be killed. So they intend to keep running and fighting until they are safe or die."

"After what's happened, I can understand how they feel."

"I must follow them, brother, slim as the hope for peace may be. But I will not ask you to come with me."

"You don't have to ask me," John said softly, reaching out to take Tall Bird's hands in his. "I'm staying with you to the bitter end. Like you said long ago, I'm part of the family now . . ."

Capable though Lean Elk proved to be in putting distance between the hostiles and the pursuing troops, he indicated his distrust of Looking Glass and his plan to seek refuge in the land of the Crows, directly to the east, by maintaining a southerly course along the base of the Bitter Root Mountains toward the land of the Shoshones. In marked contrast to their behavior while traveling up the Bitter Root Valley, where they took no goods without payment, the Nez Perces now stripped the country bare of every usable horse. Their justification for doing so was twofold, War Singer said: first, to rest the horses in their own herd; second, to deprive the pursuing soldiers of fresh mounts.

At Horse Prairie, August 13, a scouting party led by Yellow Wolf approached the Montague-Winters ranch, where seven white men were living. Because of the danger from Indians, the women and children had been sent to nearby Bannack City for safety.

An impetuous man named William Flynn had loaded his shotgun and declared he would "settle with the damned Indians" if they appeared. He attempted to do so, discharged his shotgun, and was shot dead on the kitchen floor of the ranch house. Two more men were killed in a nearby field where they were loading hay. Five miles up the valley another man was killed, while his companion escaped. At both places all the horses capable of traveling were taken.

At Bannock Pass the Nez Perces turned west, passing over a low ridge of mountains into the land of the Lemhis, a small band of Shoshones led by a chief named Tendoy.

Though a Shoshone, Chief Tendoy had always been a man of peace, and was respected by the white settlers who lived in the Lemhi Valley. Lean Elk hoped he could be persuaded to intercede with the military on behalf of the nontreaty Nez Perces and bring this hopeless conflict to an end. But Chief Tendoy's reception to the fleeing Nez Perces was cold. Making it clear that he did not want the Nez Perces in his part of the country and that he would give them no aid, comfort, or assistance in returning to their homeland, he urged them in the strongest possible terms to keep moving east.

Reluctantly, they did so.

"From the Big Hole, Chief *Ho-to-to* was the guide and leader of the Nez Perces," *Wot-tol-en* told War Singer. "He had been all over that country, east and north, and he knew the land and the trails. The people covered many miles each sun. They were outdistancing the soldiers, gaining on them all the time. Everyone was glad."

Traveling with General Howard several days behind, John Crane also knew the country well, for in his trapping days he had traveled over it many times. Since Ad Chapman had not seen it before, John explained its geographical peculiarities—which were considerable—to Lieutenant Wood, who took a keen interest in the terrain ahead.

The Continental Divide in this part of the country took many confused twists and turns, John said. Even though the Nez Perces were now traveling in a southeasterly direction to the Lemhi Valley, they remained on the Pacific side of the divide. Though there was no difference in appearance, the range called the Bitter Roots became the Beaverhead Mountains south of Lemhi Pass, then, turning east, the Centennial Mountains, where the divide ran in an east-west rather than a north-south direction.

"Fact is, the Continental Divide gets so snarled up in the Henry's Lake area, just west of Yellowstone Park," John said, "that an east-west crossing of a low ridge takes a man from the Pacific to the Atlantic slope, rather than the other way round, which would seem logical."

"Is Yellowstone officially operating as a park?"

"Its boundaries were drawn and it was designated as a national park in '73," John answered. "I don't think much has been done to develop it yet. But it's getting a few tourists, just the same. So far, the bears and buffalo probably outnumber them."

So far as the Nez Perces following Lean Elk's guidance were concerned, it was of no importance which ocean a stream flowed toward, as long as the terrain was passable, the grass good, and food and firewood readily at hand. But in traveling south, then east, and then finally northeast toward Henry's Lake and Targhee Pass at the west entrance to Yellowstone Park, they were taking the long arc of a semicircle. The distance could be greatly shortened by the soldiers, Lieutenant Wood realized, if the soldiers cut across the upper chord.

With this possibility pointed out to him, General Howard felt he had a golden opportunity to head off the hostiles and force them into a decisive battle, once it had been determined that the fleeing bands were turning east. All he need do was march his command directly east, beat the Nez Perces to Targhee Pass, dig in there, and force them to fight or surrender. But as with so many military plans during the campaign, this one shattered on the rocks of Indian unpredictability, civilian panic, and the inability of a company commander to carry out a simple order.

By accident, a party of Nez Perce braves met a freight-wagon train bound for Salmon, Idaho, in the Birch Creek area. Containing four wagons and a trailer, the train carried a load of merchandise that included whiskey. At first the meeting was friendly enough, though the Indians indicated that they wanted the eight horses with the train. One word led to another, and then the impatient Indians started shooting. One white man escaped; two Chinese with the wagon train were released after being forced to entertain the Nez Perces by cavorting around on their hands and knees like horses; the whiskey barrels were opened, and during the ensuing drunken melee, *Ke-talk-poos-min,* the warrior who had participated in the capture of the cannon at Big Hole, was mortally wounded by a blood brother.

"The Indians were getting bad," Yellow Wolf told War Singer. "*Ke-talk-poos-min* called out, 'If soldiers come they will kill us all!' He and all the sober warriors were appointed by the chiefs to spill the whiskey on the ground. *Peo-peo Thol-ekt* was one who helped, and I, Yellow Wolf, helped.

"Two drunk Indians shot at each other, one getting his head grazed by a bullet. *It-si-yi-yi*—'Coyote with Flints'—stabbed *He-yo-om-pish-kish* [an oversized man later known by whites as 'Lame John'] under the right arm. *He-yo-om* did not grunt, did not lie down. He had a strong power and became well.

"*Ke-talk-poos-min* was shot by *Pah-ka Al-ya-nakt*—'Five Snows'—

who was mad drunk. Of course, drinking Indians did not want the whiskey spilled. *Ke-talk-poos-min* after two, maybe three suns' travel, was left at camp to die. He asked to be left. He could not hold to life. A good warrior, he had much to do with capturing the cannon-gun at the Big Hole fight."

Disgusted with the behavior of the young men, the chiefs poured out what was left of the whiskey, set the wagons and merchandise afire, and moved on. Shortly thereafter, word of the theft of two hundred horses and the killing of ranch hands on Horse Prairie, plus the looting of the freight wagons and the murders on Birch Creek, reached General Howard and forced him to alter his plans.

"He's sure that the Nez Perces are heading for Targhee Pass," Lieutenant Wood told John Crane. "But he's getting pleas for protection he can't ignore from settlements such as Salmon, Idaho, Bannack City, and Virginia City, Montana. The settlers expect him to be in six different places at once."

Time and again, John knew, groups of citizen volunteers had ridden out to meet Howard, offering to help him fight Indians, so long as he made short work of it and let them fight in their own way; demanding that he send troops to protect their property, though no hostiles were anywhere near it; and insisting that he do both at the same time without further delay, even though that meant dispatching his troops in several directions at once.

Being as much a politician as he was a general, Howard compromised. Turning back from Bannack City, where he was actually between the Nez Perces and Targhee Pass, he marched his command west toward the Lemhi Valley, into which the hostiles had detoured. That night word reached him that the Indians were on the move again, this time traveling in a southeasterly direction that would eventually take them where he had figured they were going in the first place. He ordered his command to reverse direction, going east, then south. On the other side of the Centennial Mountains the Nez Perces were riding southeast, then east.

The Indians were traveling much faster. When Howard at last passed through a gap in the range and intercepted their trail, he was exasperated to learn they now were a day's march ahead of him. In desperation he dispatched Lieutenant George Bacon with forty well-mounted cavalrymen directly overland to Targhee Pass, with orders to block the passage of the hostiles when they showed up and "hold them" there.

How such a small force could "hold" a much larger band of deadly,

desperate warriors, General Howard did not say. Fortunately no confrontation between the two forces occurred. Lieutenant Bacon reached
Targhee Pass well ahead of the Indians, waited two days, and decided
the hostiles had already gone by that point. Without waiting for further
orders he returned to rejoin the main command, leaving the vital pass
unguarded.

Later, General Howard accused Lieutenant Bacon of lacking courage
and running away from a fight. In view of the odds against him, John
Crane mused, the officer should have been complimented for his good
sense . . .

14

On the afternoon of August 19, the fleeing Nez Perces and General
Howard's command made camp only a few miles apart, the soldiers in a
marshy, well-watered area known as Camas Meadows, the Indians just
beyond a rocky ridge southwest of Henry's Lake. Each had scouted the
other's position well. When Buffalo Horn urged Howard to attack the
Nez Perces at once, Howard declined.

"The men and horses are exhausted," he said. "They need a good
night's rest."

"You will let the Nez Perces get away," Buffalo Horn said sullenly.
"We will capture no guns and horses."

"No, they will not get away. By now, Lieutenant Bacon and his
company should be in position to check them at Targhee Pass. We will
catch up with them in a couple of days."

In the camp of the Nez Perces, some of the leaders were making
audacious plans to disturb the soldiers' good night's rest. *Wot-tol-en,*
who was there, told War Singer what happened.

The night before, Black Hair, who was wounded and in too much
pain to sleep, had a vision. In it, he saw a band of warriors go back over
the trail in the darkness to a place where they had camped before and
steal the soldiers' horses. So when one of the scouts brought word that

General Howard had stopped at Camas Meadows, their old camp, Black Hair told the leaders his vision.

In council, it was determined to make a surprise attack and try to capture the horses and pack mules of the soldiers, just as Black Hair had dreamed it. The party of twenty-eight men started shortly after midnight, riding slowly and as silently as possible. When still out of earshot of the sleeping camp a little before dawn, the warriors halted to form a plan of attack, with the older, more experienced chiefs deciding how the approach should be made.

They were divided in their opinions, *Wot-tol-en* said. Looking Glass and White Bull said they should attack on horseback, while Two Moons and *Wot-tol-en* argued that they should approach dismounted.

"We will slip among the soldiers on foot," *Wot-tol-en* said. "Securing many of their guns, we will kill General Howard and his leading men. We can then whip the soldiers and drive off all their horses and pack mules."

"No, we must have our horses," Looking Glass objected, as he usually did to any plan not his own. "It will spoil everything if we go afoot."

As the whispered argument went on, *Ollokot,* Chief Joseph's younger brother and a noted warrior, rode up and said impatiently, "Breaking morning is coming! However we do it, let us go!"

Since time was growing short, the decision was made to ride horses until close to the white camp, then dismount and lead them at a walk, being careful that their hoofs were not heard striking against the rocks. Several active young men turned their horses over to holders, slipped in among the picketed animals of the soldiers, and began cutting them loose and removing the bells from the pack animals.

With Left Hand and Five Lightnings, *Wot-tol-en* was guarding a point not far from the nearest soldiers' tents. Lying close to the ground, watching the horses and mules of the whites being cut loose, he was startled to hear the report of a rifle suddenly break the silence behind him.

"Who in hell do shooting?" a Nez Perce brave shouted angrily.

"Too soon the alarm is sprung!" *Wot-tol-en* told War Singer sadly. "Our plans are now spoiled. The signal shot was not to come from that direction. It was fired by *Ots-kai,* we learned later, who was a brave warrior but always did crazy things. Nervous, he broke our plan for getting all the horses."

"*Ots-kai* was a good fighter," Yellow Wolf agreed. "But at times his head did not act right. He would do things at the wrong time. But nobody could say *Ots-kai* was afraid, that he ever hid from a fight."

In any case, complete surprise by the Nez Perce warriors was impossible now. So they simply stampeded the two hundred animals which they had managed to cut loose from the picket lines, fired a volley of shots into the camp, then galloped away whooping and yelling, leaving pandemonium behind them. When War Singer asked if *Ots-kai* had been punished for his action, *Wot-tol-en* shook his head.

"He was laughed at, made fun of, that was all. I did not hear him make any excuse for the careless shooting."

In John Crane's estimation, whatever excuse the wrongheaded Indian might have made could not have equalled the imaginative account of the raid told by General Howard and given broad circulation by the press. According to Howard, security measures taken to protect the Camas Meadows camp that night had been so tight that only a military genius of Chief Joseph's stature could have gotten to the horse herd. This was the way he did it, Howard said:

"Joseph had so organized a few of his Indians, and marched them toward camp, as to make the picket think it was Bacon's party coming back. The Indians came on by fours, steadily, and very like our troopers till challenged. Not being able to reply correctly, the picket fired upon them. This was doubtless the first sound. Then came the big firing and yelling, and then, quickly enough, the reply from our camp."

Never mind that the Nez Perces knew nothing about Lieutenant Bacon's party, that Joseph was not even in the raiding group, and that it was *Ots-kai* who fired the premature shot. General Howard's story made a very clever fellow out of that red rascal, Joseph, but not quite clever enough to learn the secret password and fool an alert picket . . .

When daylight came, General Howard ordered three companies of cavalry to pursue the Indians, bring them to bay, do battle with them, and recover the stolen animals. Acting with traditional stubbornness, twenty of the mules proved too contrary to drive, so the raiders—who disliked mules anyway—left them behind for the soldiers to recapture. So far as bringing the Indians to bay was concerned, that was no problem, for in the rock-strewn, broken country five miles northeast of the soldiers' camp a dozen or so Nez Perce warriors dismounted, hid their horses, and lay in ambush waiting for their pursuers.

When the shooting began, one company of cavalry attempted a frontal assault but got such a hot reception that it withdrew and sought shelter behind rocks, of which there were plenty in the area. The other two companies spread right and left in an attempt to flank the entrenched sharpshooters. Before they could complete the maneuver, Indian reinforcements arrived, and *they* spread right and left, outflanking the flankers and pouring such a withering fire into the soldiers that the battalion commander, Major Sanford, who was with one of the flanking companies, ordered all three companies to withdraw. His own and the other flanking company did so at once, but Captain Norwood, whose company had taken refuge in the rocks, felt that ordering his men to leave their sheltered position would be suicidal, so he kept them where they were.

Having finished breakfast at last, General Howard and the rest of his command rode forward to see how the battle was going. When Howard learned that Major Sanford had withdrawn and left Captain Norwood's company surrounded by an overwhelming force of hostiles, he ordered a charge by the entire command. Then, with Norwood's company rescued and the Nez Perces withdrawing, General Howard led all his troops back to the camp in Camas Meadows, where they rested the remainder of that day and night.

In the skirmish, the Nez Perces had not lost a man. The military losses were three men killed, five wounded, and one hundred and eighty pack mules stolen. With his men exhausted from the long campaign, their shoes worn out, their clothing threadbare and insufficiently warm for this high mountain country, General Howard knew that his command was in no condition to go on until it had been re-outfitted.

His only consolation was that Lieutenant Bacon and his forty men were awaiting the Nez Perces in Targhee Pass—or so he thought.

Disappointed though the Nez Perces were in stealing mules instead of horses, their brilliantly conceived, boldly executed venture had crippled General Howard's command so badly that John Crane doubted it would ever again get close enough to the fleeing Indians to see their dust, let alone engage them in battle. Which probably was just as well . . .

So far as John Crane and Tall Bird were concerned, enlisting the aid of the fifty loot-hungry Bannocks against the Nez Perces was an act of insensible brutality on the part of a supposedly civilized white general. Even though Chief Buffalo Horn and the Bannock warriors were under the nominal command of an army officer from the Fort Hall Reservation, Captain S. G. Fisher, they were next to impossible to discipline or restrain. Shortly after dark that evening, Buffalo Horn told Lieutenant Wood that his warriors would like to have a dance, in celebration of their recent great victory. When the aide passed the request on to General Howard, the general frowned.

"What great victory have they won recently?"

"God knows, sir. Getting put on the army payroll, perhaps. Or scalping Nez Perce corpses at Big Hole. But they do want to dance."

"Very well. Let them dance. It will give the reporters something to write about."

What with drumming, chanting, neighing of horses, and braying of mules, which kept everybody in camp awake until midnight, about all the disgruntled reporters got out of it was a headache. When it was finally over, Chief Buffalo Horn and a half blood called Rainé came to General Howard's tent, where Lieutenant Wood intercepted them.

"The general is about to retire. What do you want?"

"A small favor, if you please," Rainé muttered in a thick French-Canadian accent. "Permission to kill ze two traitors we have found in our midst."

"Traitors?" General Howard demanded, drawn out of his tent half dressed by the man's statement. "Who are they?"

"Zey are Nez Perce Indians, sir, Captain John and Old George."

"What sort of traitorous acts do you accuse them of committing?"

"Consorting with hostiles, for one zing, sir. After ze Battle of Big Hole, zey followed ze Nez Perces, caught up with zem, and had a talk. Today, after ze raid on ze mule herd, zey smiled and laughed openly at ze way ze hostiles made fools of ze soldiers. I heard zem wit' my own ears. So, please, do us a favor and let us kill zem."

"I'll do nothing of the sort!" Howard exclaimed angrily. "Now get out of here and quit bothering me!" When the Bannock chief and the half blood had stalked off indignantly, General Howard told his aide in a quieter tone, "In the morning after breakfast, Lieutenant, bring Captain John and Old George to me. I want to hear what they've got to say about this. See that John Crane is present, too, so we'll have a reliable white interpreter present."

When interrogated the next morning, both Captain John and Old George were so frank and honest with Howard that he quickly dismissed the charges against them as being completely ungrounded.

"Sure, they talked to a couple of Nez Perces in the rear guard after the Battle of Big Hole," John Crane told him, after listening to their account. "Why shouldn't they? They've both got daughters with the hostiles. They were trying to get them to surrender, but the Nez Perces were afraid they'd be killed. So far as laughing about the raid is concerned—well, General, I chuckled a bit myself. Are you going to let them kill me for that?"

"Deplorable though your sense of humor may be, Mr. Crane, it is not a capital offense," General Howard said wryly. "To tell the truth, I'm not enchanted with the Bannocks as scouts and allies. As fighters, they seem disinclined to engage the Nez Perces at any range less than half a mile."

During the week that followed, Howard had even more reason to distrust the Bannocks. After his command had been resupplied from nearby settlements such as Virginia City, and had resumed pursuit of the hostiles, he noted that even the tempting reward of many good horses was not enough to make the Bannocks fight at close quarters with their traditional enemies, even though Captain Fisher had no trouble leading them forward from the main command and putting them in position to make an attack. It was much easier to run off army mounts, they decided, defecting with forty animals belonging to Spurgin's trail-building crew. Demonstrating that he could act decisively when he had to, General Howard found a way to get the horses back.

First, he arrested ten of the Bannock scouts and placed them under armed guard. When Chief Buffalo Horn piously assured him that they had not stolen any horses, Howard made an equally pious reply.

"What you say may be true, sir, but your scouts are good at hunting horses. They follow blind trails better than white men. Send out some of your young men to look for my lost horses. I will set the prisoners free when my horses are brought back."

In a few hours a group of Bannocks drove in twenty of the missing horses. "That is all they could find," Buffalo Horn said. "Since they tried as hard as they could, will you turn the prisoners loose now?"

"No, I think they can try a little harder. When they find the rest of my horses, I will let the prisoners go. I hope it will happen soon."

Shortly before dark that evening, the rest of the lost horses somehow found their way back to camp. General Howard ordered the imprisoned Bannock scouts turned loose. But their behavior had so disgusted him, he made little use of them again . . .

15

The passage of the fleeing Nez Perces and the pursuing soldiers through Yellowstone Park between August 23 and September 6 was so erratic and confusing that both Indian and white historians puzzled for a long while afterward, War Singer and John Crane agreed, as to exactly who went where, when, how, and why. Established in 1872, Yellowstone National Park at the time of the visit of the warring factions was more wilderness than park. Almost no improvements in the way of roads, bridges, or shelters had been undertaken, and Congress had appropriated no money for its development. Even so, five hundred hardy visitors had come to see its wonders during each of the first few years of its existence; this year, the number of visitors would double.

Just five days before the hostiles entered the park, its most famous visitor to date left it. He was none other than General of the Army William T. Sherman. Well aware of the fact that the hostiles were being chased in the park's direction, Sherman was positive they would not dare enter it because the area was "to their superstitious minds associated with hell by reason of the geysers and hot springs."

Returning to Fort Ellis, northwest of Yellowstone Park, on August 18 after a fifteen-day tour, General Sherman learned how badly the war with the Nez Perces was going and took measures to improve matters by ordering new military units to join the pursuit.

Meanwhile, the Nez Perces, not in the least awed by the geysers and hot springs, entered the park, took the wrong fork of a trail into unfamiliar terrain, and for part of one day became lost. But they soon acquired a tour guide in a unique way. With his cousin, *Ots-kai,* Yellow Wolf was riding out ahead of the main band at noon one day, he told War Singer, when:

"We heard chopping. Maybe it was soldiers? We went where we heard the chopping. It was a white man doing cooking. We went to him, one on each side, in back of him. We grabbed him! He was armed but did not offer fight. *Ots-kai* understood a little English and talked with him."

Described by Yellow Wolf as "an oldlike man," John Shively was a prospector who had been on his way from the Black Hills to Montana when his horses strayed away from camp. Taken to Lean Elk, he was asked if he knew the country well. When he said that he did, he was told that if he would guide the Nez Perces back to trails with which they were familiar, he would be rewarded with the gift of a horse and would not be harmed. Within half a day he led the Indians back to a trail they knew. He stayed with them for several days, helping them with the pack animals, making himself generally useful, and gaining their respect with his friendliness and amiability. Then, taking advantage of their laxness in guarding him, he slipped away without waiting for his proffered reward, which Yellow Wolf swore would have been given to him, along with his freedom, if he had been in less of a hurry to leave.

Not so fortunate as John Shively was a party of tourists encountered by the Nez Perces a day after the prospector's capture. Consisting of seven men and two women, the group had been camping in the park for a week. Suddenly confronted by Yellow Wolf and four of his friends, the leader of the group—a man named William Dinge—had enough presence of mind to give them a friendly greeting, shaking hands with all of them.

"Because I shook hands with him put me in mind not to kill him," Yellow Wolf said. "While we were there, the leading white man gave us sugar, flour, and two good pieces of bacon. The food made our hearts friendly."

But a moment later, another man—George Cowan—came out of the tent and spoke angrily to Dinge. The gifts of food to the hungry Indians stopped. Demanding in a blunt, overbearing manner to be escorted to Chief Joseph, he was warned by Yellow Wolf that the Nez Perces were "double-minded"; that is, the more moderate older leaders might not harm them, while some of the rash, hot-headed young men might kill them on sight. Cowan would not be put off; he insisted that he and the other members of his party be taken to Chief Joseph.

"Whatever now happened to their lives, I could not help," Yellow Wolf said. "It was their own mind—their own work. At last, after we traveled part of that sun, I heard a great noise ahead of us. The other Indians had seen us. Mad, those warriors took the white people from us."

After a confused day and night of being stripped of most of their food and weapons, of accepting worn-out Indian ponies in exchange for their own mounts, of being released and then recaptured, two of the men in the party were shot while trying to escape—mortally, it appeared at the time, though eventually both of the wounded men got back to civilization and recovered from their injuries.

As the Nez Perces made their way through the thick timber and deep canyons in a northeasterly direction across the park, small scouting parties sent out in advance engaged in several skirmishes with white sportsmen and tourists. Though dispatches filed with regional newspapers and telegraphed to the Eastern press claimed eight or ten whites were killed in each engagement, only two fatalities were definitely verified—the deaths of Charles Kenck and Richard Dietrich.

Among the survivors who would tell stories of their narrow escapes for the rest of their lives, was a black man, Ben Stone, who was employed as a cook with one of the tourist parties. Hearing how tenaciously a Nez Perce had pursued Stone, who finally escaped by climbing and hiding in a tree, War Singer asked him why he had been so persistent. The young brave shrugged.

"I just wanted his scalp. Colored men's hair is good for sore ears."

Though it had no bearing on the fate of the Nez Perces, the survival saga of George Cowan was so incredible that John Crane marveled at it. First Cowan was knocked off his horse by a shot in the thigh. When his wife rushed over to protect him by throwing her body upon his, a Nez Perce pulled her away, thrust a pistol against Cowan's head, and fired. Left for dead, he came to a few hours later. His wife and the other members of the party had been taken away by the hostiles. When he started to get up he was seen by an Indian and shot again—this time in the left side.

Some hours after dark he regained consciousness again and started crawling toward Lower Geyser Basin, nine miles away. It took him three days to reach it. There, in a former camp, he found matches, gathered up spilled coffee grains and an empty can, and made coffee. Next day he crawled over to the road, where he was found by two of Howard's scouts.

They patched him up as best they could, fixed him some food, and left him by a roaring fire with the assurance that the main force would gather him up within two days. But more misfortunes were to come.

After eating a bit, he lay down and went to sleep. Toward morning he was awakened by awful heat, and found to his dismay that the vegetable mold he was lying on had taken fire and encircled him with flames. He rose on hands and knees, and, suffering terribly, crawled across the charred area to safety. His hands and legs were badly burned.

And still more . . .

Picked up by Howard's column, Cowan underwent crude candlelight surgery for removal of the bullet from his skull. When he requested that he be sent back by wagon along the relatively easy trail to Henry's Lake, General Howard refused, taking the wounded man north with the troops for an extremely rough ride over terrain so steep that a road had to be built as they went along.

Nearing Fort Ellis at long last, the wagon overturned, spilling Cowan down the hill. When finally put to bed in a Bozeman hotel, the bedstead collapsed, rolling him out on the floor. At that final indignity, he cried out in despair:

"If you can't kill me any other way, why don't you try artillery!"

Reaching home at last on October 5, he eventually recovered from his wounds, had the bullet that had been removed from his skull made into a watch fob, and several times over the ensuing years returned to the park to relate his experiences to curious listeners . . .

For the fleeing Nez Perces there was a choice of three routes through the mountain wilderness of Yellowstone Park to the open plains beyond:

1. North down the Yellowstone River.

2. East down the Shoshone River, which local Indians called the Stinking Water.

3. Northeast down Clark's Fork, which eventually flowed into the Yellowstone.

Why Lean Elk, who apparently was doing the decision making at the time, chose the route he did was never completely clear. The Nez Perces had an excellent corps of scouts, knew the country well, and had proved time and again that even with all their old people and baggage they could travel twice as far in a day's time as their pursuers. Thus, the suggestion that their avoidance of the trap being set for them was pure accident simply was not acceptable to John Crane. In his opinion, they knew exactly what they intended to do—and did it very well.

Some distance to the rear, General Howard's command was making its slow way north along the Yellowstone River toward Baronett's Bridge, where it would swing up the East Fork of the Yellowstone. Directly behind and in closer contact with the Nez Perces was Captain Fisher and what was left of his increasingly disgruntled Bannock scouts, who were as weary of living on half-rations as he was becoming tired of trying to get the soldiers and the hostiles together.

To the northeast, Colonel Samuel Sturgis was getting into position with 360 men to block a descent of the Clark's Fork, if the hostiles chose that route, or, if given a day or so advance warning, to ride southeast forty miles to block their flight down the Shoshone. Because of the ruggedness of the country and the alertness of the Nez Perce advance scouts, who managed either to kill or scare off couriers carrying messages from Howard to Sturgis and vice versa, there was little or no communication between the various military units that were attempting to trap the hostiles.

Reaching the Clark's Fork several days before the Nez Perces were due to arrive, Colonel Sturgis sent scouting details into the high country looking for unfriendly Indians. They found none. Deciding that the Nez Perces had chosen to go down the Shoshone River, Colonel Sturgis moved his command into position there, a long day's ride away. He had every reason to believe that the hostiles had chosen that route, for the most reliable scout in the area, Captain Fisher, reported:

"To the east, from the top of the divide, the enemy's trail bears off toward the southeast, which direction my Indians tell me will take them onto the Stinking Water. We are following them there . . ."

But even as Colonel Sturgis was committing his forces to move from blocking Clark's Fork to blocking the Shoshone River, Lean Elk and the Nez Perces were taking evasive action. After leaving the summit and following the trail toward the Stinking Water for two miles, the hostiles milled their horses, circling them around in every direction, then, instead of going out of the mountain basin in the direction they had been traveling, turned abruptly to the north. While the rear guard used bushy tree limbs to obliterate the real trail while leaving the false one, the band of Indians cut across the flank of a mountain so steep and heavily timbered that it appeared to be impassable, then entered a dark, sheer, narrow slot leading across the divide to the Clark's Fork watershed. This passage was so rugged that both Lieutenant Wood and General Howard called it a miracle that seven hundred people with all their possessions and horses had been able to negotiate it.

"It was like a gigantic railroad tunnel," Lieutenant Wood said in amazement, while General Howard described it as "a strange canyon, where rocks on each side were so near together that two horses abreast could barely pass." But pass through the canyon to the lower section of Clark's Fork the fleeing Nez Perces did. By the time Howard reached the same point, the hostiles were a full day's ride ahead of him. By the time Sturgis got there, they were two days ahead. In open country now, with a fifty mile advantage and no serious obstacles between them and the Canadian border, it appeared that the Nez Perces had won their race to freedom.

Still, General Howard knew his duty was clear: He must continue the chase. After conferring with Sturgis, he sent messengers to Colonel Nelson A. Miles, whose command was stationed at Fort Keogh in eastern Montana, appraising him of the situation. Since Colonel Sturgis's troops were fresher, Howard let him press on in pursuit of the Nez Perces, while his own command followed at a more leisurely pace.

Meanwhile, ahead of the soldiers, Chief Looking Glass again recalled the promises made him by his blood brothers, the Crows . . .

16

Ever since he had been replaced as leader of the *Nimipu* following the Big Hole disaster, Looking Glass had become withdrawn and moody. As his most loyal friend and unswerving supporter, Swift Bird knew how deeply he had been hurt. Though Looking Glass would never admit it, he was not a good judge of people, for he trusted them to act as he himself would have acted in the same circumstances, naively refusing to believe that another man could be any less honorable or true to his pledged word than he himself. Thus, when he had declined to join the hostiles and had led his band back to their village on the South Fork of the Clearwater, where his people were living in peace when treacherously attacked by the whites, his reaction had been one of shock.

Again, when a verbal treaty of peace had been made with the white settlers of the Bitter Root Valley, he had insisted that the Nez Perces strictly enforce that truce, taking not so much as a pound of flour without paying for it and injuring no person during their travels up the valley. Yet again treachery on the part of the whites had caused his people to suffer grievously and him to lose so much face as a leader that Lean Elk replaced him.

Because of the active role he had played in the raid on the soldiers' pack mules at Camas Meadows, he had regained some of his prestige and self-respect, Swift Bird was pleased to note. But even though the

Nez Perces were nearing Crow country now as they followed Clark's
Fork across the broad, open plains to its juncture with the Yellowstone,
Looking Glass was keeping his own counsel regarding the possibility of
the fleeing hostiles finding sanctuary in the land of their blood brothers.
Curious about his intentions, Swift Bird questioned him.

"We still have the peace pipe the Crows gave us after we helped them
against the Sioux. Will you show it to their chiefs?"

"They know we have it. I will not use it to beg them for help. But
tomorrow I will ride to their village, talk to their leaders, and see what
they intend to do."

"Do you want me to go with you?"

"No, brother. It is best that I ride alone. Do not tell the people where
I have gone, for I do not want them to be disappointed by false hopes
again. I will be back before sundown tomorrow."

During the absence of Looking Glass, a number of the young braves
had themselves some fun when they captured a stagecoach. Just arrived
in midmorning of September 13 at Brockaway's Ranch on the Yellowstone two miles downstream from its confluence with Clark's Fork, it
was carrying its driver and three passengers, John Crane heard later,
one of whom was a popular frontier vaudeville performer named Fanny
Clark. As the driver and passengers began to disembark at the ranch
station stop, the raiding party of Nez Perces was seen approaching in
the distance. Panicked, the driver, the passengers, and the men working
at the ranch ran to the brush nearby for cover. From there, they
watched as the rambunctious young men ripped open the canvas sacks,
scattered the mail, set the building afire, and then tested their skill with
the stagecoach. While a reckless young Nez Perce mounted the box,
picked up the reins, and lashed the harnessed draft animals into a run, a
dozen other warriors tied their horses behind the stagecoach, swarmed
inside and atop the vehicle, and joyfully whooped and yelled as the
novice driver performed maneuvers never seen on daily stagecoach
runs.

The Indian driver and his passengers had at first decided it would be
a great idea to take the stagecoach along during the flight northward to
Canada, and fell in behind the main body of fleeing Nez Perces as it left
the valley of the Yellowstone and moved up Canyon Creek; but news
that Colonel Sturgis and his column of soldiers had been sighted a few
miles behind caused them to abandon the vehicle. Wooden boxes on
wheels might be fine playthings, they felt, but when it came to fighting,
a war horse trained to stand and eat grass while its owner sprawled
behind the shelter of a rock with a rifle in hand was more suitable.

True to his promise, Looking Glass rejoined the hostiles two hours before they made camp. Cautioning Swift Bird to say nothing to the others, he bleakly admitted that his mission had been a failure.

"Our former brothers have become women," he said bitterly. "Neither the Mountain Crows nor the River Crows have the heart to join us in our fight. They say that the *Nimipu* cannot win."

"Have they all turned against us?"

"The Mountain Crows will be neutral, they say, neither helping nor hurting us. One of their leaders told me that if we see them riding as scouts with the bluecoats, we need not be alarmed. They will only pretend to help the soldiers, he says. If there is a fight, they will raise their rifles to the sky and shoot at empty air. But the River Crows are not to be trusted. From the way they treated me, I am sure they will turn against us for the horses and loot the bluecoats will give them."

"Then there is no question what we should do. We should keep moving north toward the land of the White Queen and the sanctuary of the great Sioux chief, Sitting Bull."

Looking Glass nodded. "Yes, brother. That is what we must do. But we have little to fear from the bluecoats now, for they cannot head us off. All we need do is maintain a strong rear guard and watch out for the Cut-Arm Chief . . ."

While the Nez Perces moved north at a leisurely pace, Colonel Sturgis pushed his troops to their limit in an effort to catch up. Near the mouth of the summer-dry wash called Canyon Creek, his advance scouts sighted the Nez Perce rear guard. Sure that a decisive battle was imminent, Colonel Sturgis gave a curiously cautious order.

He dismounted his troops and had them advance as skirmishers on foot.

Since for several miles the valley of Canyon Creek was broad, flat, and open, the mounted Indians had no difficulty keeping well out of range of their infantry pursuers, who, after slogging along on foot for three or four miles, were too exhausted to move very fast. By then Canyon Creek had narrowed and its sides had become too steep for a flanking move by mounted men or for the use of artillery, which the Sturgis command had available in the form of two light cannons. Quick to see the strategic advantage of the terrain, the Nez Perce leaders hurried the pack animals, women, children, and old people into the ever-narrowing canyon, while a few sharpshooters took cover in sheltered positions and blocked the advance of the troopers with a withering fire.

"A single Indian, *Tee-to Hoon-nod*—'Bare Legs'—manned the mouth of the canyon toward the close of the skirmishing, and held back the whole line of troopers," War Singer recalled. "The warriors were satisfied with delaying the troops, as the bulk of the tribe gained safety, and made no attempt to encourage a general engagement. They saw no advantage to be gained from a battle."

Well aware of how fiercely the Nez Perces had fought at White Bird Canyon and Big Hole, Colonel Sturgis apparently assumed that the moment the first shot was fired, they would turn on his troops and charge as they had done before. Thus, he made a defensive move by dismounting his troops in a situation where a swift mounted charge would have been much more effective. John Crane suspected that recent battles other than Big Hole and White Bird Canyon had inclined Sturgis toward caution. He had lost a son on the Little Big Horn.

Whatever the reason for his prudence, the end result was that the Army had blundered again. Exhausted and running so low on rations that some of the soldiers began killing and eating their wornout horses, the Sturgis command gave up the pursuit and went into camp, where it was presently joined by General Howard and his troops, which were in no better shape.

Disappointed with the feeble effort made by the white soldiers, a hundred or so Crows began harassing the Nez Perces, shooting at stragglers and attempting to run off horses. Yellow Wolf emphatically denied General Howard's story that the Crows only pretended to attack the Nez Perces, while actually helping them by being their guides.

"Not true! The Crows fought us. They killed one warrior and two old, unarmed men. They did not act as guides for us. We had men who knew the country, who scouted far ahead all the time. They found each day the way to go.

"Some Crows told Chief Looking Glass not to travel too fast. Said they would join and help us. But Looking Glass paid no attention. He now knew they were against us. He knew the Crows were lying, that they wanted the soldiers to catch up with us. Although they had been helped in battle by us, we all knew not to trust the Crows."

After a couple of days of ineffectual skirmishing with the Nez Perce rear guard, the Crows abandoned the chase and went home, having taken no more than thirty or forty horses. For the next six days, the Nez Perces moved north without molestation by red or white attackers, reaching the south bank of the Missouri River at a place called Cow

Island Landing. It was now September 23 and the river was at its lowest stage of the year. Even for shallow-draft steamboats, this was as far upriver as a loaded craft could go. Consequently, a large supply of food, utensils, and other items needed by government survey crews and the military was stored in a depot on the north bank, protected by tents and guarded by a dozen soldiers and two civilians.

To the seven hundred tired, hungry, poorly clad hostiles, who had lost, mislain, or worn out a great deal of their camping gear during their three-month trek through the wilderness, the well-stocked supply depot was almost too good to be true. In a council of chiefs, it was decided to send twenty warriors across the river as guards, swim the pack animals and people to the north bank, then set up camp two miles or so from the depot.

"If the soldiers do not fire on us," Lean Elk said, "we will do no shooting."

Faced with such overwhelming odds, the soldiers forted up and waited to see what the Nez Perces would do. When the band of warriors rode toward the depot, a civilian employed by the agent in charge of Cow Island came out to greet them. They refused to talk to him, asking to speak to the leader of the soldiers. Sergeant William Moelchert came out and asked them what they wanted.

Politely, the warriors asked him to give them supplies from his ample stores. Politely, he refused. They offered to buy what they needed. He still refused. Would he give them something to eat? Grudgingly, he gave them a side of bacon and half a sack of hardtack. Sending that meager present back to camp, the Indians decided that if the needed supplies would not be given or could not be bought, they must be taken. Shortly thereafter, the shooting began.

Having the good sense to fort up behind wagons and river-bank bluffs well removed from the supply depot, the defenders did not force the hostiles to dispose of them before getting to the supplies—which the Nez Perces could have done easily enough. For most of the night and part of the next day token shots were exchanged in a token attack and resistance, with a token Indian and two token whites receiving minor wounds. Meanwhile:

"We took whatever we needed," *Peo-peo Thol-ekt* said. "Flour, sugar, coffee, bacon, and beans. Anything whoever wanted it. Some took pans and pots for the cooking. We figured it was soldier supplies, so set fire to what we did not take. We had the privilege to do this. It was in the war."

Ironically, John Crane noted later, getting supplies to troops in the field had been a major problem for the army quartermaster, for it was difficult to predict where deposits of rations, ammunition, and clothing should be made along a rugged, mostly roadless route extending more than a thousand miles through several military districts. But as far as the Nez Perces were concerned, the service was great.

Next morning the Indians moved on, well fed and well supplied. In this northern land the late September nights were becoming cold, the days were getting shorter, and the older people were growing weary of the never-ending traveling. Now that the Missouri River had been crossed, nothing lay between the exiles and their goal but the rolling grassland of the high plains.

Canada and freedom were less than one hundred miles away . . .

Toward noon, some ten miles north of Cow Island Landing, the Nez Perces were given another opportunity for looting when they encountered a slow-moving wagon train drawn by oxen and loaded with supplies. Killing three of the teamsters while the rest escaped into the hills, the Indians took what they wanted, in the process of which they discovered that part of the cargo was whiskey. At that critical moment, soldiers were sighted riding over a ridge to the south. Forgetting the firewater, the hostiles put torch to the wagons, mounted their horses and rode back to do battle with the newcomers.

This was a contingent of thirty-six mounted volunteers, commanded by Major Guido Ilges, from Fort Benton. Knowing that the Indians were in the area, Major Ilges was leading his company on a cautious scout, seeking information he could pass on to Howard or Miles. Reaching Cow Island Landing that morning, he had observed the damage done there, then set out on the trail of the Indians. He caught up with them just in time to watch them overwhelm the freight-wagon train.

With his small force there was nothing he could do about it. After a brief exchange of shots, in which one of the volunteers was killed, he broke off the skirmish and rode back to Cow Island Landing, from which he dispatched couriers to Howard and Miles.

Shortly after the attack on the wagon train, Looking Glass and Lean Elk had an argument. Many Wounds said:

"Looking Glass upbraided Lean Elk for his hurrying, for causing the old people weariness; told him that he was no chief, that he himself was a chief and that he would be the leader. Lean Elk replied: 'All right, Looking Glass, you can lead. I am trying to save the people, doing my best to cross into Canada before the soldiers find us. You can take command, but I think we will be caught and killed.' "

After their long trek, everybody was tired, War Singer said. The horses were footsore and jaded. There was good grass in this part of the country and many buffalo. So far as the Indians knew, the only army troops in the area were those with General Howard, who was far behind. Why not take their time? By starting late each morning, traveling slowly during the day, and making camp early each afternoon, the horses could be given a chance to regain their strength and the young men time to hunt and bring in meat they would need for the winter.

No doubt Lean Elk was as disgusted with having constantly to urge laggards to move along as they were sick of the sound of his scolding voice. No doubt the series of victories won over the whites since Big Hole had made many of the Indians forget that disaster and had restored faith in Looking Glass. No doubt a glaze of fatigue dulled minds and clouded judgments after 113 days and 1,300 miles of flight.

In any case, Lean Elk was out as leader now, and Looking Glass was in. Confidently, he took the people north in easy stages, following a route across rolling grassland turned brown by early autumn frost, passing between broken hills called the Snowy Mountains and the Judith Mountains, the Little Rockies and the Bear's Paw Mountains. Hunters ranging ahead killed a number of buffalo the morning of September 29. At noon Looking Glass ordered a halt so that camp could be made, fires built, and a good meal cooked.

In this land of great distances and far horizons, the site selected for the camp was not very attractive. There were no trees, the creek which ran through the low swale was sluggish and small, and the view was cut off by surrounding ridges. But buffalo chips could be gathered in quantity for the cooking fires, the ridges blocked out the cold night breeze, and the water in Snake Creek would fill their needs.

The Canadian border lay just forty-five miles to the north. An easy two days' travel. Before undertaking the final segment of their journey, they would rest awhile here . . .

1 7

Realizing after the Canyon Creek skirmish that the chances of his
weary troops catching the Indians were very small, General Howard
sent another message to Colonel Nelson A. Miles at Fort Keogh:

"The Indians are reported going straight toward the Musselshell. I
earnestly request you to make every effort in your power to prevent the
escape of this hostile band, and at least hold them in check until I can
overtake them."

Major Luke Crane was with Colonel Miles when the courier arrived
on September 17. He knew exactly what the colonel meant when he
exclaimed, "By heaven, Major, this is it! A once-in-a-lifetime chance!"

"I'd like to go with you, Colonel. I have a lot of debts to settle with
the Indians."

"Why not? You're combat trained and tested—and I may need an
officer with your skills. Here's how we'll organize . . ."

An ambitious, energetic commander who knew a golden opportunity
for a brigadier generalship when he saw one, Colonel Miles wasted no
time. With Major Crane's able assistance, he spent the entire night
ferrying troops across the Yellowstone River, where he put together a
wagon train filled with rations for thirty days. By the time marching
orders were given next morning, he had assembled a force of six hundred men, consisting of a mixed bag of infantrymen mounted on captured Sioux horses, two battalions of cavalry on army horses, a Hotchkiss gun, and thirty Cheyenne and Sioux auxiliaries.

From Luke Crane's knowledge of him, Miles not only was an energetic commander, he was a lucky one. *Just as my friend George Custer
was,* Luke thought bleakly, *until that day on the Little Big Horn when
his luck finally ran out.* Given this chance to cut off the fleeing hostiles
before they could cross the border into Canada and join forces with
Sitting Bull and the two thousand Sioux exiles reputedly living there
with him, Colonel Miles and all the soldiers in his command could take
their long-awaited revenge against the killers of their friends during the

Nez Perce War and restore the Army's lost prestige in the eyes of the American public.

"What if the hostiles cross the border before we catch up with them?" Luke asked Miles. "Will we dare follow them?"

"We'll deal with that eventuality if and when it arises, Major. But we'll exert every effort to catch them this side of the border."

Colonel Miles's luck held, though he needed several fortunate happenings to put his troops in the right place at the right time. Moving at a forced-march rate, his command covered two hundred miles in twelve days. Despite the fact that he sent scouts five to twenty miles in advance and to the flanks, his information regarding the whereabouts and route of the hostiles was so outdated that he almost missed them.

Nearing the Missouri River some sixty miles downstream from Cow Island Landing the evening of September 23, he conferred with Major Luke Crane, who agreed that the assistance of a river steamer in crossing part of the command to the north bank was imperative. Ordering Lieutenant Biddle to mount a detail, ride ahead, and locate a handy steamboat to help them, he asked Luke's opinion as to whether a steamer would likely be found upriver or downriver.

"It's so late in the season the chances of finding a boat this high on the Missouri are mighty slim," Luke answered, shaking his head. "But the best bet is upriver, for if a boat has gone below, his detail won't catch it on horseback."

As luck would have it, the detail led by Lieutenant Biddle reached the south shore of the Missouri River just as the last regular steamboat of the season, the *Western Star,* Captain William Baldwin, Master, thrust its bow around a bend half a mile upriver. In response to the lieutenant's urgent signaling, Captain Baldwin halted his shallow-draft stern-wheeler inshore, cheerfully agreed to take on the troop-ferrying chore, and remained, awaiting the arrival of the main command.

Thinking that the Nez Perces were still fifty or sixty miles south of the river, Colonel Miles had a battalion of the Second Cavalry under Captain Tyler transferred to the north bank by the steamer.

"Your duty will be to prevent the Nez Perces from crossing at any of the ferries above," Miles told Captain Tyler. "The rest of the command will march upriver along the south bank, probably making contact with the hostiles before they reach the river."

Since there appeared to be no further need for the steamer, Colonel Miles thanked its accommodating master, Captain Baldwin, and bade him a pleasant farewell. The steamer headed downriver. There then occurred another lucky break for the ambitious colonel.

As the main body of the command was preparing to march to the west, with the steamer a short distance away but moving rapidly, three men in a small boat appeared floating downriver, shouting an urgent message as soon as they came within earshot. Learning that they were from the Cow Island Landing depot sixty miles upriver, where the Nez Perces had attacked after crossing the Missouri (without needing a ferry), Major Luke Crane realized the same instant that Colonel Miles did that the services of the *Western Star* had been dispensed with too soon.

"Good Lord, Major! The hostiles are north of the river! Can a rider on a fast horse catch up with that steamer?"

"Not a chance, sir! But there's another way!" Motioning to Sergeant McHugh, whose piece of artillery was resting not far away, Luke cried out, "Sergeant, train your piece on the bluffs downriver just ahead of the boat! Show us how much noise you can make in the next thirty seconds!"

"Yes, sir!"

The reverberations of the Hotchkiss cannon, which could fire a three-inch, fourteen-pound, exploding projectile upward of three miles, along with the bursting of shells in the air on the left bank, made a noise that could be heard for a long way, accomplishing the purpose for which it had been intended. Although the *Western Star* had disappeared around a bend by the time the cannonading ended, a few minutes later billowing black smoke from its twin stacks became visible again, its bow hove into sight, and it came puffing its way back upriver.

"By heaven, Captain Baldwin is a thorough soldier!" Colonel Miles exulted. "The moment he heard the cannon, he knew it was a signal we needed him!"

With the help of the steamer, the entire command was quickly transferred to the north side of the river. Thanks to the information supplied by Major Ilges, Colonel Miles now knew exactly where the hostiles were, where they were headed, and the route they would take to get there. Conferring with Major Crane, his staff, and his scouts, with a map of the area spread out before them, he blocked out his strategy.

"Gentlemen, our present position and the nature of the terrain give us an excellent opportunity to approach the Indians without being detected. We are here. A few days' march to the north, the Little Rocky Mountains extend northwest and southeast for fifty miles or so. Beyond their northern point ten miles is a range known as the Bear's Paw Mountains, with a low ridge connecting the two ranges. My information is that the Nez Perces have taken a course that will bring them through this pass between the ranges. If, instead of going to the west of the Little Rockies, as they are doing, we stay to the east, there's a good chance their scouting parties will never see us."

"So far as they know, the forces pursuing them are directly to their rear," Luke said, nodding agreement. "Which would be to the south."

"Exactly! By keeping the mountains between us, moving fast, making no campfires, and disturbing no herds of buffalo by prohibiting all hunting, we should be able to get ahead of the hostiles, then make a surprise attack on their camp from an unexpected direction—the northeast."

"The wagons are slow and noisy, sir. Should we leave them behind?"

"A good point, Major. We'll travel as light as possible, with the wagons, tents, camping gear, and supplies following at a slower pace."

Transferring the supplies to pack animals carrying a minimum of rations and ammunition, marching from dawn to dark for four straight days, disturbing the buffalo herds as little as possible by prohibiting the firing of rifles, the command camped on the northeast side of the Little Rockies the night of September 29. According to reports brought in by Sioux and Cheyenne scouts, who had cautiously prowled among the rocks of the ridges affording a view to the southwest, the hostiles had gone into camp in a low swale at the base of the Bear's Paw Mountains, just eight miles away. From their actions as they set up shelters, built fires, cooked meals, and loose-herded their horses over the grassy flats, they had no suspicion that white soldiers were anywhere near them.

"We'll hit them tomorrow morning," Colonel Miles told Luke Crane. "By heaven, Major, we'll strike a blow that will make the whole country take notice!"

"What about the Sioux and Cheyenne auxiliaries, sir? Are they to be trusted?"

"Under ordinary circumstances around a military post, I wouldn't trust a one of the rascals with a skillet of hot grease," Colonel Miles said. "But the prospect of loot and horses is driving them wild. My guess is, they'll fight like devils. In any case, since they've given good service as scouts, there's no way to justify keeping them out of the battle."

Like most career army officers, Luke Crane had little use for Indians. During his first tour of duty at Fort Gibson down in Indian Territory, later at Fort Riley in eastern Kansas, at Fort Lincoln in North Dakota, and currently at Fort Keogh in southeastern Montana, he had found the hordes of Indians living around these posts to be dirty, lazy parasites with neither the ambition nor the intelligence to do anything for themselves. True, they were tame Indians, removed by treaty or force from their native environment. Until the Custer disaster, he had been willing to tolerate them as a kind of human refuse that must be accepted as part of the process of conquering and civilizing the West by a superior race. But so many of his fellow officers and close friends had died in that debacle that the only feeling he had toward wild Indians now was the most bitter hatred.

According to dispatches released by General Howard and given wide circulation in the national press, Chief Joseph, the Nez Perce leader, was a wily master of strategy, able time and again to evade traps set for his people because of his knowledge of the wilderness country through which they were traveling. When he was forced to do battle, he apparently had no scruples against turning every man, woman, and child in his band into a formidable warrior willing to fight to the death before surrendering. That was why the element of surprise played such an important part in the strategy formulated by Colonel Miles.

An amazing change in behavior and appearance had come over the Sioux and Cheyenne scouts from the moment the camp of the hostiles had been sighted. During the twelve days' forced march, they had worn old, dirty, ragged clothes, ridden their poorest horses, and let their hair fly loose and uncombed. Now, they were casting old clothes aside, cleansing themselves, painting their faces and upper bodies, donning their best clothes, bringing their finest horses into camp to curry and groom and paint in as gaudy a style as they were painting themselves. Though they obeyed the strict orders against drumming, dancing, and howling, their excitement was evident in their flushed faces and glittering eyes, and they were constantly chanting quietly in their own tongues.

Years ago, Luke recalled, when his father had first come to visit him in St. Louis during the period when he was guiding wagon trains from Independence to Oregon, he had talked about the Nez Perces, telling his credulous, horse-loving son what fine riders they were and what excellent horses they bred, implying from the way he talked that they were a superior breed of Indian. Later, when his father had come to Washington with the delegation of chiefs in 1868, for whom he had been acting as an escort and interpreter, Luke met three of them—Lawyer, Timothy, and Jason—and was favorably impressed by their dignity, good manners, and intelligence, though like all Indian chiefs he had met when they were dressed in their most elaborate buckskin costumes and were encountered in warm rooms, they emanated a strong odor of imperfectly tanned hides.

The last letter he had received from his father had been in early June.

Still living on his ranch in the Wallowa country, which was part of the disputed area whose ownership had caused the war, his father had written:

Though the Nez Perces feel they have been treated badly, it now appears that they will make the move to the Lapwai Reservation without incident by the June 14th deadline set by General Howard. The whole quarrel between them and the local white settlers has been blown out of all proportion by politicians and press. In a country as big as this, there's no reason why whites and Indians can't live together in peace. But the problem seems settled for now . . .

Settled? Not quite, Luke brooded. *But by this time tomorrow it will be.* While he respected his father and understood why he sympathized with a tribe of Indians for whom he had worked as a subagent and among whom he had lived for years, the kind of life that had suited wild, free-roaming Indians, just as it had suited wild, free-roaming mountain men and wagon-train guides, was done. The restraints of civilization now must be imposed upon them both. It was his duty to stop the rebellious hostiles and bring peace to the land.

In command of a Corps of Engineers battalion, with three officers, eight noncoms, and ninety enlisted men under his orders, Luke's current projects were scattered over a wide area of the West. After overseeing the building of Atlantic coastal fortifications, new posts on the frontier, roads, bridges, and other works, his current labors were piddling stuff, requiring no great expenditure of expertise or energy, just as they received no great allowance of funds during this dollar-conserving post-Civil War period.

Of the twelve-man detail at Fort Keogh, he had left six privates and a sergeant to carry on there, while he, a corporal, and four men had come along with Colonel Miles. As Engineers had done from the inception of the Corps, he and his men were prepared to build or fight, as the occasion required. All were armed with revolvers and carbines, which Luke made sure were kept in good condition and ready for instant use. While it was not required that an officer of his rank be prepared to take part in combat, his personal arms and ammunition were always near at hand. As darkness fell on the subdued, quiet camp, which was without shelter tents or hot food because the wagons had been left some distance behind, Colonel Miles strolled over, eyed the carbine Luke was reassembling after meticulously cleaning and lubricating it, squatted down beside him, and smiled.

"That weapon is not official infantry or cavalry issue, Major."

"Neither am I, Colonel."

"The 50-50 Spencer was Custer's favorite gun for Indian-fighting, I've been told, even though Ordnance equipped the Seventh with the Springfield '73 before Little Big Horn."

"Actually, Custer's Spencer was a 56-50 caliber, which he used both for hunting and fighting. But if the Seventh had used the Spencer instead of the Springfield at Little Big Horn, the battle might have turned out differently. Even the top men in Ordnance admit that the Spencer can be loaded and fired faster, with less chance of jamming, than any other carbine the Army has ever used."

"Yes, I know. But it does have that 'fool-killer' magazine in the butt."

"Any weapon is dangerous if it's abused, Colonel."

The argument was one that had been going on among soldiers since the middle years of the Civil War. With a large, musket-type hammer and weighing a little over seven pounds, the Spencer carbine had a seven-shot, tubular metal magazine that slid into the butt end of the weapon, upward into the stock. The rimfire copper-cased cartridge was fed forward into the breech by a coiled spring. The downward action of the trigger guard lever dropped the breechblock, extracted the empty case, and moved a cartridge out of the magazine, into the chamber.

The approximate rate of fire for the carbine was ten rounds per minute. Without the tubular magazine or using the Stabler cutoff, it could be fired as a single-shot carbine. The single-leaf rear sight, with a sliding V-notch elevating bar, was graduated to 800 yards. Ordnance stated that the arm was sighted for 1,000 yards, with an effective range of 400 yards. Battle range was from 200 to 300 yards, with a six-inch group at 100 yards. Reloading rate using preloaded tubes was ten to twelve seconds.

It was a matter of historical record, Luke knew, that at Gettysburg, 3,500 Spencers were in the hands of federal cavalrymen. J. E. B. Stuart's Confederate cavalry, ten thousand strong, met with four regiments of the Michigan Brigade led by Major General Judson Kilpatrick, on June 30, 1863, at Hanover, fourteen miles south of Gettysburg. Custer, who had recently been promoted to brigadier general, led his Spencer-armed Fifth and Sixth Michigan regiments against Stuart's gray-clad soldiers. The volume of fire poured into the rebels from Custer's Spencers sent Stuart's men reeling back, forcing them to swing wide of Lee's main army, not reaching Gettysburg until late evening of July 2, too late to turn the tide for the Confederacy.

A number of officers today, Major Luke Crane among them, bitterly blamed Ordnance for the poor performance of the arms used at Little Big Horn. The only drawback to the Spencer, as Colonel Miles had mentioned, was the way the cartridges nested in the magazine, nose to tail. If a trooper carelessly dropped the carbine butt first to the ground, the shock could discharge one or more shells—with disastrous results. Calling the possibility a "fool-killer," Ordnance had given up on the weapon and sought something safer and better.

Under Brigadier General Alfred Terry, a board had been convened in 1872 to select a breech-loading system for rifles and carbines. Over one hundred different arms were examined, including some developed in European countries. After reviewing the reports, the board voted to adopt the single-shot, trap-door loading, 45-70 Springfield. By September 30, 1874, all companies of the Seventh Cavalry at Fort Lincoln were in possession of the carbine.

Almost immediately, use under field conditions revealed major faults in the Model 73 Springfield. One of the main drawbacks was the breech-block. When the loaded piece dangled at the side of a mounted man, the block was liable to be thrown open and the cartridge lost. Thus the soldier would be uncertain if his weapon were loaded when his horse was in motion. The ejector spring often failed to eject the cartridge shell, leaving it partially pulled out. Should the ejector spring cut through the head of the cartridge, or the head become detached from the shell after the piece was fired, the soldier was left powerless until he picked the empty shell out with the point of a knife, if he happened to have one.

Another contributing factor to the failure of extracting shells was in the shells themselves. During rapid fire, the breech became foul and greasy, with cartridges often swelling in the bore and jamming. The basic cause was the poor and soft quality of brass used in the cartridge due to government cutbacks in expenditures. Following the Custer battle, Major Marcus A. Reno severely criticized the Springfield 73.

"Out of the 380 carbines in my command, six were rendered unserviceable by failure of the breech block to close, leaving a space between the head of the cartridge and end of the block, and when the piece was discharged and the block thrown open, the head of the cartridge remained in the chamber, where with the means at hand it was impossible to extract it. I believe this is a radical defect and in the hands of hastily organized troops would lead to the most disastrous results.

"An Indian scout who was with that portion of the regiment which Custer took into battle, in relating what he saw, says that from his hiding place he could see the men sitting down under fire and working at their guns, a story that finds confirmation in the fact that officers, who afterwards examined the battlefield as they were burying the dead, found knives with broken blades lying near the dead bodies."

Still another advantage of the Spencer carbine, in Luke's opinion, was the Blakeslee patent cartridge box, which was issued toward the end of the Civil War. Containing ten removable tinned tubes, each holding seven cartridges, making a total of seventy in the light, leather-covered, wooden box, it was the quickest loading device ever invented. Combining the old army adage that "rank has its privileges" with the ingenuity of a Corps of Engineers veteran scrounger, Luke had managed to equip himself with a Spencer and a cartridge box soon after the defects of the 73 Springfield had become evident. He did not intend to give up the weapon.

"Am I correct in assuming, Colonel, that you'll want me with you tomorrow at your command post, rather than taking part in the charge?"

"That's right, Major. I'd like to have you standing by. My plan is to cut the hostiles off from their horses with one section of the charge, while the other section overruns their camp. My guess is, the fight won't last very long . . ."

18

To the *Nimipu,* the name of the place where they were camped was *Tsanim Ali-kos Pah*—"Place of Manure Fire." It was called that because only a little scarce brushwood could be found to burn, but buffalo chips were plentiful. With the horses' feet lame and tender, lots of grass, and fresh meat to be cooked and eaten, Chief Looking Glass ordered:

"We will camp here until tomorrow forenoon."

Behind them, young warriors were stationed on buttes and ridges, watching to see if enemies might be near. They expected none, for they knew that the Cut-Arm Chief was at least two suns back on their trail and traveling so slowly that it would not be hard to keep ahead of him.

Next morning, September 30, not too early, while some of the people were still eating breakfast, two scouts came galloping down from the heights, calling loudly as they drew near:

"Stampeding buffalo! Soldiers! Soldiers!"

Some families had packs partly ready and horses caught. But Chief Looking Glass, who was now the head man, mounted his horse and rode around ordering:

"Do not hurry! Go slow! Plenty, plenty time. Let the children eat all wanted!"

This slowed the people down, even though *Wot-tol-en* had told them he had dreamed soldiers were coming and would attack that morning. About an hour later another scout was seen coming from the same direction, running his horse as fast as it could go. On a high bluff above the camp he rode in a circle, waving the frantic blanket signal:

"Enemies right on us! Soon the attack!"

Now a wild stir hit the camp, with great hurrying everywhere. Coming out from under the slanting canvas shelter he had rigged for his family since leaving the skin tepee and poles at Big Hole, Chief Joseph could be heard shouting:

"Horses! Horses! Save the horses!"

As Swift Bird grabbed his rifle and cartridge belt and ran with other Nez Perces toward their horses, he saw a number of armed warriors hurrying toward the bluffs to meet the soldiers. A rumble like stampeding buffalo filled the air. Reaching the high ground north of the camp, he looked back. Hundreds of soldiers were charging in two wide, circling wings, surrounding the encampment. Sioux and Cheyenne Indians were ahead of the soldiers. Rifle fire was crackling, spooking the horses so that he could not catch one. Giving up, he dropped prone on the ground, took careful aim, and fired. He saw the bluecoat he shot at fall out of the saddle.

A short distance away, several Nez Perce women who had managed to catch horses were trying to lead the pitching, squealing animals to their men. A Cheyenne scout with the soldiers was swinging his war club at the women, apparently trying to kill them. *Hey-oom Ik-la-kit*— "Grizzly Bear Lying Down"—who was proficient in sign language, shouted at him, got his attention, then threw him the command:

"Stop right there! You are helping the soldiers. You have a red skin, red blood. You must be crazy! You are fighting your friends. We are Indians. We are humans. Do not help the whites!"

The Cheyenne stopped swinging his war club at the women. He answered by signs: "Do not talk more. Stop right there! I will never shoot you. I will shoot in the air. There are twenty more of us down below here."

Ending the sign-talking, *Hey-oom Ik-la-kit* called reassuringly to the Nez Perces, "He is our friend and will not shoot us. He will shoot in the air!"

Hey-oom Ik-la-kit left his horse and moved up the slope toward the soldiers. Swift Bird saw him, walking brave and fearless, like a man who knew he was going to die but would not turn away from it. The soldiers killed him before he had gone fifty paces. Swift Bird saw him fall.

He saw, too, that the Cheyenne scout had lied to *Hey-oom*. Riding only a little way from where they had been talking, the Cheyenne met a mounted Nez Perce woman. Before she could get away, he seized the bridle of her horse, lifted his six-shooter, and killed her. Angered by the Cheyenne's treachery, Swift Bird lifted his rifle and triggered three quick shots at him. But the scout's protective medicine was strong, and he rode away untouched.

From what Swift Bird could observe, one wing of the initial attack had swept between the horse herd and the camp, separating some of the horses and a number of *Nimipu* who had been trying to catch and mount the animals from the camp. Now these soldiers were driving the horses away, while others were chasing and fighting groups of Nez Perce men, women, and children who were fleeing north, trying to escape and reach safety in Canada. *This is good,* Swift Bird thought, *for if they make it across the border, they will ask Sitting Bull and his Sioux warriors to come to our aid.*

Directly before him, the soldiers who had come charging down the slope toward the camp itself had been stopped by the steady, accurate fire of warriors like himself, Looking Glass and others, who were dismounted and not wasting a single shell. Though there were only twenty or so *Nimipu* fighters spread along the low, brush-covered ridge on which they had chosen to make their stand, they were strong in the battle, trading the soldiers bullet for bullet, and holding them back from advancing.

Even as the white soldiers reined their horses around and rode back up the slope, breaking off the fight for the moment, Chief Joseph's young warrior nephew, *He-mene Mox-mox*—"Yellow Wolf"—who had caught and mounted a horse, rode up behind the line of dismounted Nez Perce skirmishers, waved a hand at the camp in the swale below, and shouted:

"The Cheyenne and Sioux are heading toward our camp! We must go back and save our women!"

His own wife and three of their children had been killed at Big Hole, where his sister Singing Bird had lost her husband and two of their children; now, Swift Bird's eight-year-old son, his sister, and her six-year-old daughter and four-year-old son were all the family he had left with the *Nimipu*.

He would fight to the death to protect them. But it was a bitter thing to know that because of the greed of people of his own race, he must fight to save his family from other Indians.

With Yellow Wolf leading the charge and Nez Perce warriors returning to the camp from all directions as the soldiers withdrew to the ridgetops, the attack of the Sioux and Cheyenne scouts was soon routed, the treacherous Indians being driven away like cowardly, skulking dogs. *Why do they fight us?* Swift Bird wondered in anguish. *We do not make war on them. Our war is with the whites. Started by General Howard at the Lapwai council and made worse by the attack of the soldiers on our peaceful village where Looking Glass took his people to keep them out of the fighting. Why the Sioux and Cheyennes are helping the soldiers, I cannot understand.*

Much to his relief, he found that Singing Bird and the children had not been harmed by the hail of bullets sweeping through the camp, for with the initial charge they had stretched out on the ground, burrowed into the damp brown grass, and made their bodies the smallest possible targets. Without being told, they were now doing as they had done at Big Hole, scooping out holes in the soft earth in which they could hide from the bullets which they knew would soon begin pouring down into the swale along Snake Creek; the soldiers were taking sniping positions on the surrounding heights, settling down for a long siege. Using camas hooks, butcher knives, pans, and even their bare hands, women, children, and old people were digging pits, trenches, and caves with the single-minded ferocity of blind gophers caught above ground whose only hope for survival was to disappear into the earth. Having often seen his own children play cave-digging games in the wet sandbars along the banks of the Clearwater, Swift Bird almost smiled at the memory. Then he remembered that three of his children were dead now, and the smile failed to come.

Until this day's fighting ended and War Singer could make the rounds, learning who had been killed or wounded, no one could say how many casualties the *Nimipu* had suffered in the attack. Swift Bird did hear that fifty people had escaped and were fleeing toward Canada, though a band of soldiers led by Cheyenne scouts was pursuing them and would perhaps prevent them from getting away. While the women,

children, and old people dug shelters along both banks of Snake Creek
in the center of the grassy swale, the warriors lay behind bushes and
rocks along the slopes rising toward the bluffs that rimmed the depres-
sion, their accurate fire making the soldiers keep back a respectable
distance.

The battle continued all that sun, mostly around the camp. Swift Bird
did what he could on the outer perimeter with other warriors. The
Nimipu fighters dared not charge the soldiers, Looking Glass told him.

"There are too many of them for us. Also, they have the big gun,
which they are starting to use now, though the exploding shells have
not hit us yet. For some reason they are falling far away."

As daylight began to fade and the chill of the early autumn darkness
grew, reports of casualties were totaled by War Singer and circulated
about the camp. They were grim. Twenty-two *Nimipu* had been killed,
while a large, unknown number had been wounded. Death had claimed
many of the leading chiefs and bravest warriors. *Ollokot,* leader of the
young men and Chief Joseph's brother, had been killed early in the
fighting. So had tough old *Too-hool-hool-zote,* the "cross-grained
growler." In the confusion of the first encircling attack, a bad mistake
had been made by *Hush-hush Cute,* Yellow Wolf said.

"Three brave warriors, *Koy-eh-kown, Kow-was-po,* and *Peo-peo Ips-
ew-ahk,* were in a washout southeast of camp. They were too far toward
the enemy line. *Hush-hush-Cute* thought them enemy Indians and
killed them all. He had a magazine rifle and was a good shot. With
every shot he would say, 'I got him!'

"Lean Elk was also killed by mistake. A Nez Perce saw him across a
small canyon, mistook him for one of the enemies, and shot him."

The soldiers had suffered heavy casualties, too. In the judgment of
Major Luke Crane, the surprise attack by mounted soldiers with what
seemed to be overwhelming superiority in numbers and firepower
against a camp containing women, children, and old people, as well as
warriors, had failed miserably.

Once again, incredibly, the Nez Perces had struck back with a stun-
ningly fierce resistance.

During the first charge, Colonel Miles's command had managed to
capture one third of the Nez Perce horse herd, amounting to six or
seven hundred animals, cut off a number of families from the camp, and
inflict most of the casualties suffered by the Indians during the battle.
But the soldiers had paid a bitter price.

"Captain Hale, Lieutenant Biddle, and twenty-two enlisted men have been killed," Colonel Miles told Luke bleakly. "Four officers and thirty-eight enlisted men have been wounded. It's plain to see that further cavalry charges would incur great losses. The only alternative is to lay siege to the camp."

Holding the higher ground and encircling the Indian camp so that none of its occupants could escape, Colonel Miles ordered the Hotchkiss gun brought up and the encampment shelled. That proved ineffectual because the muzzle of the piece could not be depressed sufficiently to bear on the valley below, where the Indians were digging shelters in the soft, moist earth.

Miles then tried to cut the Nez Perces off from water by sending two troops of cavalry down the hill to take and hold the creek, but heavy gunfire from the hostiles forced the soldiers back.

As darkness fell, turning a chilly, rainy day into a cold, snowy night, the troops kept watch on the heights; Nez Perce warriors dug rifle pits on the middle slopes; and down in the bottom of the valley old men, women, and children excavated a protective network of caves, tunnels, and underground living quarters that in the next few days and nights became amazing in extent.

By morning, October 1, five inches of snow covered the ground, and the weather was very cold. In a way the soldiers suffered more than the Indians. Until their wagon train arrived with tents and supplies, they had no shelter or fuel—they did not know about the ample store of buffalo chips underfoot. The Indians, on the other hand, knew the chips were there, could feel them with their feet through the blanket of snow, and could use them to make small fires in their trenches.

Even so, the women did not do much cooking. Singing Bird and the other mothers handed dried meat around, giving it to the children first, not eating themselves. Children cried with hunger and cold. Old people suffered in silence. Misery was everywhere, Singing Bird mourned. Cold and dampness all around. In the small creek, there was water, but the people could get it only at night due to the shooting of the soldiers. Because of the cold and the crying of the children, she slept only in naps, sitting in the deep shelter, leaning back against the dirt wall. Like the other warriors, Swift Bird stayed in a rifle pit dug into the middle slope.

Because so much history was being made that must be remembered and passed on, War Singer welcomed the help of *Wot-tol-en,* who was already something of a tribal historian, and of *Ala-hoos,* who also had a good memory. Yellow Wolf called him:

"An oldlike man who was still strong. *Ala-hoos* made announcements of all incidents and events each day. All knew him and reported to him who had been wounded or killed in battle, who was missing or had disappeared. The names of all were known throughout the land."

In the morning, Colonel Miles raised a white flag and had a man call out in Chinook Jargon that he wanted to talk with Chief Joseph. From General Howard's statements to the press, he assumed that Joseph was the tribal leader. Neither White Bird nor Looking Glass, who were the ranking chiefs now, objected to letting Joseph be their spokesman, for they deeply mistrusted the soldiers and still hoped either to escape to Canada or be aided on this side of the border by Sitting Bull and the two thousand warriors reputed to be under his command.

Because Chief Joseph was his uncle and leader of the Wallowa band for which he was pledged to fight to the death, Yellow Wolf made himself a close observer of the meeting between Chief Joseph and Colonel Miles.

"I did not go where they met," he told Swift Bird afterward. "I looked around. There was a hollow place off a distance in the ground. I went there and lay down. I could see Colonel Miles where Joseph met him. I could see plainly where they stood. I was saying to myself, 'Whenever they shoot Chief Joseph, *I* will shoot from here!'

"There was talk for a while, and Chief Joseph and Colonel Miles made peace. Some guns were given up. Then there was a trick. I saw Chief Joseph taken to the soldier camp a prisoner!

"The white flag was pulled down!

"The white flag was a lie!

"The warriors came back, and right away a soldier officer rode into our camp. Chief Yellow Bull yelled a warning and grabbed him. I could see him take the officer to the main shelter pit. When I saw all this— Chief Joseph taken away—I ran to where the captured soldier was being held. Held that Chief Joseph might not be hurt. He had on a yellow-colored outside coat to keep off the wet. A strong-looking young man, he did not say much. Looked around, but seemed not much afraid.

"The chiefs instructed the warriors to guard him. Ordered: 'Treat him right! He is one of the commanders!' "

Exactly what happened during the abruptly ended talks under the white flag, Major Crane did not know, for as soon as the state of siege developed, he had vented his frustration, rage, and grief for his close friends killed and wounded by the hostiles—he had positioned himself behind a clump of rocks on high ground overlooking the battle site and sniped from a range of three hundred yards at every Nez Perce warrior seen below. The night before, Colonel Miles had been in a state of shocked disbelief at the way in which his strategy had failed and the terrible casualties his troops had suffered. Though the detail of Cheyenne scouts and soldiers sent north yesterday morning to cut off and capture the band of Nez Perces fleeing toward Canada had managed to round up a dozen stragglers, the rest had gotten away. If Sitting Bull and his formidable force of Sioux warriors should respond to their plea for help, a disaster comparable to the Custer affair might be in the making.

Discovering that a cannon capable of throwing an exploding projectile three miles was useless at a range of six hundred yards was frustrating Colonel Miles, too, though Sergeant McHugh promised that sooner or later he would find a way to put the piece on target—even if he had to use it like a howitzer.

But the principal worry for Colonel Miles just now was how soon General Howard and his command would reach the scene where the hostiles had at long last been brought to bay. Two days? Three? Four? Having caught the Nez Perces after a twelve-day forced march and attacked them with so many factors in his favor, the extent of the casualties suffered by his command could be justified only by a total victory—which meant unconditional surrender.

That was the sticking point in the truce talks.

"Joseph says he is willing to surrender all the hostiles under his direct authority," Colonel Miles told Luke. "But he claims he cannot speak for all the chiefs, who will do whatever they want to do. What kind of surrender would that be?"

"Not much of a one, I agree."

"Furthermore, if he does surrender, he wants me to promise that the Nez Perces will be allowed to return to their reservation in Idaho. All I could say to that was that I would do my best to effect such a return. He also insists that his people be allowed to keep half of their rifles, instead of giving them all up. They will be needed for hunting, he says."

"What was your answer to that?"

"That his people must give up all their rifles, trusting in the government to feed them. He refused to accept that without first going back and conferring with his people. I felt he was stalling. So I detained him."

Just how Chief Joseph had been detained was a matter whose truth Major Luke Crane never discovered positively, for he had gone back to his sniping post when the talks broke up and did not personally observe what happened. Since none of the accounts reflected favorably on Colonel Miles's sense of honor, he did not dare question the commander himself. One story said that Chief Joseph was seized, bound, rolled in a blanket, and tossed in among the picketed mules to spend a cold, wet night on the ground. Another was that he was housed in the colonel's tent, which had arrived with the supply wagons that afternoon, was served hot tea and food, and treated with respect. But whatever the quality of his treatment, one fact was crystal clear: he was detained overnight against his will—after coming into the camp under a flag of truce.

Equally unclear was why the young cavalry officer, Second Lieutenant Lovell Jerome, happened to wander into the heart of the hostile camp at the same time Chief Joseph was being taken prisoner. Colonel Miles later claimed he had asked Lieutenant Jerome to "go see what the Indians are doing." Meaning that he should ride to the rim of the bluffs overlooking the Indian camp, eyeball it, then return and report what he had seen. Misunderstanding, Lieutenant Jerome, apparently thinking peace had been declared, had ridden on down into the midst of the Indian camp, where the Nez Perces seized him as a counterhostage. Colonel Miles was thus put in the uncomfortable position of risking a subordinate's life in a questionable cause.

Whatever the case, Lieutenant Jerome was treated very well. In fact, the lieutenant wrote a note to his commander next morning, which said:

"I had a good supper, good bed. I had plenty of blankets. This morning I had a good breakfast. I am treated like I was at home. I hope you officers are treating Joseph as I am treated."

According to Yellow Wolf, Joseph was not treated right.

"Chief Joseph was bound hands and feet," he told Swift Bird angrily. "They took a double blanket. Soldiers rolled him in it like you roll a papoose on a cradle board. Chief Joseph could not use arms, could not walk about. He was put where there were mules, not in soldier tent. That was how Chief Joseph was treated."

Understandably, Colonel Miles later glossed over the incident. According to him, it was the Nez Perces who asked for a truce, pretended to surrender their arms, then reneged on their agreement. Whatever the sequence of events, Chief Joseph was not held until the hostiles surrendered, as Colonel Miles desired, nor was Lieutenant Jerome killed in an act of revenge, as a rash young Nez Perce warrior named *Chus-lum Hih-hih*—"White Bull"—wanted. Instead, they were taken to the "halfway ground," shook hands, were exchanged, and returned to their people.

The white flag was lowered.

The fighting resumed.

"Some warriors talked to charge the soldiers," Yellow Wolf told Swift Bird when he brought him a handful of cold, cooked buffalo meat Singing Bird had saved for him and sent to the rifle pit he had not left for three days and nights. "If we whipped them, we would be free. If we could not whip them, we would all be killed and would have no more trouble."

"That is true," Swift Bird said. "If it would save the people, I would be willing to die."

"But others said, 'No! The soldiers are too strong. They have the big gun, the cannon gun. If we are killed, we leave women and children, old people, and many wounded. We cannot charge the soldiers. We must keep fighting to the end. Perhaps Sitting Bull will come to help us.' "

On the morning of the fifth day of the siege, the soldiers finally scored a hit with the cannon, when they at last managed to bring it to bear on the floor of the grassy swale. It was toward noon that a bursting shell struck and caved in a shelter pit, burying four women and several children. When the Nez Perces at last managed to dig into the collapsed pit, they were saddened to discover that a girl of twelve snows, *Atsi-pee-ten,* her grandmother, *In-te-tah,* and three other people were dead.

The others, Yellow Wolf told Swift Bird sadly, were his sister, Singing Bird, her six-year-old daughter, Spotted Fawn, and his own eight-year-old son, Lone Rabbit. Because he had been sheltered by the body of his mother, which had given him an air space in which to breathe until the diggers got to him, his sister's four-year-old son, Little Bird, had survived.

Is there no end to death in my family? Swift Bird grieved. *Who is left to mourn?*

"If I live, I will take Little Bird to Canada," he told Yellow Wolf in a low, choked voice. "I will raise him as my son, teaching him to hate white men as I have learned to hate them. He will live free—or die."

"Many of us feel as you do, brother. No matter what Chief Joseph does, we will never surrender. We plan to slip through the soldier lines under cover of darkness—"

"Yes, I know. My warrior blood brother, Looking Glass, who knows my death-song as I know his, has told me. But before the fighting is over, *He-mene Mox-mox,* there is one special white soldier my *Wy-a-kin* tells me I am destined to kill, just as he has been trying to kill me. He is nestled behind a clump of rocks up there—" Swift Bird pointed out the spot. "That is the place, brother. Shooting a rifle that speaks many times in only a few heartbeats, he already has killed or wounded many of our warriors. So I have vowed to kill him—even if I have to crawl up the hill on my hands and knees to the very edge of his shelter to do it . . ."

19

On the night of October 4, General Howard and a dozen of his men arrived at the Bear's Paw siege site. At first, Colonel Miles gave the general a cool reception. Then, upon being assured by Howard, "I have no desire to assume immediate command—finish the work you have so well begun," Miles greeted his old comrade in arms in a much more friendly manner.

With Howard were the Nez Perce scouts, Captain John and Old George. At the general's suggestion they went into the hostile camp under a white flag. Pleased to hear that both their daughters were still alive, the two scouts urged the Nez Perces to surrender. Howard's main command was only a day's march away, they said, and when it arrived further resistance would be useless. Surrender would involve no trials or executions, General Howard promised. Those who surrendered would be given food, clothing, medical care, and honorable treatment as prisoners of war. Furthermore, it was the expressed intention of the military that when the Indians were captured they were to be returned to the Nez Perce Reservation in Idaho.

"How safe will we be there?" Swift Bird asked bitterly. "We were living peacefully in our village on the South Fork of the Clearwater when the soldiers attacked us without reason and forced us to go to war."

"If you surrender, the war will be over," Captain John said. "There will be no reason to fight."

"Will surrender bring back my wife and children? Will it bring back my sister, her husband, and their three dead children? Will it restore a family to my sister's son, Little Bird, who now has no family left but me? Will surrender wipe the blood from the wounds of the dead and bring them back to life?"

"No, it will not do that," Old George said gently, shaking his head with a deep sadness in his eyes. "But it will bring peace. This will please your father, Tall Bird, and his white brother, John Crane."

Swift Bird scowled. "What do they know of the war?"

"A great deal, for they have been traveling with us ever since the fighting began, in hopes they could help end it."

"My father and his brother are with the Cut-Arm Chief, you say?"

"Yes. They are with the main body of troops, which will be here tomorrow."

"Good! You can give my father a message, in case I am not here."

"Whatever you want me to tell him, I will."

"Tell him I hate the white blood in my veins, just as I hate the white men who have destroyed my people," Swift Bird said bitterly. "Tell him it was an evil thing his mother and my grandmother, Moon Wind, did when she let the white man lie with her and begin a mixed-blood family. Tell him I will die cursing her memory . . ."

Even on the terms offered by Howard and Miles, Chief White Bird would not surrender. Though in his seventies now, he made it clear to Chief Joseph that he would rather die in a desperate attempt to reach freedom in Canada than go back to Lapwai as a prisoner of the white man.

Looking Glass felt the same way. "I am older than you," he said to Chief Joseph. "I have my experiences with a man of two faces and two tongues. If you surrender, you will be sorry. In your sorrow you will feel rather to be dead than suffer that deception."

"Many of our people are out in the hills, naked and freezing," Joseph replied, wearily shaking his head. "The women are suffering with cold, the children crying with the chilly dampness of the shelter pits. For myself, I do not care. It is for them I am going to surrender."

"I will never surrender to a deceitful white chief," Looking Glass declared. "Let there be no more words between us . . ."

By tradition, arguments among the Nez Perce leaders always ended with each chief going his own way, taking the people who believed as he did with him. A short while later, Looking Glass joined Swift Bird in his rifle pit midway up the slope toward the bluffs where a number of soldier sharpshooters were still keeping watch, now and then making their presence known by firing at any Indian foolish enough to expose a portion of his body. Lighting pipes, the two lifelong friends smoked and talked.

"Joseph is going to surrender," Looking Glass said. "But White Bird thinks we have a chance to escape to Canada. When it grows dark, we will try."

"Have you given up hope that Chief Sitting Bull will bring Sioux warriors to help us?" Swift Bird asked.

"If they were coming, they would be here by now. He has had time—" Suddenly Chief Looking Glass broke off, raised his head, and cupped a hand to his ear. "Listen! Do you hear that rumble?"

"Yes! Like the hoofs of many horses!"

"Could it be the Sioux?"

Before Swift Bird could answer or lay a restraining hand on his arm, Looking Glass leaped to his feet, scrambled atop the rock which protected the front of the shelter pit, and shaded his eyes as he gazed to the north through the gray autumn day. Excitedly, he called down to Swift Bird:

"It is them! It is them! They are riding like the wind, in a long black line of horses—"

The sound of a rifle shot shattered the air. Struck squarely in the forehead by a high-powered bullet, Chief Looking Glass collapsed, the blood from his instantly fatal wound pouring over Swift Bird's hands and arms as he caught the body of his warrior brother and lowered it to the ground.

Kneeling over it, he began keening the death-song of his friend, making sure that its deeply felt words would reach the Spirit Land before the soul left the body and began the long skyward journey from which there would be no return—not until the day promised by believers in the Dreamer faith when all the Indians who had ever lived on the earth would arise and live again. Swift Bird chanted:

> *"Ko-na ip-ne lu-nik te-tu"*
> ("There he names himself in light")
> *"Il-a-ka wes-pa we-tes-pe"*
> ("In the bright land")
> *"Eys-ni-ku hi-le-se-te-tum"*
> ("Most joyful it rings")
> *"Ko-lal-ko-lal il-a-ka wis-pa we-tes-pe"*
> ("Rings in the bright land")

In the Spirit Land toward which the soul of his friend was on its way, all the honored dead of the *Nimipu*—"the People"—who had ever lived during the ten thousand years that had passed since coyote created the tribe out of the heart's blood of the slain monster, and placed it in his most favored land—all these people would be waiting to greet him and praise him for the way he had fought for his people, his way of life, his home, and his freedom. Until the last day, he would dwell among them in a state of perpetual glory.

Releasing the body gently, Swift Bird checked his carbine to make sure that its magazine was fully loaded. With a twenty-inch barrel and a magazine that would hold twelve cartridges, the .44 caliber Winchester 73—for which he had traded three good horses to a merchant in the Bitter Root Valley just two years ago—was the finest weapon he had ever owned. He found that the magazine was full. To make sure that he would have plenty of ammunition for what he intended to do, he hung a cartridge belt, which he had recently filled, over his right shoulder and left side, freeing his right arm and hand for action.

As he cautiously peered over the rocks fronting the rifle pit, hoping to get a glimpse of the white sharpshooter who had killed Looking Glass and who he had vowed to kill himself, he heard several nearby Nez Perce defenders shouting at one another. Alerted by the exuberant cry from Looking Glass that Sioux warriors were coming, they were gazing more carefully in the indicated direction through the gray, hazy forenoon; now that the long black column he had seen was drawing nearer, it was bitterly evident that he had been wrong.

"A herd of buffalo running from hunters!" a warrior cried in disappointment. "That is what he saw!"

"Could the Sioux be chasing them?" another shouted.

"No, the hunters are not Sioux. From what I can see of them, they are a small party of Cheyenne scouts and soldiers. I fear Sitting Bull will not come."

Whether help came in any form did not matter to Swift Bird now, for as he crawled over the rocks in front of the rifle pit and started snaking his way up the slope toward the spot where his personal enemy lay, his *Wy-a-kin* told him he would be given only enough time to permit him to do what he had to do. From brief glimpses he had gotten of the soldier during the cat-and-mouse duel in which they had engaged during the siege, he knew that the white man was one of the commanders, for he had seen the glint of golden oak leaves on the shoulders of his uniform when one side or another had been briefly exposed. Once, when the white man had raised his hat and waved it derisively in a gesture of defiance, he had seen that the man's hair was red, curly, and almost as long as a woman's. To less honorable Indians like the Cheyenne and the Crow, such a crown of abundant red, curly hair would be a scalp trophy to be treasured. But Swift Bird had no interest in trophies. All he wanted to do was kill the man who had killed his friend.

Between the rifle pit midway up the slope and the bluff where the red-haired sniper lay were two hundred paces of wet hillside, thinly covered with dead grass, low shrubs, and a scattering of rocks. Making himself as small a target as possible, moving erratically, changing his course to the right and to the left in order to take advantage of every piece of cover, Swift Bird began stalking his prey.

With his adversary shooting downhill, his body would not be an easy target, he knew, even for an expert marksman. But it would be exposed. The trick would be to show a portion of himself just long enough to tempt the bluecoat commander to rise a bit from behind his cover in an attempt to get off a good shot, thus briefly exposing his own body. If timed right, the sniper's shot would miss its target, while one quickly fired in return would strike home.

Hearing him chant his death-song as he crawled, Nez Perce warriors in pits along the slope understood what he was attempting to do. In order to give him cover, they opened up an intense fire against the other soldiers entrenched on the bluffs, forcing them to lie low, confining the contest to a personal duel between Swift Bird and the red-haired commander.

He did not feel the dampness or the cold. His heart was on fire, his blood hot for killing. He felt as if he were dreaming. Chanting his death-song, he had memories of youthful, happy scenes. Of the Wallowa country where he had been born. Of a time when only the *Nimipu* lived there. Of tepees along a winding river. Of the clear blue lake, and wide meadows filled with horses. Of treks to the buffalo country with hunting parties and brave comrades. Of his wife and children and life in the village on the South Fork of the Clearwater. Of the way all those he loved had been taken by death on a long journey to the bright land— where he soon would join them.

He kept moving up the slope . . .

From behind his rock shelter on the bluffs, Major Luke Crane stared down into the Indian encampment, amazed at the stubborn tenacity of the Nez Perce resistance. Would they never give up? Since the dreadful casualties on both sides during the wild charges and countercharges on

the first day of the battle, the main body of Indians had dug entrenchments so impervious to bullets that their occupants could not be dis-
lodged. Nor were they seriously disturbed by exploding shells from the
Hotchkiss cannon, which, though it appeared to have finally made a hit
or two, was so awkward and ineffectual that Colonel Miles had at last
ordered its use discontinued.

Ringing the encampment in the grassy swale were the rifle pits on the
middle slopes, dug and manned by what appeared to be a moderate
number of Nez Perce warriors but proved veritable hornets' nests when
probed by scouting details. Never again would Major Crane believe the
cliché that wild Indians were poor shots because their weapons were
usually inferior and they did not take care of a good one when they had
it. In all his combat experience, he had encountered no marksmen with
the skill the Nez Perces had shown. At any reasonable range, their fire
was deadly—and they seemed to know exactly what that range was.
Furthermore, they were equipped with more repeating carbines and
rifles per capita than the soldiers, possessed plenty of ammunition, and
seldom wasted a shot. Now he understood why the casualties suffered
by regulars and volunteers since the uprising began had been so appall-
ing.

Because of the arrival of General Howard and his advance detail the
previous night, with the news that his command was only a day's march
away, capitulation of the surrounded hostiles was only a question of
time, Major Crane knew. Still, the Nez Perces were stalling, urging
Joseph to hold out for better terms. Suspecting that a substantial portion of the tribe was plotting to break and run for Canada under cover
of darkness, Colonel Miles had asked Major Crane to take command of
two companies of sharpshooters, whose task would be to contain the
hostiles, while he continued to put pressure on Joseph to surrender.

"Don't ask the men to expose themselves or charge the camp," Colonel Miles said. "And don't let them communicate or get friendly with
the Indians, as Lieutenant Jerome did. We can't afford to give them
another opportunity to take hostages."

To keep the force of sharpshooters alert, Major Crane had given
orders that each shot from the rifle pits of the hostiles should be answered by at least three shots from the shelters of the soldiers, and that
each time a body was seen exposed several bullets should be fired in its
direction. Setting an example, he himself had spent considerable time as
a sniper, getting off a dozen or so shots during the day. At least one shot
had taken effect, he knew, for when the Indian leaped atop the rock in
front of his rifle pit and pointed at something in the distance, all the

sharpshooters except Major Crane were so taken by surprise that he alone had fired. From the way the Indian collapsed and fell, he was sure the shot had been fatal.

"Great shooting, Major!" shouted a sergeant at the other end of the shelter. "That'll teach the red bastards to keep their heads down!"

For a brief while it did have that effect, with not a patch of hair or skin to be seen along the long line of hostile rifle pits. That the Indian he had killed had been a man of importance was indicated by the howls of grief and rage from pits nearby, followed by a rising and falling wailing and keening on an eerie, unnatural musical scale, the words between a chant, a dirge, and a prayer.

"Do you hear that, Sergeant?" Luke Crane called to the noncom, who as a member of the Seventh Cavalry was a veteran of Indian campaigns.

"Sure do."

"Any idea what it means?"

"It's a death-song, Major. Chanted by one warrior for a blood brother."

"Listen! It's changed!"

"Yeah, it has. Likely the first song was that of the booger you just killed. Now his blood brother is chanting his own death-song, pumping up his courage to avenge his friend."

Incredible though it might be, Major Crane saw that an Indian had crawled out of the rifle pit and was snaking his way up the slope. In reply to shots fired at him by sharpshooters on this sector of bluffs, a hail of bullets crackled all along the line of hostile rifle pits, forcing the snipers to keep low and respond to the fire directed at them. After getting off a couple of shots, the noncom muttered quietly, "No question about it, Major. The booger figures to get you or die trying. It'll take a bullet to stop him."

"So be it," Luke Crane said grimly. "If that's what he wants, I'll oblige . . ."

Half a dozen times as he moved up the slope, Swift Bird drew shots from the shelter where the red-haired commander lay. He would show an elbow, a shoulder, or a portion of his head for a fleeting instant, then fling himself to the opposite side of his cover; triggering a bullet in reply to the piece of uniform or flesh briefly exposed as the commander raised up to fire at him he would blister splinters of rock into the face and over the person of his adversary. With the distance closing to one hundred paces now, it was inevitable that sooner or later he or the commander would place an effective shot.

Just ahead, an eroded wash furrowed the slope. Three feet deep and its lower end the width of a man's body, it pinched down toward its upper end, which was only twenty paces from the rock shelter and bluffs where the commander lay. If he rose, ran, and dove into the lower end of the wash, Swift Bird decided, the commander would be given only a fraction of a second to aim and shoot at a target moving rapidly sideways before him. His chance of hitting it would be slim, though he would no doubt get off a shot. Then the commander would wait, eyeing the lower end of the wash, expecting his next glimpse of his opponent to be near the spot where he had just disappeared. But Swift Bird would not be there. Instead, he would snake rapidly along the floor of the wash from the moment he dove in, move up it ten paces or so to a place much nearer the bluff shelter than the commander would look for him to be, and there, with a clear, open view into the shelter, he would rise and fire the shot he hoped would pay his debt to Looking Glass.

Committing his fate to his *Wy-a-kin,* he gave a wild, piercing, shrill cry, rose, ran, and dove for the wash.

He heard the crack of a rifle. He felt the sting of a bullet grazing his left hip, and he knew that, as he had expected, the commander had failed to follow his movements quickly enough. Landing in the wash, he crawled rapidly upward over the wet, slick earth of its floor. Ten paces from the spot where he had leaped into it, he stood erect, the muzzle of his carbine trained on the near end of the rock of the rock shelter. There, exposed for a clear shot, he got a split-second glimpse of the red-haired commander. Taken by surprise, he seemed frozen, for a single instant unable to move.

Swift Bird shifted his weight toward his left side as he started to fire. Suddenly, for no reason, his left leg collapsed, dumping him to the ground. Dazed, he rolled over, stared down, and realized that what he had thought to be only a grazing shot had actually pierced deeper, cutting the nerves that controlled the leg muscles, with the shock masking the damage until he had tried to use those muscles. No matter. He would still do what he had to do.

Struggling awkwardly erect, his weight now carried on his right side, he swung the muzzle of the carbine back toward the red-haired commander. But the delay proved fatal. Lifting his own gun, the commander fired. Swift Bird felt himself driven backward as a powerful blow struck him in the breast. He groveled on the wet earth, his face down and buried in it. Blackness was closing in. Only two or three breaths were left him, he knew. Only two or three heartbeats.

As if from far away, he heard cheering. In the rifle pits atop the bluffs the soldier sharpshooters who had been watching the duel were yelling their approval. In response to their vocal praise, the red-haired commander straightened up, took off his hat, and waved it in their direction.

Only one heartbeat and one breath are left now, Swift Bird's *Wy-a-kin* whispered. But they would be all he needed. For a fraction of a second, his vision cleared, his hands steadied, and the resolve within him burned like brightest flame.

He fired.

The red-haired commander fell.

And Swift Bird, the debt to his blood brother paid, died . . .

20

Shortly after they arrived at the battlefield with Howard's command, next day, War Singer, carrying out his duty as tribal historian, told Tall Bird and John Crane how their sons had died.

"God in heaven!" John murmured hoarsely. "They killed each other!"

"No, brother," Tall Bird said, putting a gentle hand on his arm. "It was the war that killed them. They both died fighting for their people."

Because their sadness was too deep, the two men could find no more words to say. As for grief, there was much to be shared by both red men and white men, now that the long, cruel war and the last terrible battle were over.

Of the more than seven hundred Nez Perces who had begun the epic flight, 118 days before and 1,300 miles away, ninety-six had been killed during the campaign, thirty-six of them women and children, John Crane learned. When deaths of white soldiers and civilians were finally totaled, he suspected that they would prove to be even greater.

During the night, under cover of darkness and a snowstorm in which the exhausted soldiers failed to maintain a close guard, White Bird and an estimated one hundred and forty men and boys, along with ninety-three women and girls, slipped out of their shelters in the grassy swale and headed toward Canada. Most of them were members of the Looking Glass or White Bird bands. There were a few exceptions, individuals or groups cut off from the Snake Creek camp by the first attack, widows whose husbands had been members of bands choosing to surrender while their sisters still had living husbands belonging to a band choosing flight, or simply persons to whom freedom at any cost appealed more than surrender. One of those who fled was *Ollokot*'s widow, *We-ta-ton-mi.* Later she recalled sadly:

"It was in the night when I escaped with Chief White Bird and his band, all afoot. It was lonesome, the leaving. Husband dead, friends buried or held prisoners. I felt that I was leaving all that I had. But I did not cry . . ."

Typical of a group whose flight north had been more accident than design was that of Wounded Head's wife, who, with ten women, a few children, and some men, had been able to flee moments after the first cavalry charge.

"We mounted horses and left. Only one blanket, I rode bareback as did the rest. Going quite a distance, we stopped. There we stayed till the evening drew on. Not only ourselves, but Chief Joseph's older wife and daughter were with us. But people were scattered everywhere, hungry, freezing. Almost naked, they had escaped from the camp when the soldiers came charging and shooting."

Somehow evading notice by the detachment of Cheyenne scouts sent out by Colonel Miles, the group traveled north through the bitter cold and the falling snow, with nothing to eat for four days. On the fifth day they found and killed a buffalo; the next day they met a band of friendly Chippewa Indians, who gave them moccasins, food, and shelter.

Not so fortunate were other groups of refugees. On October 6, General Howard wrote:

"Miles received information at 2 P.M., from the Red River half-breeds, of thirty Indians, twenty of them wounded in Miles' fight, who had escaped across the boundary. Also, from scouts, of six killed by the Assiniboines, of two or three killed by the Gros Ventres."

The last Nez Perces to flee the Bear's Paw camp and head for Canada was Yellow Wolf, Chief Joseph's nephew. Before the surrender, he said:

"Near morning came, and Chief Joseph said to me, 'You better go find your mother and my daughter. Bring them here.'

"That would be good, I thought, seeing my mother. The first sun of the fighting, my mother and my uncle's daughter made their escape. Yes, I would go find them.

"I stood with blanket about me, with rifle inside my legging. Not a long rifle, this that I fought with. I had both cartridge belts under my shirt. I would not stay. I would not go with the people, wherever the soldiers took them. Nor would I hide myself about that battlefield.

"During the night, soldier guards were all about us. Only the guards, all other soldiers sleeping. I waited until just breaking morning. My mind was made up what to do. I would not hide myself. I would walk out past those guards. They would see me, and if they tried stopping me, that would be good. I would kill them both."

Slipping past the guards without being challenged, Yellow Wolf walked through several inches of snow in his badly worn moccasins to a canyon where he knew a horse was hidden. Finding it, he mounted and rode north all day through a blinding snowstorm that completely obscured all trails. Toward evening he stumbled upon an Indian camp that he was sure must be hostile, but with his magazine carbine and two well-filled cartridge belts, he thought, *I am the same as ten men!*

Riding boldly into the camp, he found that these were Nez Perces, the very people he sought.

"We all then went. I would not take my mother and Chief Joseph's daughter back to the soldiers."

A few days later, they met the Sioux . . .

The possibility that Chief Sitting Bull and the two thousand Sioux exiles living in Canada might get together with Chief Joseph and his seven hundred Nez Perces and do battle against American troops had deeply worried General Howard and Colonel Miles, just as it greatly intrigued the newspaper-reading public, which was following the campaign as if it were some kind of game—with many of the readers pulling for the Indians. If such a thing had happened, the results would have been interesting. According to Indian accounts, their dream almost came true.

The first group of Nez Perces to reach the Sioux were some of the older men, who could communicate only in sign language. In attempting to tell the Sioux that their people were being attacked south of the border on a stream called Snake Creek, the Nez Perces made the sign meaning "water" or "stream." Thinking they meant the Missouri River, which was too far away for a rescue effort to be practical, the Sioux felt unable to help.

When a larger group arrived, a better means of communication was established. With the proximity of the battlefield now understood, the Sioux organized a war party led by Sitting Bull and containing several hundred braves, which started south next morning. Before it had gone far it met some of White Bird's refugees, who told them about Joseph's surrender. Realizing it was too late to help, most of the war party turned back, escorting the refugees to the Sioux camp.

"But a small company of Sioux and ten Nez Perces went on to see where the fighting took place," Yellow Wolf said. "Everything was still. Nothing living was seen anywhere on that field. But we found some of our dead who were unburied, and buried them as best we could. There was nothing to be done, and we returned to Chief Sitting Bull's village. The Sioux talking about the location of the battlefield said, 'This would have been no distance for us to ride. It was just from head to pillow.' "

Which was to say, if the Sioux had known such a great battle was taking place only a day's ride away, they would have picked up their arms and gone to the aid of their blood brothers.

The hospitality shown the Nez Perces by the Sioux exiles was warm, friendly, and generous.

"The meeting of the two chiefs for the first time was one of vivid contrasts," Yellow Wolf recalled. "Sitting Bull with his proud and undefeated warriors, his six racehorses beside him. White Bird afoot with his band of frozen, hungry people. The war paint and fine horses of the Sioux next to the Nez Perce women and children who had only pieces of blanket wrapped around their feet. But Sitting Bull dismounted from his fine pony and led his warriors in wailing and crying when told what had happened to the Nez Perce resistance."

Another nephew of Chief Joseph, who was ten years old at the time, also remembered the great kindness with which Chief Sitting Bull greeted the refugees.

"He came up to each and every one of us, man, woman, and child, and shook our hand. With even the youngest children, he did that— came up and shook our hand . . ."

For a time, at least, the 233 people in Chief White Bird's band had found freedom, friends, and a home in which they felt reasonably comfortable.

But for the more than 400 people in Chief Joseph's band, their search for these same things was just beginning . . .

2 1

Though the official surrender ceremony would not take place until two o'clock in the afternoon, October 5, 1877, all hostilities had ceased by nightfall the day before. Next morning, cooking fires were built in the soldier camp, meals were prepared, and the Nez Perces were invited to partake in the first hot food they had tasted for five days, with the children being fed first. Blankets and coats were provided for those who needed them, medical attention was given the wounded, and the Indians reluctantly gave up all their rifles and horses not needed for transportation.

"Will the captives be taken back to Lapwai, as promised?" Tall Bird asked John Crane, who had discussed their fate with General Howard and Lieutenant Wood.

"It's too late in the year for that now," John said, shaking his head. "As I understand it, they'll be escorted to Fort Keogh and sustained there for the winter by Colonel Miles. But next spring, Howard says, they'll be returned to the Nez Perce Reservation. His orders are to hold them in the Pacific Military District."

"The Cheyenne and Sioux scouts are bragging that each of them is to be given five good Nez Perce horses as their reward for killing their brothers," Tall Bird said bitterly. "Can't this act of thievery be stopped?"

"Afraid not. The spoils of war . . ."

With no tribal leaders left now except Joseph, Yellow Bull, and *Hush-hush Cute,* the weary band of people surrendering numbered 87 men, 184 women, and 147 children. Ironically, among the survivors to give up his rifle and be taken prisoner was the seventy-one-year-old half-blood son of William Clark, whose Nez Perce name was *Ha-lah-too-kit* —"Daytime Smoke"—along with his daughter, *Il-tolkt,* and her baby. John wondered if Clark, who during his long, honorable career as Superintendent of Indian Affairs for the Missouri and Snake River country had been the best friend the Indians had, ever knew he had left a son with the Nez Perces.

The remains of all the soldier dead had been sewn into canvas shrouds and loaded into wagons, with the enlisted men to be buried in military cemeteries at Fort Keogh or Fort Lincoln, while the bodies of the officers would be shipped down the Missouri and interred with full honors at Fort Leavenworth or St. Louis; if the survivors so desired, the remains would be taken to Washington, D.C. for burial in Arlington National Cemetery. Both General Howard and Colonel Miles were lavish in their praise of Major Luke Crane as an officer and man.

"He was one of the best I ever served with," Colonel Miles said fervently. "The kind of officer who never would ask the men in his command to risk a danger he would not risk himself. That was why he was with the sharpshooters."

"He was destined for a great future in the Corps of Engineers," General Howard said. "Without question, he would have reached the rank of Brigadier General before he retired. Did you see him often?"

"No, I'm afraid not. The last time was in '68, when I went back to Washington, D.C., with a party of Nez Perce chiefs. But we corresponded regularly."

"He and Custer were classmates and friends, I understand."

"Yes," John said, tight-lipped. "He pulled all sorts of strings so that he could get out of Washington and join Custer. But we never foresaw this."

"Do you have any idea as to what his widow's wishes will be for the site of his burial?"

"My guess is she'll choose Arlington National Cemetery. But I won't presume to speak for her. She and the children are living in St. Louis."

"How much of a family did he leave?"

"A son and a daughter. Let's see, Peter would be twenty-two now, with Abigal eighteen."

Staring bleakly out over the now silent battlefield through the gray, overcast day, General Howard shook his head, a deep sadness in his face. "What a pity! What a waste! So much misery, pain, and bloodshed for people of both races. Let us pray there will be no more."

Even though Howard and Miles offered to provide shrouds for the Nez Perce dead and transport the remains to Fort Keogh for temporary interment, after which army transport would take them to Lapwai or whatever other burial place the Indians might choose, the *Nimipu* insisted upon the old custom of their people—digging graves near the spot where the dead had fallen, wrapping each one in a single blanket, then placing it in the ground in an unmarked site, where the Earth Mother quickly would claim it as her own.

John Crane helped Tall Bird lay Swift Bird's body in the rifle pit from which he had defended the encampment. Taking only a beaded choker from around the neck of his son and the rawhide medicine bag in which he had kept the secret tokens acquired at the time of his *Wy-a-kin* quest, Tall Bird wrapped a blanket around the body, lowered it into the pit with John's help, then together they filled the grave with earth topped by what few rocks they could find nearby.

Standing erect, John moved back a step, too deeply shaken by the grief in Tall Bird's face as he knelt beside the newly filled grave to speak. Without looking up, Tall Bird murmured, "We have lost our sons, brother."

"Yes."

"Can your white man's God tell us why?"

"I don't have the heart to ask Him."

Starting to rise, Tall Bird stumbled, and John moved forward to catch him by the arm and steady him. Tall Bird gave him a grateful smile.

"We've ridden a long, bitter way together, John. I'm glad you were with me."

"So am I."

"What do you plan to do now?"

"Go back to Wallowa and look after the ranch—if I'm not needed here. What about you?"

"First, I must find a family to take care of Little Bird, who will need someone to look after him. Chief Joseph says he will help me. He does not trust the white man hired by General Howard as a scout and interpreter—Ad Chapman."

"He's dead right there. In my book, Chapman is a liar, a coward, and a scoundrel."

"I have promised Joseph that wherever he and his people go, I will go with them and do whatever I can to help them. It is the least I can do."

John shook his head. "It's too great a sacrifice for you to make, brother. If you go with them, you'll be a prisoner—just as they are. You'll be listed as one of the hostiles who took part in the war, with all the penalties they will bring for the rebellious Nez Perces for all time to come. You will be foolish if you do it."

"What would you have me do?"

"Come back to the Wallowa with me. We'll share the ranch and what few years are left us living there in peace."

"My people were driven out of the Wallowa, John, by the white man's law. How can I go back there to live?"

"You're half white, brother, with legal papers to prove it. Under your white name, Mark Crane, you filed a claim on a square mile of land years ago, proved up on it, and own it free and clear. No man can deny your right to it—or to full citizenship."

"So all I have to do is make a choice. Do I want to live as a white man or as an Indian? Is that what it comes down to?"

"For now, I suppose it does," John said uncomfortably. "Certainly, if you come back to the Wallowa with me, it would be wise for you to use your white name, dress in white clothes, and live as a white man does for a few years. Among the people who suffered losses during the war, there are going to be a lot of bitter feelings against the hostiles for a while. But once they're back on the Lapwai Reservation and absorbed into the general Nez Perce population there, it will gradually ease off."

"You wish only the best for me, I know," Tall Bird said gently. "But I cannot turn my back on my people. Where Chief Joseph goes, I shall, go. This I have promised . . ."

So far as Ad Chapman's reputation was concerned, Lieutenant Charles Erskine Scott Wood agreed with Joseph, Tall Bird, and John Crane that the man was a rascal. Waiting with the two dozen or so reporters, staff officers, and scouts on the bluff where the official surrender ceremony was to take place that gray, cold, early autumn afternoon, Lieutenant Wood muttered to John, who was standing beside him:

"How well do you know Ad Chapman?"

"As well as I want to know him. Among the Nez Perces, he has a bad reputation."

"That's what I've heard. And somehow I can't put much trust in an interpreter who is a functional illiterate—as Chapman is—in his own language. How can such a man possibly understand the shades of meaning of an Indian tongue as complicated as you tell me the Nez Perce language is?"

"Compared to Chief Joseph, Lieutenant, he's the village idiot."

"So I would say. Stand by, John, and give me your interpretation of what Chief Joseph says. I want to record it accurately."

Watching the surrender party move up the slope from the grassy swale to the bluffs, John saw that only Chief Joseph was mounted, while the three Nez Perces accompanying him walked alongside on foot. All were bareheaded, wearing gray, black-striped blankets, with their hair hanging in long twin braids. As they drew nearer, he recognized two of the walking Indians as *Hush-hush Cute*—"Naked Head"—and *Chus-lum Mox-mox*—"Yellow Bull"—who were the only other chiefs left. Though the third walking Indian looked familiar to John, he did not at first recognize him. He appeared to be an old man, very tired and somewhat crippled, for he limped badly as he walked, partially supporting himself by resting one hand on the horse's withers.

Then, as he raised his head and said something to Joseph, with the leader of the Wallowa band leaning down to listen, John suddenly realized that the old man was his half brother, Tall Bird. Discarding his rancher's coat and black broad-brimmed hat, which he customarily wore, and letting his hair, which he usually kept up under the hat, drop to below his shoulders and be confined in twin braids, he had donned a blanket and become as Indian as the others. From this day on, John suspected, his personal fate would be joined to that of the Joseph band.

Chief Joseph carried a rifle across the pommel of his saddle. It was only a symbol, John knew, for Tall Bird had told him that during the long campaign, Joseph had done little fighting. But as the last chief left alive he would go through the ceremony of surrender to bring peace to his people.

Reaching the spot where the white men waited, Chief Joseph stopped his horse and dismounted. He took a step toward General Howard, held out the rifle, and offered it to him. Howard murmured something in so low a voice that John could not make out what it was, shook his head, and motioned toward Colonel Miles. Walking to Miles, Chief Joseph handed him the rifle. Then he stepped back, adjusted his blanket to leave his right arm free, and began to speak. Lieutenant Wood flipped open his notebook, pencil poised.

"Ew-in a-tom-na-no ecu-kwe-ney-se ip-ne ti-me-ne . . ."

"Tell General Howard I know his heart. What he told me before I have in my heart. I am tired of fighting. Our chiefs are killed. Looking Glass is dead. The old men are all killed. It is the young men who say yes or no. He who led the young men is dead. It is cold and we have no blankets. The little children are freezing. My people, some of them, have run away into the hills, and have no blankets, no food; no one knows where they are, perhaps freezing to death. I want time to look for my children and see how many of them I can find. Maybe I shall find them among the dead. Hear me, my chiefs. I am tired; my heart is sick and sad. From where the sun now stands, I will fight no more forever . . ."

22

Through newspaper accounts and letters from Tall Bird as he moved with the captives during the long months and miles of their travels, John Crane learned that every promise made to the hostiles who surrendered was broken by the federal government.

Because winter was at hand and the mountain passes to the west soon would be choked with snow, General Howard decided it would not be practical to return the Indian prisoners to the Lapwai Reservation just then. He issued an order to Colonel Miles:

"On account of the cost of transportation of the Nez Perces to the Pacific coast, I deem it best to retain them all at some place within your district, where they can be kept under military control until spring. Then unless you receive instructions from higher authority, you are hereby directed to have them sent under proper guard to my department, where I shall take charge of them and carry out the instructions I have already received."

The instructions which had come from General McDowell in San Francisco stated unequivocally that the nontreaty Nez Perces, when finally subdued, were to be returned to the Idaho reservation. Despite this commitment, Howard apparently sensed that the original plan might be changed. In his report of the campaign, he wrote:

"But as I had made arrangements with Colonel Miles respecting the Indians, which he and I deemed most important, and as we feared without a full and proper explanation to General Sheridan that we might be overruled, we thought it best for the public interests that I should go through to Chicago and see General Sheridan."

So while Colonel Miles and his troops escorted the prisoners overland to Fort Keogh, General Howard hurried east to Chicago. Traveling with the overland party were eleven hundred captured Nez Perce horses. As a reward for the loyal service of the Cheyenne and Sioux scouts, Colonel Miles kept his promise to them.

"I directed the officer in charge of the Nez Perce herd to give each of them five ponies as a reward for their gallant service."

But Miles did not keep an implied promise made to General Howard, who had generously let him stay in command of the Bear's Paw operation and accept Joseph's surrender. Although one version of his report —which he showed Howard—mentioned the one-armed general's presence, this was not the version that reached General Sheridan and the press. That message, dated October 5, totally ignored Howard's presence at Bear's Paw, reading:

"We have had our usual success. We made a very difficult and rapid march across country, and after a severe engagement and being kept under fire for three days, the hostile camp under Chief Joseph surrendered at two o'clock today."

Learning of the slight when he reached Fort Lincoln a week later, General Howard was so incensed that he authorized Lieutenant Wood to write and release to the newspapers the *true* version of the surrender. Before it appeared in the Chicago papers, Colonel Miles sent in an amended report, in which he did mention Howard's presence.

When Howard arrived in Chicago he found Sheridan very angry over the fact that Lieutenant Wood's report had been released without his permission, for it made it appear that his officers were bickering and headline-hunting. Indignant words were exchanged, and Howard walked out before a full discussion of the real problem—what to do with Joseph and his people—could be held.

Actually, to General Philip Sheridan the problem was not people, it was supply. Subsisting the Nez Perces at Fort Keogh would be too expensive, he felt, so in November he ordered them moved downriver, first to Fort Lincoln, near Bismarck, North Dakota, then to Fort Leavenworth, in eastern Kansas, where the four hundred weary exiles arrived November 27, 1877. Here they were to be held as prisoners of war until the following spring.

"The camping place selected by the commandant," Tall Bird wrote, "was in the Missouri River bottom, about two miles above the fort, between a lagoon and the river, the worst possible place that could have been selected. Sanitary conditions among us soon proved that. The physician in charge said that one half of the people were sick at one time, and all of us were affected by the poisonous malaria of the camp."

During the first six months that the exiles were held in the Fort Leavenworth pesthole camp, twenty-one deaths occurred. Obviously, the Indians could not be held as prisoners of war forever. Neither could they be sent back to their homeland, for every community through which they had passed had drawn up indictments against them. The simplest solution appeared to be to send them down to Indian Territory, which since the 1830s had been a dumping ground for tribes uprooted by relocation or war.

"This will be no hardship to them," one commissioner wrote with abysmal ignorance, "as the difference in temperature between that latitude and their old home is inconsiderable."

Chief Joseph did not agree. Comparing the miserable, humid, malaria-infested lands assigned to the Nez Perces on the Quapaw Reservation to the high, cool, healthy Wallowa Valley from which he and his people had been driven, he said:

"I think very little of this country. It is like a poor man; it amounts to nothing."

By October 1878 forty-seven more captives had died. Ironically, the white man who had precipitated the war by firing the first shot at White Bird Canyon, Ad Chapman, had gone to work for the government as an official interpreter for the Nez Perces. In exile with them, he found the climate so bad that during a full day's delay in a sweltering railway station while making a transfer to the new reservation home, he was prostrated with the heat. So were Chief Joseph's wife and three Nez Perce children—the latter died during the journey.

Though the location and conditions of living on the new reservation were better, Chief Joseph continued to plead with officials in the federal government to let him come to Washington, D.C., and state his case for the return of his people to the Lapwai Reservation. At long last, his plea was granted. In an urgent letter written to John Crane in February 1879, Tall Bird said:

Permission has been given Chief Joseph to go to Washington in late March or early April. Yellow Bull and I are authorized to go with him, along with Ad Chapman as interpreter. Unfortunately, my health has failed to such a degree that I do not feel I can make the trip. None of us trust Chapman. To make sure that Chief Joseph is understood by the officials and the press, could you come to Indian Territory in time to go with him? Money for your expenses will be available here, if you can get this far on your own. Sell horses or cattle if you need to—with my consent. By rail, I understand, the trip can be made in three or four days. *Please come.*

Concerned as much over the state of Tall Bird's health as he was with the plight of the Nez Perces and the mission to Washington, John made the trip, marveling at the way the long, weary crossing of mountains and plains could be made in comfort these days and how small what had seemed in his younger days an immensely wide continent had become.

He found the March weather in Indian Territory pleasantly cool and healthy, but conditions under which the exiles were living depressed him. Their housing was poor, their farms small and not very productive, and their general attitude one of hopeless despair. Living in a canvas tepee pitched behind a dilapidated board-and-batten shack occupied by one of Chief Joseph's cousins and his family, who were caring for him as best they could, Tall Bird was shockingly thin, shaky, and hollow-eyed.

"Brother," he murmured in a husky voice, "I am glad to see you. How are things in the Wallowa?"

"Fine. How is Little Bird?"

"Healthy and growing like a weed," Tall Bird said, then shook his head. "But unhappy in school, where they're trying to make him forget he's an Indian."

As John had expected, Ad Chapman resented his presence with the delegation during the trip to Washington, and watched him with surly suspicion during the three weeks Chief Joseph spent making the rounds and talking with officials in the Indian Bureau, congressmen, ministers, and members of the press. Clearly, Chapman did not care nearly as much about making sure that Joseph was understood as he did about holding on to his government job, in which, Tall Bird had claimed, his opportunities for petty graft were substantial. But after learning that John knew the workings of federal bureaucracy far better than he did and would not intrude on his position as official interpreter, Chapman became less hostile. After making a clumsy pass at putting Chief Joseph's eloquent statements into understandable English, Chapman did not object when John lingered after the interview was over to explain in more subtle detail what Joseph had said.

Of all the interviews with the news media, the two hours spent with an extremely sympathetic writer from the influential, widely respected magazine, *North American Review,* was in John's opinion by far the most worthwhile. Explaining that the magazine had requested that he conduct the interview because of his experience as a missionary bishop to the Sioux, the tall, gaunt, middle-aged man—whose name was William Hare—smiled apologetically.

"I have no special knowledge of the history of the Nez Perces, so I hope you'll be tolerant of my questions. The Indian mission where I served was in Niobrara, Nebraska, not far from Yankton, South Dakota. Ever been in that part of the country?"

"Back in my trapping days, I passed through it a couple of times," John said. "As I recall, Niobrara is a small stream that flows into the Missouri River from the south."

"That's right. The Santee Sioux Reservation is located there."

After asking Chief Joseph to give him a complete background of the causes of the Nez Perce War from the Indian point of view, then to express his feelings as to what should be done to create better relations between the Indians and the whites, Bishop Hare sat patiently taking notes while Joseph talked and Chapman interpreted. By the time Joseph was done, Hare had filled at least twenty pages with notes so detailed that they approached being a verbatim shorthand account of everything Joseph had said.

"It's a shorthand only I can read," William Hare told John with a self-deprecating smile after the interview had ended and Joseph and Chapman had gone. "But it serves its purpose. After years of interviewing Indians, I've learned the wisdom of reporting what they mean to say, rather than what was actually said."

"That makes sense."

"From the way you and Chief Joseph exchanged remarks now and then, I gather you speak his language?"

"I've lived with the Nez Perces for years. At one time, I worked with the Indian Bureau as a subagent and interpreter."

"Then why aren't you acting as an interpreter for Chief Joseph, instead of that ignorant clod, Ad Chapman?"

"Because he wanted the job and was hired," John said with a shrug, "while I didn't and wasn't."

"I don't know a word of Nez Perce," Hare said, scowling down at the hastily scrawled pages of his notebook. "But Chief Joseph impresses me as an eloquent man. I can't believe that Chapman interpreted him very well."

"He didn't. If there are any points you want clarified, I'll be happy to help you."

"By heaven, I'll accept that offer! Are you free this afternoon?"

"Yes."

"I'll treat you to lunch. Then we'll spend the rest of the day going over my notes line by line. When we're finished, I'll edit the interview, pull galley proofs, and have you go over the articles before it's published in the *Review*. I've got a feeling this is a story that will touch the national conscience . . ."

As John had anticipated, Constance Crane had agreed that her husband's remains should be brought to Washington and buried with full military honors in Arlington National Cemetery. Without telling her that he arrived at the battlefield the day after Luke had been killed, he had written her a brief letter of condolence, saying how much he grieved with her for the loss. In return, she had penned a short, formal note of thanks, in which she said she and the children had gone to Washington for the re-burial service.

She had sent no news of his grandchildren and given no indication that she or they had any interest in seeing or hearing from him again. He could understand that. As a father, he had not been of any use to Luke during his formative years. Though a reconciliation between them had developed later to the extent that they corresponded regularly, John had seen his son's wife and their two children only during his brief stay in Washington back in '68. In her mind then, he knew, was the suspicion that someday he might attempt to take legal steps to acquire part of the substantial fortune Luke had inherited from his grandfather. Now that she was a widow, that suspicion had no doubt become stronger.

But it's not my son's fortune I want, he mused bitterly. *It's my son.*

While waiting for the *North American Review* writer to get back to him with galley proofs of the Chief Joseph interview, he hired a hack and drove out to Arlington National Cemetery to visit the site of his son's grave. The spring day was sunny and warm. Finding the grave, he took off his hat, bowed his head, and stood for long silent moments in wordless grief, barely able to read the marker through the haze of tears glazing his eyes.

MAJOR LUKE CRANE
September 3, 1832–October 4, 1877
"He Gave His Life for His Country"

That was true. But how much did the country care? Sure, it cared enough to create this beautiful cemetery where its honored dead could be put to rest as a reward for their services. But two thirds of a continent away in a bleak, unmarked hollow a day's ride south of the Canadian border lay the dead of a different race who had given *their* lives for *their* country. For what noble purpose or cause had his son and Tall Bird's son, who had never met until that final exchange of bullets, fought and died?

It had taken John many years of living to gain maturity enough to understand his father, who in his youth had engaged in the adventure of his life with the Lewis and Clark Expedition. In the Nez Perce country, his father had met Moon Wind, loved her, and fathered a son whom he yearned all his life to meet but never did. Years later, John recalled, his father told him, "I've always hoped that you and he would meet some-day, and learn to love each other."

Eventually, they had. Both he and Tall Bird had hoped that someday *their* sons would meet and come to love each other. They had met. Not in a spirit of love, but of blind, unreasoning, racial hate.

And now they both were dead . . .

Blindly, he turned away from the grave, found his way to the waiting hack and rode unseeing back into the city . . .

Scheduled to be published in the April issue of the *North American Review,* the long statement by Chief Joseph as edited by William Hare, was a masterful piece of writing. After reading it, John agreed that it would affect the conscience of every person in the nation. The article began with Joseph's explanation of why he had chosen to surrender even though at that time the battle was a draw:

"General Miles had promised that we might return to our country with what stock we had left. I believed General Miles, or I never would have surrendered. I have heard that he has been censured for making the promise to return us to Lapwai. He could not have made any other terms with me at that time. I could have held him in check until my friends came to my assistance, and then neither of the generals or the soldiers would have left Bear Paw Mountain alive.

"I was told we could go with General Miles to Tongue River and stay there until spring, when we would be sent back to our country. After our arrival at Tongue River, General Miles received orders to take us to Bismarck. The reason given was that subsistence would be cheaper there.

"General Miles was opposed to this order. He said, 'You must not blame me. I have endeavored to keep my word, but the chief who is over me has given me the order, and I must obey it or resign. That would do you no good. Some other officer would carry out the order.'

"General Miles turned my people over to another soldier, and we were taken to Bismarck. Captain Johnson, who now had charge of us, received an order to take us to Leavenworth. At Leavenworth we were placed on a low river bottom, with no water except river water to drink and cook with. We had always lived in a healthy country, where the mountains were high and the water was cold and clear. Many of my people sickened and died, and we buried them in this strange land. I cannot tell you how much my heart suffered for my people while at Leavenworth.

"During the hot days we received notice that we were to be moved farther away from our country. We were ordered to get into railroad cars. Three of my people died on the way to Baxter Springs. It is worse to die there than to die fighting in the mountains.

"We were moved from Baxter Springs, Kansas, to the Indian Territory, and set down without our lodges. We had but little medicine, and we were nearly all sick. Seventy of my people have died since we moved there.

"We have had a great many visitors who have talked many ways. Some of the chiefs from Washington came to see us, and selected lands for us to live upon. We have not moved to that land, for it is not a good place to live.

"The Commissioner Chief came to see us. I told him, as I told everyone, that I expected General Miles's word would be carried out. He said it could not be done; that white men now lived in my country and all the land was taken up; that if I returned to Wallowa, I could not live in peace; that law-papers were out against my young men who began the war, and that the government could not protect my people.

"The Commissioner Chief invited me to go with him and hunt for a better home than we have now. I like the land we found better than any place I have seen in that country, but it is not a healthy land. There are no mountains and rivers. The water is warm. It is not a good country for stock. I do not believe my people can live there. I am afraid that they will die.

"Then the Inspector Chief came to my camp and we had a long talk. He said I ought to have a home in the mountain country north, and that he would write a letter to the Great Chief in Washington. Again the hope of seeing the mountains of Idaho and Oregon grew up in my heart.

"At last I was granted permission to come to Washington and bring my friend Yellow Bull and our interpreter with me. I am glad we came. I have shaken hands with a great many friends, but there are some things I want to know which no one seems able to explain. I cannot understand why so many chiefs are allowed to talk so many different ways, and promise so many different things. I have been to the Great Father Chief, the next Great Chief, the Commissioner Chief, the Law Chief, and many other law chiefs, and they all say they are my friends, and that I shall have justice, but while their mouths all talk right I do not understand why nothing is done. Good words do not last long unless they amount to something.

"Words do not pay for dead people. They do not pay for my country, now overrun by white men. They do not protect my father's grave. They do not pay for all my horses and cattle. Good words will not give me back my children. Good words will not make good the promises of your War Chief General Miles. Good words will not give my people good health, and stop them from dying. Good words will not get my people a home where they can live in peace and take care of themselves.

"I am tired of talk that comes to nothing. It makes my heart sick when I remember all the good words and all the broken promises. There has been too much talking by men who had no right to talk.

"If the white man wants to live in peace with the Indians he can live in peace. There need be no trouble. Treat all men alike. Give them all the same law. Give them an even chance to live and grow. All men were made by the same Great Spirit Chief. They are all brothers. The earth is the mother of all people, and all people should have equal rights upon it. You might as well expect the rivers to run backward as that any man who was born a free man should be contented when penned up and denied liberty to go where he pleases.

"If you tie a horse to a stake, do you expect he will grow fat? If you pen an Indian up on a small spot of earth, and compel him to stay there, he will not be contented, nor will he grow and prosper. I have asked some of the great white chiefs where they get their authority to say to the Indian that he shall stay in one place, while he sees white men going where they please. They cannot tell me.

"I only ask the government to be treated as all other men are treated. If I cannot go to my own home, let me have a home in some country where my people will not die so fast. I would like to go to the Bitter Root Valley. There my people would be healthy; where they are now they are dying. Three have died since I left my camp to come to Washington.

"When I think of our condition my heart is heavy. I see men of my race treated as outlaws and driven from country to country, or shot down like animals.

"I know my race must change. We cannot hold our own with the white men as we are. We only ask an even chance to live as other men live. We ask to be recognized as men. We ask that the same law shall work alike on all men. If the Indian breaks the law, punish him by the law. If the white man breaks the law, punish him also.

"Let me be a free man—free to travel, free to stop, free to work, free to trade where I choose, free to choose my own teachers, free to follow

the religion of my fathers, free to think and talk and act for myself—
and I will obey every law, or submit to the penalty.

"Whenever the white man treats the Indian as they treat each other,
then we will have no more wars. We shall all be alike—brothers of one
father and one mother, with one sky above us and one country around
us, and one government for all. Then the Great Spirit Chief who rules
above will smile upon the land, and send rain to wash out the bloody
spots made by my brothers' hands from the face of the earth. For this
time the Indian race are waiting and praying. I hope that no more
groans of wounded men and women will ever go to the ear of the Great
Spirit Chief above, and that all people may be one people.

"*Hin-mah-too-yah-lat-kekt* has spoken for his people."

During Chief Joseph's well-publicized stay in Washington, the dignity of his bearing, his eloquence, and his appeal for justice had aroused
a tremendous wave of sympathy in Congress, in the press, and in the
hearts of the American public, John knew. When this article was published, as it soon would be, he suspected that Congress and the Indian
Bureau would be bombarded with petitions demanding that the Nez
Perce exiles be permitted to return to their home.

Already working in their behalf were General Howard, General
Miles, and Howard's brilliant, outspoken aide, Lieutenant Charles Erskine Scott Wood. Wood, after serving in a brief, brutal campaign
brought on by an uprising of the Bannocks in 1878, had gotten a law
degree at Columbia while serving as Howard's assistant during his term
as Superintendent of West Point; he then resigned from the Army and
was now planning to establish a private law practice in Portland.
Whether all the former hostiles would be permitted to return to Lapwai
was questionable, for there among the Nez Perces who had taken no
part in the war, feeling still was running high, as was the animosity of
whites living in the area who had suffered family or property losses
during the conflict. But it seemed clear that sooner or later, Chief Joseph and his people would be permitted to return to the Pacific Northwest.

Heading back to Indian Territory with the delegation in late April
1879, John Crane was pleased by Chief Joseph's promise that if Tall
Bird were well enough to travel, there would be no objection to John's
taking him back to Wallowa with him on the train. Once at home on the
ranch, the pure, cool mountain air, the clean, cold mountain water, and
the knowledge that he had done all he could possibly do to effect the

return of his people to their homeland, would be the best medicine Tall Bird could be given.

"Take him home," Joseph said with a gentle smile. "Perhaps I can pay you a visit soon and see the valley I love . . ."

23

In St. Louis, John left the delegation, rented a rig and horse, and drove out to the former Samuel Wellington estate, which his son had inherited and now was the home of his widow and children. Three weeks ago, John had written Constance that he was in Washington and that he hoped to stop off in St. Louis and see her and the children on his way west. He had received no reply, which did not particularly surprise him. Whether she felt no answer was required or just plain did not want to see him hardly mattered. He intended to see her and his grandchildren, whatever her feelings, for in all probability this would be his last trip East.

Parking the rig in front of the beautiful, southern antebellum style house, he walked up on the portico to the massive polished oak door, found the button of the door bell in the adjoining panel, and pressed it. Distantly within the house, musical chimes sounded. After what seemed a long while, John heard slow, deliberate steps as someone approached the door, then it opened. A tall, dignified, elderly Negro stood just within the threshold, regarding him without warmth.

"Yes, suh?"

"I am John Crane, the late Major's father. I wrote Mrs. Crane a few weeks ago from Washington that I would be paying her a call."

"Yes?"

"Is this a convenient time for her to see me?"

"If you'll wait, suh, I will ask her."

Closing the door firmly without suggesting that he wait inside, the old Negro servant was gone for a long while. At last he returned, opened the door, and bowed stiffly. "She will see you in the drawing room, suh. But please make your visit brief. She has not been well."

"I understand."

Taking off his hat as he entered the house, John followed the servant through the entry hall and into the large, exquisitely furnished drawing room, whose drapes were closed. Beyond the tall windows, John recalled, lay a well-groomed garden filled with beautiful flowers. But in the drawing room now the light was very dim, the atmosphere heavy and funereal. Sitting stiffly erect in a straight-backed Victorian chair and not rising to greet him, Constance Crane looked thin and drawn, appearing to have aged by at least twenty years since he last had seen her, rather than by the eleven that had actually passed. In silence she gazed at him, no warmth in her eyes, no expression on her face. After waiting a few moments for the Negro servant to withdraw, then finally realizing that the servant did not intend to do so, John inclined his head respectfully and spoke.

"It is good to see you, Constance."

"Oh."

"I've spent the past several weeks in Washington. While I was there, I went out to Arlington National Cemetery and visited Luke's grave. For whatever consolation it may be to both of us, it is a beautiful place."

"Yes. I have seen it."

"You have not been well?"

"No."

"Then I won't impose on you long. But I would like to see the children."

She arose then, swayed as if feeling faint, then steadied herself, turned away from him, and walked to the draped windows. With her back to him, she at last spoke in a low, broken voice.

"That won't be possible, Mr. Crane."

"They're not here?"

"No. They are not here. Nor will they ever be again."

Puzzled, he took a step toward her, then stopped. "I'm afraid I don't understand."

Whirling around, she spoke with a strained harshness, as if the very fiber of her inner being were being torn apart.

"Two months ago, Peter and his wife, with Abigal and the young man she planned to marry, went downriver to New Orleans on a holiday. Coming home, the steamboat they were on got into a race with another boat. Too much pressure was put on the boilers. They exploded, the boat caught fire and sank, with a great loss of life. They were among the people killed."

"Oh, no!" John breathed. "Not the children, too!"

As he stared at her in horror, the heavy silence of the house was broken by the sound of a door slamming, running feet, and a child's peal of laughter. Awkwardly pursued by a large, kind-faced Negro woman of middle age, a little girl dressed in an ankle-length white pinafore burst into the room. Clutching a bunch of flowers in both hands, she ran to Constance Crane, and lifted the bouquet for her approval.

"Aren't they pretty, Grandmother? I picked them just for you!"

"Yes, dear. They're very pretty." In response to the unspoken question in John's eyes, Constance put her hands on the child's shoulders and held her protectively. "This is Peter's daughter, Ruth. She stayed with me when the young people went on their holiday. She is all the family I have left."

"How old is she?"

"Four." Looking pale and drawn, Constance sank into the straight-backed chair, while the matronly Negro woman took the little girl by the hand and led her away. "Please excuse me, Mr. Crane. It's more than I can bear."

As much as he wished to, he could not impose on her grief by insisting that he be given at least a few moments to talk to his great-granddaughter. His brief glimpse gave him an impression of a pert oval face, bright brown eyes, and curly auburn hair. But it was obvious that Constance did not intend for him ever to know the child or for the child to know him.

Blindly turning away, he stumbled across the room, along the hall, and out the door. She was beyond any comfort he could give her. For that matter, only the therapy of movement, of being forced to go on to Tall Bird, tell him the good news about going home, and try to get him in shape to travel, was taking John's mind off the tragedy of having lost both his son and his grandchildren . . .

But when John reached Indian Territory, one look at Tall Bird as he lay gasping for breath on the canvas floor of his tepee bleakly told him that his brother would not live long enough even to start the journey home, let alone complete it. During the month the delegation to Washington had been gone, he had failed badly. Without assistance he could not even lift his head. He listened attentively as John told him about the trip and passed on the good news that a large number of influential people were now marshaling all their forces to effect the return of the exiles to their home; but the way his eyes frequently glazed and the lids often closed made it clear that he was having difficulty focusing his mind on what John was saying. At last, John said lamely:

"I asked Joseph if I could take you home. He said I could. So as soon as you feel better, we'll go."

"No, brother," Tall Bird whispered. "I will never leave *Eekish Pah.* I will die in the Hot Country soon, as so many of my people have died since we were brought here. You must go back to Wallowa without me. I ask only one last favor."

"Anything you want, brother. Anything at all."

"Go to the school and get Little Bird. Then . . . then . . . home . . ."

Lapsing into the Nez Perce tongue as he had done, in which it was difficult at times to distinguish meanings of action words unless they were accompanied with gestures, which Tall Bird now was too weak to do, John was not sure whether Tall Bird had said "take" or "bring."

"You want me to go get him, then bring him here?"

"Not here, brother. Home. To *Nimipu* country."

"Will they let me?"

"Ask Joseph to help you. He will. If you have to, steal the boy and spirit him away with you. But take him home. Raise him as if he were your own grandson."

"Oh, God, brother, how I wish I could! But I'm an old man now, with not a notion in the world as to how to raise a child."

"Don't you want him?"

"Of course I want him. Next to you, he's the closest blood kin I've got." After a moment's silence, John nodded and murmured, "It could work out, at that. I could take him to Lapwai, where your daughter and her family live, or to Alpowa, where your son and his family live, and ask them to raise him."

"Any *Nimipu* family would take him, whether blood kin or not. Among the *Nimipu,* all men are brothers. But I do not want him raised by an Indian. I want him raised by you."

"Why by me?"

"Because you are the only man I know who understands the world of the *Nimipu* and the world of the white man. Only you know what is good and what is bad in each world. Only you can teach him the many things he will need to know. Will you do this for me, brother?"

"Yes," John said huskily. "I will do it."

With an effort, Tall Bird picked up a worn buckskin bag lying beside him and handed it to John. The items it contained, John knew, were the things most treasured through Tall Bird's lifetime: a picture stone acquired on his *Wy-a-kin* quest; the many-bladed knife sent to him by the white father he never met; Swift Bird's neck choker; and the New Testament given him long ago.

"Give him the knife as soon as you are sure he can use it without cutting himself," Tall Bird whispered. "But save the rest until he returns from his *Wy-a-kin* quest."

"I'll do that, brother. And I'll tell him how jealous I've always been of you because that fancy knife our father gave you was so much better than any knife he ever gave me."

"It was a token of his love, I was told. I'm sure he loved us both—as we came to love each other." Closing his eyes, Tall Bird lay still for a long while, laboriously fighting for breath. Then he opened his eyes, smiled weakly, and said, "Do not stay and watch me die. Go and get Little Bird. Take him home. Take him home . . ."

When John Crane told Chief Joseph what he had been asked to do, Joseph nodded and said, "The boy is in school at Chilloco, which is near the Ponca Reservation just south of Arkansas City. The Nez Perces will be moving there this summer. I will ask our agent to write a letter for you, saying Little Bird's grandfather is ill and you are there to take him home. Both these things are true."

"Yes, they are."

"Which home you are taking him to is your business. I'm sure you will have no trouble getting a half-fare ticket for him on the train. Of course, before you can put him on the train, you may have to grab his ankle, pull him out from under the bed where he may be hiding, blindfold and tie him hand and foot. Or you could put him in a gunnysack."

John laughed. "Will he be that scared?"

"Some of the children are, for to them steam engines and railway cars are fearful things. But they soon learn."

Loaned a wagon, a team, and a teenage Nez Perce boy to drive him to Chilloco and Arkansas City, then bring the team and wagon back, John made the 180-mile trip west from the Quapaw to the Ponca Reservation over poor, muddy roads in a spine-numbing four days. The director of the school accepted the note without question, sent for Little Bird, and told him to go to the boy's dormitory and pack. Though it had been two years since John had seen the child, who at Bear's Paw had been just four years old, Little Bird nodded when John asked him if he knew who he was.

"Yes," the boy said shyly in Nez Perce. "You are a *Pe-ke-lis.*"

"That's right," John said in the same tongue. "I'm a grandfather. And I'm going to take you home."

By the time they reached the railroad station in Arkansas City, it was two o'clock in the afternoon. There was a passenger train going north at four-thirty, the agent said, which would get them to Junction City at nine that evening. There they would change to a Union Pacific train due to head west at ten o'clock. It would get them to Pendleton, Oregon in two and a half days.

"Which you got to admit is mighty fast traveling, mister, even for these modern times."

"Quite a bit faster than we traveled the first time I made the trip," John admitted.

"When was that?"

"Before you were born. Back in '32."

"Say, you are an old-timer, ain't you!" Handing him a full and half-fare ticket, taking his money, and then making change, the agent eyed the chubby, wide-eyed little Indian boy dubiously. "What're you doing with him?"

"Taking him home."

"You with the Agency?"

"In a way."

"Well, I hope he don't have lice. Makes passengers mad when they find lice in the seats of the cars."

"It'd make him mad, too. We'll be careful where we sit."

Because Little Bird did remember him vaguely as a grandfather and because John spoke the Nez Perce tongue as well as his Indian elders did, the child had not been in the least afraid of being taken out of the school and transported to Arkansas City, or of the puffing engine and metallically clanking train. The only outward sign of apprehension he showed was to cling like a shadow to John's side, seeking his hand and holding tightly to it, glancing up now and then in round-eyed wonder to make sure that this particular grandfather was still there, steady and calm, prepared to protect him from any possible danger.

By late afternoon, next day, they had become great friends, the boy trusting him so completely and showing so much of Singing Bird's sunny disposition that John began to love him as he had loved the child's mother. Far to the west as the train thundered north across the high plains of Colorado, John could see a faint blue line of mountains rising. As had happened the first time he had seen the Rockies so many years ago, his spirits lifted and his heart began to beat a little faster. Cradling Little Bird's shoulders with his left arm, he raised his right hand and pointed out the window, against which the child's face was pressed.

"Do you know what those are, Little Bird?"

"No. What?"

"Those are the Rocky Mountains, boy. Not bad, as mountains go. But wait till you see the ones we've got in our backyard at home. Ain't none as beautiful as the Wallowas."

"What does 'Wallowa' mean, Grandfather?"

"Well, the way *Speelyi* explained it to me, it means 'Land of the Winding Waters.' He says it's the most beautiful place on earth. He's proud he made it."

"Were you there when he made it, Grandfather?"

"Not that day, no. But I got there the day after. You see, he was having some trouble with the monster and wanted me to help him."

Little Bird squirmed with delight, for he thought he knew what was coming. "Is this a grandfather tale?"

"You could call it that, yes. But if you want me to tell it, you've got to sit still and listen."

"I will, Grandfather. Truly, I will."

Ignoring the white passengers in the half-filled coach, who were eyeing the white-haired old man and the dark-eyed Indian boy with perplexity, John switched to the special tone of voice which elderly Nez Perce myth-relaters used when telling grandfather tales.

"Wa-qo na-qe tit-wa-tis tit-wa-tit-ya-as hit-tew-ye-cine," he began . . .

"Now I will tell a story about myth people, when only myth people were living. About Speelyi, *the Coyote Spirit who made the world ten thousand snows ago. About how he killed a monster and made all the Indian tribes out of pieces he cut up and threw to the four winds, saving the best people of all, the* Nimipu—*who were made out of the heart blood of the monster —for the last. And in all of* Nimipu *country, the most beautiful spot is the Wallowa . . ."*

ABOUT THE AUTHOR

For many years a regular contributor to *Liberty, The Saturday Evening Post, Esquire,* and *Collier's,* BILL GULICK has published sixteen novels, several of which have been turned into movies, such as *Bend of the River, Road to Denver,* and *Hallelujah Trail.* His first nonfiction book, *Snake River Country* in 1971, was given the Pacific Northwest Booksellers Award as the best Nonfiction book of the year.

He has written and produced three historical outdoor dramas: *The Magic Musket* in 1953; *Pe-wa-oo-yit: the First Treaty Council* in 1955; and *Trails West* in 1976 and 1977, which was selected by the United States Department of Commerce as one of America's top ten family spectaculars for 1976.

Making his home in Walla Walla for the past thirty years, he has worked with the Nez Perces, Umatillas, Walla Wallas, Cayuses, and Yakimas on a number of projects to bring about a better understanding of Indian rights. In 1976 he was project director for a $24,000 Washington State Humanities Commission Grant given *Trails West,* in conjunction with Whitman College and the Whitman Mission National Historic Site, to pay Indian advisers and actors performing in the production and to hold eleven public forums in which Indian and white experts discussed Indian treaty rights.

His wife Jeanne, who assists in research, secretarial, and editing work, has just retired from her position as a research librarian at Penrose Library, Whitman College, where most of the material Gulick has gathered over the years now is deposited. He is past president of the Western Writers of America, Inc. Two of his *Saturday Evening Post* stories have won that organization's prestigious Spur Award as best Western short story of the year.

In 1983 he was given the Levi Strauss Saddleman Award by the Western Writers of America "for an impressive career writing fiction, nonfiction, and drama of the West."